EM.

Dr Andrew Jeffrey studied at the University of St Andrews and has written widely on military and maritime history. He has authored a trilogy of books on Scotland's role in the Second World War and his media work has included research and on-air contributions for British, Dutch and French documentaries. Glasgow-born, Dr Jeffrey is a former sea fisherman, Royal Navy reservist and RNLI lifeboatman.

A TASTE
FOR
TREASON

ANDREW JEFFREY

BIRLINN

First published in 2022 by
Birlinn Limited
West Newington House
10 Newington Road
Edinburgh
EH9 1QS

www.birlinn.co.uk

ISBN 978 1 78027 788 2

British Library Cataloguing-in-Publication Data
A catalogue record for this book is available from the British Library

Designed and typeset by Initial Typesetting Services, Edinburgh
Printed and bound by Clays Ltd, Elcograf, S.p.A.

Contents

The greatest peacetime spy ring in history
– FBI Director J. Edgar Hoover

Go ahead, investigate the cocksuckers!
– US Secretary of State Cordell Hull to J. Edgar Hoover

There is no doubt whatever that Jordan is a member of the German espionage organisation at Hamburg
– MI5, January 1938

Intercept has created a tremendous impression in the Deuxième Bureau and French naval circles
– MI5, October 1938

Movie exposes work of Hitler stooges in U.S.
Chicago Tribune on *Confessions of a Nazi Spy*, May 1939

Preface

A Taste for Treason

They came for him in the still, silent hour before dawn.

Capitaine de vaisseau Pouech woke the young officer and said, 'Aubert, votre recours en gràce est rejeté. Habillez vous. C'est l'heure de la penitence.' (Aubert, your appeal for mercy has been rejected. Get dressed. It is time for repentance.)

Enseigne Marc Aubert had spent the seven weeks since his court martial refusing to wash or shave and shouting rambling confessions at the drab, indifferent walls of his cell. It had been the madness of the condemned. But the new day would bring atonement and, resigned to his fate, he heard Mass, gave naval chaplain l'abbé Fabre a last letter for his mother and waited, chain-smoking, until the escort arrived.

Normally a hive of activity even at that early hour, Toulon Naval Dockyard was eerily quiet that fine spring morning. Gendarmes patrolled the streets to keep the morbidly curious away while, beneath the walls of Fort Malbousquet, 700 soldiers and marines had formed up in silent, serried ranks around a wooden post backed by a bank of earth. A truck drew up and Aubert was escorted towards the post. He stopped briefly to embrace the priest, then waited patiently while an officer read the sentence of the court martial.

'. . . la peine de mort par fusillade' (the penalty of death by shooting).

The German military intelligence service Abwehr's top spy in France for more than a year, Aubert's treachery had gone undetected until an American Nazi agent's letter, intercepted in Scotland, triggered an international spy hunt. Among those identified by MI5 and

FBI investigators was a German widow living in Dublin, Eire, and an intercept on her mail revealed that she was in contact with another Nazi spy code-named Charles, apparently a French naval officer. Identifying Charles from among thousands of Marine Nationale officers was not going to be easy, yet the rapidly mounting international tension in the summer of 1938 lent the search immense urgency.[1]

The Japanese had marched into the Nationalist Chinese capital, Nanjing, in December 1937 and massacred perhaps as many as 200,000 Chinese civilians in six weeks. As the rest of the world looked on, unable or unwilling to intervene, more than 20,000 women and girls were brutally gang-raped, pregnant women had foetuses torn from their bodies and babies were skewered on swords. To place the depraved Rape of Nanjing in perspective, British civilian deaths for the entire six years of the Second World War totalled 67,000, a third of the Chinese civilian death toll at Nanjing. And, in an alarming portent of what was to come, British and American river gunboats evacuating Western civilians were deliberately targeted by marauding Japanese aircraft. One, USS *Panay*, was sunk.

In Africa, Italian dictator Benito Mussolini had unleashed 100,000 troops and deadly clouds of chemical weapons on defenceless Ethiopia. Here, as in Nanjing, thousands of women were raped, hospitals were bombed and, in one three-day killing spree following an attempt on the life of an Italian general, around 6,000 Ethiopian men, women and children were shot, bayoneted or burned alive. In all, some 275,000 Ethiopians died as Mussolini pursued his ridiculous quest for a latter-day Roman Empire. The rest of the world, indifferent to the fate of a few thousand black Africans, paid no heed as deposed Ethiopian ruler Haile Selassie warned, 'It is us today. It will be you tomorrow.'

As if to bear out Haile Selassie's grim prediction, a deadly miasma of ferocious small wars was already spreading across Europe. The Spanish Civil War was plumbing new depths of bestial savagery as the militarist right and hitherto pacifist left from around the world weighed into a bloody proxy war that would cost more than half a million lives before the fascists, ably assisted by Nazi Germany, claimed victory in 1939. Britain and France contented themselves with pointless moralising from the sidelines, then professed weary surprise when it transpired that nobody was listening.

Taking his cue from the feeble international response to the Italian invasion of Ethiopia, Hitler had reoccupied the demilitarised Rhineland in 1936 and annexed Austria in 1938. Six months later, in a rabble-rousing tirade at a Nazi rally, he demanded that Czechoslovakia evacuate the disputed Sudetenland border region within days or face invasion. Wehrmacht and Luftwaffe units were heading for the Czechoslovak border, German terrorists were murdering Czechoslovak policemen, the Red Army was massing on Poland's eastern border, the French, Romanians, Yugoslavs and Hungarians were all mobilising, Italy had ordered all Jews out of the country and air-raid drills were being rehearsed in London and Paris.

It was abundantly clear to all but the most wilfully myopic that Hitler was an amoral, racist thug at the head of a militarist cult hell-bent on, at the very least, continental domination. Yet, having colluded in the destruction of Czechoslovakia at Munich in September 1938, British Prime Minister Neville Chamberlain boasted, albeit while accelerating British rearmament, of 'peace for our time'. French Prime Minister Edouard Daladier, a more astute judge of Hitler's character than Chamberlain, entertained no such conceit and returned to Paris wretched at having danced to the British appeasement tune. 'Don't have any illusions,' he said, 'this is only a respite, and if we don't make use of it, we will all be shot.' As Daladier recognised, Hitler was unappeasable and Munich had merely delayed the inevitable.[2]

This was the fraught background against which the hunt for the French naval officer spy 'Charles' began. And it was a search that assumed even greater urgency when the British intercept on the Dublin agent's mail revealed that 'Charles' was handing his delighted Abwehr spymasters a treasure trove of French naval ciphers, blueprints and technical reports. Anglo-French strategy for a sea war against Germany and Italy was being comprehensively betrayed and the vital Mediterranean route to Suez and the Middle East oilfields was in jeopardy. Even the mobilisation orders issued to the French

Mediterranean Fleet during the September 1938 Munich Crisis were in German hands, decrypted, almost as soon as they reached their intended recipients. By then, however, the MI5 intercept had yielded the vital clue that would lead the Deuxième Bureau to enseigne de vaisseau Marc Aubert.

Caught in the act of copying yet more documents for his Abwehr spymasters when he was arrested aboard the destroyer *Vauquelin*, Aubert was tried by court martial in January 1939. The proceedings were largely held in camera, but the left-leaning press saw enough of the accused to draw unfavourable comparisons between his treachery and endemic French government corruption. Others on the right were unequivocal in their condemnation, *L'ouest-éclair* thundering that he was 'un des plus abominables criminels qui aient souillé l'uniforme d'officier francais' (one of the worst criminals ever to soil the uniform of a French officer). He had, suggested one observer, acquired 'un goût pour la trahison', a taste for treason.[3]

Two months later, on that March morning in Toulon, Aubert got to his knees and was tied to the post, his only show of emotion an emphatic shake of his head when a sailor stepped forward with a blindfold. But this was judicial killing up close and personal and staring into the pleading eyes of a condemned man could easily upset even the most cold-blooded marksman's aim, so it was applied anyway. Quietly reminding his men to aim for the heart, the officer in charge glanced at his watch, raised his sword and, at precisely 6 a.m., brought it smartly down again.

Twelve bullets, each preceded by a shock wave 30 times its own volume, slammed into Aubert at close on 2,000 feet per second. Soft tissue turned instantly to boiling jelly and vital organs were shredded before the volley burst out of his back in a spray of blood, flesh and splintered bone to kick up puffs of dirt in the earth bank behind him. As startled birds scattered noisily into the still morning air, a sailor stepped forward and blew the young officer's brains out with an automatic pistol. One of France's most damaging traitors was dead and the whole gruesome ritual had taken less than four minutes.

At the very moment German spy Aubert faced one firing squad in Toulon, British spy and former Italian naval officer Antonio

Scarpa was being tied to a chair with his back towards another in an army base near Rome. Part of a network run by Tom Kendrick, the Secret Intelligence Service (MI6) Head of Station in Vienna, Scarpa had been spying on Italian naval rearmament and meddling in the Spanish Civil War. But Kendrick's wafer-thin cover as Passport Control Officer fooled nobody and his networks were rounded up in August 1938, a few weeks after the *Anschluss*, the German annexation of Austria. Kendrick, his wife and his driver were bundled out of Vienna in a blaze of publicity and four other members of the British spy ring received long prison sentences. For Scarpa, however, there could only be one outcome and the timing of his execution to coincide with Aubert's was no accident.

Yet another firing squad assembled a few days later at a rifle range near Nancy in north-western France to shoot 26-year-old gardener Hellmuth Gruneberg, an Abwehr spy caught snooping around the Maginot Line, France's supposedly impregnable barrier against a German invasion. Three weeks later, Georg Froch and Matthias Glaser were dragged to the death house in Berlin's Plötzensee Prison and guillotined for spying for France. Many others would make that grim journey during that last summer of peace, though not naval architect and British spy Dr Karl Krüger. Betrayed by Folkert van Koutrik, a Dutch double agent employed by MI6 who had sold out to Nazis, Krüger is believed to have cheated the Plötzensee headsman by hanging himself in his cell.[4]

In Britain, Abwehr agent Else Duncombe had committed suicide, four others were serving lengthy jail terms and yet more were under MI5 surveillance. Spies were also being unmasked in Panama, Czechoslovakia, Turkey and France, among them Paris beautician Lucienne Gané, whose body would be discovered in the Seine in February 1940. She had been strangled by her officer husband after he discovered that she was peddling military secrets to the Japanese.

It was a dangerous, often fatal, time to be a spy.

* * *

Today, the place where Marc Aubert faced his executioners lies in the shadow of an autoroute flyover, the roadside ditch where his shattered body lay now covered by a neat pavement. It is an unremarkable spot, yet what took place there on that spring morning in 1939 was the culmination of a seven-year duel between Abwehr's spies and the British, American, Canadian, French, Belgian, Czech and Irish security services.

It was a duel shot through with all the spy fiction staples of alluring femmes fatales, Nazi thugs, sinister spymasters, glamorous film stars and seedy traitors. For the Austrian playboy cavorting with a Côte d'Azur nightclub dancer in a champagne bath, the 'Swiss Mata-Hari' seducing French naval officers, the German lawyer spying on British airfields with his teenage mistress and the Belgian electrician whose well-paid treachery would precipitate the 1940 Dunkirk evacuation, espionage had its compensations. For others, among them the French beauty queen driven to suicide on a Moroccan beach, the Berlin society hostess ritually beheaded with an axe and the Hollywood moguls forced to brave pro-Nazi intimidation, spying would prove anything but amusing.

Europe might have been awash with spies of all hues, but most European nations had long since developed security services like Britain's MI5 and the French Sûreté Nationale to counter the threat. In the United States there was no shortage of evidence that Nazis and their American fellow travellers were bent on political subversion, yet until 1936 there was no US government body charged with counter-espionage and most Americans still clung to the naïve view that spies were a uniquely European problem. That was until Nazi espionage plots in the United States and Britain converged with the interception, in a Scottish post office, of a letter detailing a plan by Abwehr spies to forcibly relieve a US Army officer of secret plans for the defence of America's east coast.

In the months that followed, a joint British and American counter-intelligence operation would unmask yet more Nazi agents in the United States, Britain, Canada, Ireland, Panama, Czechoslovakia and France. Told in full for the first time, this is the story of that operation and the breaking of what FBI Director J. Edgar Hoover, albeit never one for self-effacing understatement, would describe as 'the greatest peacetime spy ring of all time'.

Yet that letter intercepted in Scotland did much more than unmask Nazi spies across Europe and North America; it led directly to the formation of an intelligence and security alliance of unequalled power and reach, an alliance that hastened Allied victory in the Second World War, that held the line in the Cold War and, for better or worse, still underpins Anglo-American relations in the 21st century. Quite simply, that letter helped shape the modern world.

Chapter 1

The Mad Major

Herzlich Willkommen an Arsch der Welt – A Warm
Welcome to the Arsehole of the World

Sign at a secret German training airfield, Russia, 1922

Tower Bridge, London, 30 September 1931

At first the silver wings of the little de Havilland Puss Moth were
all but invisible against a leaden grey sky. Then it swooped down,
lined up on the twin Gothic towers of Tower Bridge and shot
through the gap between the roadway and the iron tracery of the
walkway above. As astonished motorists and passers-by looked on,
it continued upriver, passing low over the next seven bridges before
darting through the central arch of Westminster Bridge and climbing
away towards Brooklands aerodrome.

Daredevil pilot, wartime fighter ace and 'resting' actor Major
Christopher Draper told reporters on landing that the flight had
been a publicity stunt, partly to get work for himself and partly
to highlight the plight of other jobless ex-servicemen reduced to
penury by the global recession. The dramatic one-man protest
led to an appearance in court charged with dangerous flying and
flying without a valid pilot's licence. A policeman claimed that the
Puss Moth had dropped to within seven feet of the Tower Bridge
roadway and that Draper and his cameraman passenger narrowly
escaped death as the bridge was about to be raised to allow a ship
to pass through. This was nonsense, as Paramount News footage
of the flight showed, and Draper was let off with a stern warning.
But it was music to the ears of a resting actor dubbed 'The Mad

Major' by a delighted press as it brought welcome offers of work including a starring role in *Aces of the Air*, a nationwide tour by wartime British and German airmen delivering homilies on peace and the future of aviation to cinema audiences about to be thrilled by Howard Hughes' new aviation comedy, *Sky Devils*.

In the audience when *Aces of the Air* opened at London's Plaza cinema on 24 June 1932 was the tour's promoter, Colonel William Francis Forbes-Sempill. A scion of one of Scotland's oldest aristocratic dynasties and a wartime Royal Naval Air Service veteran, the Master of Sempill had been spying for the Imperial Japanese Navy since leading a naval aviation mission to Tokyo in 1922. Seduced by the militarist fascism of the ultra-nationalist Kōdōha (Way of the Emperor) faction and motivated to treason by an eye-watering bank overdraft, this clever, pushy, egocentric aristocrat was a keen supporter of British fascist organisations like the stridently anti-Semitic National Political League and the Royal Empire Society, a peculiar group that advocated stemming the tide of imperial decline with a programme of 'planned' emigration that would increase the Anglo-Saxon gene pool in fractious colonies. Sempill was also, in 1931, one of the founding principals behind the Anglo-German Fellowship, an organisation so rabidly right-wing that Soviet mole Kim Philby joined as effective cover for his own brand of treachery.[1]

Sempill had begun planning the *Aces of the Air* tour after one of his regular visits to Germany and his shrill advance publicity trumpeted 'Personal Appearances by Four Famous Air Aces!' This was certainly warranted in the case of German Eduard Ritter von Schleich, the wartime 'Black Knight' who had a *Pour le Mérite*, or Blue Max, and 35 victories to his credit. 'Mad Major' Christopher Draper, fresh from his London bridges flight, had nine victories, so he too could be considered an ace. But Sempill was lying when he tried to pass off army officer Günther von Richthofen as a brother of the late Red Baron, Manfred von Richthofen, and an illustrious airman in his own right. Günther von Richthofen was really only a distant cousin of the Red Baron and no airman. The other British ace, Major Allan Bridgeman, was actually just a shy and unremarkable wartime pilot down on his luck after a messy divorce. It is telling that this was to be a purely Anglo-German affair; no airmen from Britain's wartime allies, or from Germany's for that matter, were invited.[2]

Aces of the Air ran for 151 packed performances with the charismatic 'Teddy' von Schleich, his black uniform aglow with medals, the star turn. A fierce anti-communist who had narrowly escaped death while resisting an attempted Bolshevik coup in Bavaria, von Schleich had been among the first recruits to the nascent Nazi Party and, as Christopher Draper writes:

> From him I learned a great deal about the National Socialist Party, and we had long and most interesting discussions, especially because one of our party, who accompanied the tour as a sort of business manager, was a very English Jew. As can be imagined, he and Teddy had the most heated arguments ... Teddy used to tell me time and again: 'Christoph, eet eez only a question of time before my Hitler eez zee power.'[3]

Draper subsequently went to Germany as von Schleich's guest and, on 15 October 1932, was introduced to Hitler at Munich airport. The Führer seemed bored at first, but brightened on being told by his press agent Ernst Hanfstängl that Major Draper would be making a case for the Nazis in influential circles in London. Quite where 'Putzi' Hanfstängl got the idea that a cash-strapped, unemployed actor could wield pro-Nazi influence in Britain's corridors of power is unclear. Perhaps Draper's association with Sempill had something to do with it and, while this may only be a coincidence, Sempill had visited Germany just a week before Draper arrived in Munich.

Whatever really happened in Germany, Draper was by no means the first gay man to find the Nazis' pantomime rituals and homoerotic male bonding strangely appealing and, on 19 March 1933, the *Sunday Despatch* reported that Major Christopher Draper, recently returned from Munich where he had met Herr Hitler, was organising a nationwide series of talks on behalf of the Nazis. At the end of April, an MI5 mail intercept on Dr Hans Thost, the London correspondent of the Nazi Party newspaper *Völkischer Beobachter* and a known low-level German spy, turned up an invitation to a meeting in Hampstead at which Draper would speak on the future of fascism in Europe.[4]

Thost recruited Draper as a Nazi agent; that much is clear. But the two men offer radically different accounts of how they met and the circumstances surrounding Draper's recruitment. Thost's version is that, in August 1932, towards the end of the *Aces of the Air* tour, he took Draper and von Schleich to lunch at London's fashionable Oddenino's restaurant and encouraged the Englishman to write pro-Nazi letters to the press. About a year later, Draper told Thost that he was 'prepared to work on behalf of Germany, that he was very short of money and that he would like to assist the German Luftwaffe'. Thost replied that Draper would first have to meet intelligence officers in Hamburg and, after some haggling over who should pay the fare, Draper agreed to go.[5]

Draper's autobiography, *The Mad Major*, published in 1962, makes no mention of the lunch at Oddenino's and claims that Thost invited him to his Wimbledon home on several occasions in 1933 and, after one particularly boozy lunch, proposed that he should become a German spy. Draper says that he asked for a couple of days to think it over as he was anxious 'to get in touch with MI5 as quickly as possible, for I realised that here was the most wonderful opportunity to double-cross the Hun'. He maintains that he told an acquaintance, one Baron K. de Trirop, of the approach and, two days later, met a 'Major X' and 'Sir Percy Sillitoe, the head of MI5', who instructed him to go along with everything the Germans asked of him, but to keep MI5 informed of his every move.

Draper then says that he boarded a Lufthansa flight from Croydon to Hamburg on Sunday, 23 July 1933, and, on landing, was taken to the Atlantic Hotel and left to his own devices for the evening. A young German called for him the next morning and led him to a café where, in a scene that might have come straight out of one of his own low-budget movies, the only customer was a pasty-faced man seated at a corner table with the light behind him, wearing dark glasses and a hat pulled low over his eyes. Coffee was served and the spymaster, who gave his name as Degenhardt, said he wanted intelligence on military aircraft, aircraft factories and RAF squadrons. Draper replied that he could get this information and, perhaps a little over-eagerly, asked how much he would be paid. The German replied that payment would be by results and gave Draper two mail relay addresses, one in Hamburg and the other in Rotterdam, through which he was to send intelligence. Letters to Draper, ostensibly about stamp collecting, would be couriered to Britain and posted there. The meeting over, Draper returned to the Atlantic, packed and left for home.[6]

That, at least, was Draper's version of events, yet neither Draper nor Thost was telling the whole truth. Thost's account was given to Allied interrogators eleven years later, in 1945, so he can be forgiven some confusion over dates. It was also by then in his interest to downplay his role as an influencer and talent spotter. But Draper's story that he contacted MI5 immediately Thost tried to recruit him, and that the Hamburg trip was undertaken with their sanction, is nonsense. MI5 records show that they were already aware of Draper's links to Thost, but that his first meeting with MI5 actually took place on 3 August 1933, a week after his return from Germany. Draper made no mention of a café, dark glasses or a hat during the interview, merely stating that Degenhardt had been 'a German, aged about 35, rather Jewish and . . . not a man who had served as an officer in the forces'. Moreover, he certainly did not meet Sir Percy Sillitoe, who was then Chief Constable of City of Glasgow Police and only became head of MI5 in 1946; he was actually interviewed by Colonel Sir Vernon Kell, the Director General of MI5 and his deputy, Brigadier Oswald 'Jasper' Harker.[7]

Kell probably took part in the interview because MI5 had been monitoring Thost and his contacts with senior Nazis including Göring, Goebbels and Hess since his arrival in Britain in 1931. But his distrust of the flamboyant, homosexual Draper is all too evident in Harker's minute of the meeting. The MI5 officers rightly concluded that the Englishman had considered becoming a German agent, but had changed his mind on realising that he was playing with fire and was now trying to rehabilitate himself by stringing the Germans along. Harker wrote that 'there is no doubt that he is prepared to play', but noted ruefully that, cash-strapped as ever, Draper had demanded to know whether he could keep any money the Germans sent him. MI5's German specialist Edward Hinchley Cooke was assigned the role of case officer and, on 28 September 1933, gave Draper an innocuous Air Ministry document to send to Louis Fischer, Berglustaan 51a, Hillegersberg, Rotterdam, the Dutch cover address that he had been given while in Hamburg. This was returned without comment the following month and a small sum in Dutch florins was posted to Draper's London flat a few weeks later.[8]

So if Draper really had considered becoming a German spy and only went to the authorities on returning from Hamburg, what had changed his mind? There was then certainly no shortage of evidence of the risks attached to the spying game in the early 1930s. Italian naval rating Ugo Traviglia had been shot for stealing documents for his 'dark-eyed beauty' French lover, while French engineer Professor Charles Eydoux and his secretary, Georgette Bonnefond, had been caught and jailed for espionage in Italy in February 1933. A Czech Army officer had killed himself after being lured into a honeytrap by a German nightclub singer, two Polish officers caught spying for the Soviet Union had been shot, a Yugoslav officer caught spying for Hungary had been hanged, two Frenchmen had been jailed for selling naval secrets to the Japanese and six British engineers were languishing in a Moscow jail awaiting trial for espionage.[9]

These cases were widely reported, but the contemporary spy case that must have concentrated Draper's mind had begun with a British Army officer brazenly asking a Berlin hotel porter for the address of German military intelligence. Tipped off by a mysterious Russian, MI6 Head of Station in Berlin Frank Foley discovered that the British officer was one Lieutenant Norman Baillie-Stewart of the Seaforth Highlanders and an MI5 intercept on Baillie-Stewart's mail turned up, in November 1932, a letter from a Marie-Luise [sic] in Berlin:

My Dear Boy!

I often think of the nice days we spent together in Berlin last summer. I hope you are very well and you have not forgotten me. You were so kind in lending me some money. You remember my father stopped giving money to me because he did not wish that I should continue studying. Meanwhile, he has altered his opinion and it is all right. Unfortunately I cannot pay you back the whole sum at once, but I hope I may be able to send you the rest before Christmas. I look forward to seeing you again next year. Please write me again if you can come. With very kind regards, yours, Marie-Luise.[10]

The text of the supposed love letter was wooden and ambiguous, but the £50 enclosed with it, ostensibly as part-repayment of a loan, was downright suspicious. Baillie-Stewart had a substantial bank overdraft and was in no position to be lending large sums of money to anyone, least of all a German girlfriend he had only just met.

Baillie-Stewart's reply to the Marie-Luise [sic] letter was intercepted before it left Britain. Addressed to one Otto Waldemar Obst in Berlin, it read:

Dear Friend,

Thank you very much indeed for your letter and the prompt way in which you settled our small debt.

It is very good of you to ask me to stay with you and I shall do my utmost to take a holiday then, but I am afraid it is still too early for me to make any definite statement as to when I can get away. At the moment I think I should be able to manage at the beginning of March, but I shall let you know for certain later.

When you write to me in future may I make a suggestion that you use much smaller seals as such large ones are apt to arouse the curiosity of unscrupulous people. I say this because from the appearance of your letter I should imagine someone had opened it to have a look inside, before it reached me at my home address.

The weather here is not too good at the moment and nearly everyone seems to have colds. I hope you are faring better in Berlin. I shall look forward to hearing from you soon and to seeing you in the spring.

Again many thanks. Yours ever, Alphonse Poiret.[11]

The reference to the first Marie-Luise letter having been tampered with caused some consternation until the Post Office confirmed that one of two wax seals on the envelope had actually been broken in transit from Germany, probably through being crushed. And the French-sounding signatory Alphonse Poiret led to some head-scratching in MI5 until Edward Hinchley Cooke pointed out that 'Poiret' meant a small pear in French, 'Marie-Louise' was also a type of small pear and 'Obst' was German for fruit. Hinchley Cooke had also learned that, since returning from Berlin, Baillie-Stewart had borrowed mechanised warfare training manuals from the garrison library at Aldershot and had snooped around the Mechanical Warfare Experimental Establishment at Farnborough.

Another 'Marie-Louise' letter, this time with £40, was intercepted a month later and, with the evidence against him mounting, Baillie-Stewart would normally have faced a court martial. But his ham-fisted approach to the Germans and his palpable lack of success as a spy would make it hard to portray him as a credible threat to national security. So he was confronted by Lieutenant Colonel Frederick Syms of the Judge Advocate's Office and Captain William Phillips of MI5, handed two closely typed pages detailing his treachery and given the opportunity to quietly resign in exchange for information on his dealings with the Germans.

Anyone with a grain of common sense would have leapt at such an easy way out of a treason charge, but not Norman Baillie-Stewart,

a conceited buffoon whom David Niven, a Sandhurst contemporary before becoming an actor, recalled as 'a singularly unpleasant
piece of work'. He considered the offer for a few minutes in awkward silence, then petulantly turned it down. The Provost Marshal
formally charged Baillie-Stewart with offences under the Official
Secrets Acts and, six days later, on 26 January 1933, he was bundled
into a car and:

> I soon recognised that we were on the London road. All
> my wonders and doubts again came back to me. Where the
> devil was I being taken? Was it to the War Office itself for
> further examination? In what seemed a very short while
> we were driving through the thick of the London traffic
> in parts that I did not know. Then suddenly a notice: 'To
> the Tower of London'. Good heavens, I thought, can it be
> possible that I am being taken there of all places?[12]

The Tower might have been the most secure detention barracks in
London, but it was also one of Britain's most popular museums and
tourists were soon flocking to gawp at the 'Officer in The Tower'
cutting a dash in the tartan trews and Glengarry bonnet of the
Seaforths as he took his daily exercise.

The court martial opened on 20 March 1933 with Baillie-Stewart
admitting that he had gone to Berlin, but claiming that, while
sitting alone in a café, he had met an Otto Waldemar Obst who
offered to introduce him to a girl who would show him the sights.
The attractive blonde, whom Baillie-Stewart said he only knew as
Marie-Louise, promptly fell for his charms and they had energetically consummated their relationship in woods beside Wannsee, a
lake in the south of the city. He strenuously denied giving away
secrets and, much to the amusement of the packed public gallery,
portrayed himself as a sexual athlete whom women would gladly
pay for his expert favours, hence the £90 from a suitably apprecia-
tive Marie-Louise.[13]

Baillie-Stewart's brother Eric confirmed that 'Women are on his
mind the whole time', and a visibly distressed Mrs Suzanne Hickey,

the French-born wife of a fellow officer, admitted that she had spent the evening with him in London on Saturday, 27 August 1932, then saw him off from Liverpool Street Station on his first trip to Holland. German girl Lotte Geiler, discreetly identified in court only as Miss D, described meeting Baillie-Stewart on the boat train that same night and tearfully confirmed that, 'Yes, we got very friendly,' during the ferry crossing. A court official was overheard commenting wryly that Baillie-Stewart had 'made the most of his short acquaintance of her'. Indeed, such was the accused's growing fame as a latter-day Casanova, the War Office was being deluged with gushy letters from women pleading for his release. One woman admirer even offered to die for him, while a Belgian woman ran a bizarre fan club, Les Amis du Baillie-Stewart, for her 'cher petit Norman'. Mme de Renoz had, of course, never met the object of her distant admiration.

Appearing as Major A, Edward Hinchley Cooke told the court that the Berlin contact address Baillie-Stewart had given his regiment before leaving for Germany was actually that of Kaufhaus Nathan Israel, a department store. A search of the accused's room had revealed a scrap of paper with the Berlin telephone number of the Reichswehrministerium, the high command of the post-1918 German Army, another scrap of paper between the pages of Baillie-Stewart's driving licence with a Berlin address for Otto Waldemar Obst, photographs of an experimental British tank and several restricted British Army manuals including one entitled The Tactical Handling of Army Tank Battalions.

Baillie-Stewart tried to pass this off as study material for promotion and, amid hoots of derision from the public gallery, maintained that he only had the Reichswehrministerium phone number because he planned to offer himself as a liaison officer between the Reichswehr and the British Army. Backtracking furiously when Hinchley Cooke pointed out that he had also found, stuffed into the pocket of a brown tweed jacket in his wardrobe, a list of information that the Germans wanted on British tanks, Baillie-Stewart then tried to claim that he had actually gone to Berlin to pull off an intelligence coup that would so impress the British intelligence services that they would at once offer him a job.

The defence did their best, but their suggestion that only a complete fool would have kept such damning evidence of espionage in his quarters did not have quite the intended effect as few now doubted that Baillie-Stewart was indeed a very complete fool. They did pull one rabbit out of the hat in the form of bandleader Victor Silvester who said that a 'pretty, young and fair' Marie-Louise, who claimed to be 'very fond of ze Eengleeshmen', had accosted him in the ballroom at Berlin's Eden Hotel on 19 August 1932, the same night Baillie-Stewart had left the city. But most observers agreed with prosecutor Major Henry Shapcott when he snarled at the pale and trembling accused, 'I am not mincing words, the prosecution contend that Lieutenant Baillie-Stewart sold his country for £90.' On 13 March 1933, he was found guilty, cashiered and sentenced to five years in jail.[14]

In Berlin, meanwhile, a small army of journalists was hot on the trail of the mysterious Marie-Louise. Reports all too obviously planted to throw the journalists off the scent suggested that she had died of pneumonia, then Sefton Delmer of the British *Daily Express* tracked down one Olga Israel, an attractive Berlin Jewess who admitted that she had gone dancing with Baillie-Stewart but vigorously denied that she was 'Marie-Louise' or that she had, as he was now claiming, spent a day with him at a nudist colony.[15]

And there the trail would have gone cold were it not for two seemingly unrelated events in France. First, even as the former Lieutenant Baillie-Stewart, now prisoner B.1.13, joined the admissions queue at Wormwood Scrubs on that March afternoon, French newspapers were reporting that there could be a link between him, the still enigmatic Marie-Louise, a German spy known as 'La Belle Sophie' and a French Army officer and suspected German agent named Georges Frogé. 'La Belle Sophie' was actually a German-born woman named Sibela Drosd who ran a seedy café and brothel in the northern border town of St Avold. Intriguingly, Sibela Drosd's husband, Joseph, an odious creep who pimped underage girls, admitted under interrogation that he was a German courier and claimed that he had made several trips to Britain. There was also a striking similarity between the Marie-Louise letters sent to Baillie-Stewart and letters sent by one 'Germaine' to Frogé.[16]

Then, just as the La Belle Sophie story broke in the French press in October 1933, German courier and French double agent Wilhelm Gustav Geissmann told his Deuxième Bureau handlers that he had seen Parisian woman Lydia Stahl with German officers at Lindau in southern Germany. Whether there was any truth in Geissmann's tale about the Russian-born Stahl's contacts with the German military is unclear, but it turned out that she had spent several years as a Soviet agent in New York and was now part of a network spying on the French military for the Soviet military intelligence directorate, Glavnoye Razvedyvatelnoye Upravleniye (GRU).[17]

Rounding up the Stahl ring in December 1933 proved simplicity itself as its members were invariably stupid. Despite an anonymous telephone tip-off, 'Prenez garde! Vous êtes Americains? Oui? Eh bien, vous feriez fort bien de quitter Paris . . .' (Take Care! You are Americans? Yes? Well, you would be well advised to leave Paris). American communists Gordon and Marjorie Switz still had stolen documents and a wad of cash hidden behind the wardrobe when detectives burst into their Paris hotel room. New York City-born Vassar graduate Marjorie simply refused to answer questions about the photographic negatives that had been rolled up in the cigarettes she was furiously chain smoking while detectives searched the room. Not that the Sûreté needed the smouldering evidence in the ashtray; both Gordon's and Marjorie's fingerprints had been found in a packet of films intercepted in Switzerland while en route to Russia.[18]

It was all thoroughly embarrassing for the Soviets, not least because Gordon Switz, the ring's paymaster, wasted no time in handing over his detailed account books in exchange for an early release, thus compromising Soviet agents and sympathisers across Europe. Worse still for the Soviets, the French had passed copies of intercepted correspondence between Lydia Stahl and Helsinki-based GRU agent Ingrid Bostrom to the Finnish state security police, Etsiva Keskuspoliisi (EKP), and this led the EKP to another 30 GRU spies operating in Finland, among them one Marie-Louise Martin.

Initially at least, both the Finns and the French suspected that the Marie-Louise languishing in a Helsinki prison might be the same

Marie-Louise with whom Norman Baillie-Stewart had allegedly cavorted in the Wannsee woods the previous summer. This raised the intriguing prospect that, if the girl now locked up in Helsinki and the blonde who had supposedly entertained Baillie-Stewart in Berlin really were one and the same, then Baillie-Stewart, who was many things unsavoury but no communist, had been duped into joining a Soviet spy ring. But neither Baillie-Stewart nor Victor Silvester recognised the Helsinki Marie-Louise's photograph and it turned out that she was really a Latvian farmer's daughter, former Riga barmaid and low level GRU asset named Marija Emma Schul who just happened to be using the alias Marie-Louise Martin.[19]

So now there had to be two Marie-Louises, one a Soviet agent languishing in a Finnish jail, the other a German agent still at large. Once again, however, the trail went cold until, in December 1936, several newspapers named Marie-Louise as civil servant's daughter Marie-Louise Bäckendorff. It seems, if the newspaper accounts are to be believed, that she had seduced British spy Robert Wendell, a German-born engineer of British descent who was handing MI6 details of fortifications on Heligoland, an island fortress off the entrance to the River Elbe. Marie-Louise found the evidence needed for Wendell's conviction, but had fallen in love with her target and, after Wendell was executed, fled to a Swiss convent.[20]

* * *

With so much espionage-related mayhem splashed across newspaper front pages, it is hardly surprising that Christopher Draper took an attack of cold feet, abandoned his plan to spy for Germany and turned British double agent. Yet, just as MI5 officers Oswald 'Jasper' Harker and Edward Hinchley Cooke had suspected, there was much more to Draper's story than he was letting on, and it is now possible to piece together what really happened.

Early in 1933, Draper, fellow RAF veteran 'Captain' Guy Nugent and business associate Baron Martin Kristensen de Trairup had hatched a crazy get-rich-quick scheme that involved setting up an air taxi service in the Labrador goldfields, bribing miners to steal choice nuggets and mooring a large yacht off the tiny Inuit settlement of Rigolet ready to make off with the loot. Another even more far-fetched scheme involved flying stolen Inca gold out of South America.

Neither Draper nor Nugent had any money while de Trairup was on the brink of his second bankruptcy and in no position to finance their plans. But one of them seems to have realised that, thanks to his Thames bridges flight, his friendship with von Schleich, his meeting with Hitler and his connections to right-wing British airmen like the Master of Sempill, Draper would be able to pose as a convincing spy in return for Nazi cash to finance the gold smuggling enterprise. A company rather indiscreetly named Inca Aviation (Overseas) Ltd was formed and, in a letter intercepted by MI5 at the end of June 1933, more than a month before his interview with Harker and Hinchley Cooke, Draper contacted Thost, who had indeed lunched with him and von Schleich at Oddenino's the previous year, to offer his services as a spy.

De Trairup, a half-Russian, half-Danish one-time minor functionary at the court of the last Tsar whom MI5 suspected of involvement in illegal arms trading, was right about the Germans being interested in the RAF. But, as Kell and Harker had guessed, Draper must have had second thoughts once he considered the prison sentence that awaited him if caught, not a pleasant prospect for anyone, but infinitely worse for a homosexual man like him. One thing is certain: while MI5 was aware of his links to Thost from the latter's intercepted mail, Draper's trip to Hamburg was not, as the MI5 official historian has suggested, made with their foreknowledge and approval; the dates simply do not match.[21]

Espionage was not, thanks to Degenhardt's insistence on payment by results, going to be the money-spinner that Draper and his accomplices had hoped it would be, so de Trairup contacted MI5 and a contrite Draper was able to clear his yardarm by becoming a double agent. Guy Nugent, who handled the Canadian end of the scheme, turned up in a Los Angeles courthouse a few weeks later charged with passing counterfeit $20 bills and only escaped a prison sentence by claiming to be a war hero with a British DSO and a French Légion d'Honneur when he was actually just an undecorated, non-commissioned despatch rider. Inca Aviation was put into liquidation only to be reborn as Plane Publicity Ltd, a legitimate banner-towing concern that once again failed to prosper and collapsed in 1938.[22]

As for Draper's recruiter Hans Thost, he was kept under close surveillance with one MI5 informant, Thost's barber at Harrods department store in London, reporting that the German was oddly curious about fellow customers including senior staff at the Foreign Office and US Ambassador Robert Bingham. Thost was booted out of Britain 'in the public interest', in November 1935. But who was Draper's Hamburg spymaster Degenhardt, who was he working for, and why was Germany, supposedly demilitarised after the First World War, trying to steal British military technology?[23]

* * *

The First World War had fostered at least as many problems as it resolved. Not least of these was that the weak post-war German government, in hock to the victorious Allies for war reparations, printed shoals of money to buy off its own embittered extremists. As many Western governments would rediscover a century later following the coronavirus pandemic, ill-judged, panic-driven fiscal stimuli inevitably trigger dangerous levels of inflation and the German economy was already in freefall when, in December 1922, beleaguered Berlin ministers decided to test Allied resolve by defaulting on reparations shipments of coal and timber. The French, itching to avenge their vast losses in the war just ended, promptly sent 60,000 troops on a smash-and-grab raid amid the industrial riches of the Ruhr. Overnight, Germany's communists and nationalists, workers and industrialists alike, were united in common cause and passive resistance brought her staple industries shuddering to a standstill. Tax revenues collapsed, the mark plummeted to an eye-watering 4.2 trillion to the dollar and unemployment rocketed to 30 per cent.[24]

Berlin had gambled with Germany's economy and lost. But they had been right about one thing; the grand alliance that had won the First World War was falling apart under the new strains of peace.

London and Washington had refused to get involved in the Ruhr occupation, the enormous cost of which was now crippling an already ailing French economy. Worse still for Paris, everyone from the Vatican to the Kremlin was condemning French atrocities against German workers and, in just a few days, Germany had gone from a nation of belligerent militarists responsible for a war that had cost 16 million lives to the plucky victim of ruthless French aggression. A humiliated Paris was finally forced to accept an Anglo-American exit strategy, the Dawes Plan, that set a timetable for withdrawal, rescheduled reparations and, much to Gallic disgust, granted a substantial American loan to Germany.

It was victory of a sort for Berlin, but millions of ordinary Germans had been ruined, the country's embryonic democracy had been dealt a fatal blow and the only ones to profit were extremists whose paranoia found an audience amid the misery. Communists were first to the barricades, though their Moscow-orchestrated uprising in Hamburg was a fiasco. At the other end of both Germany and the political spectrum, membership of the Nazi Party in Munich shot up to 35,000 and, thus emboldened, Adolf Hitler and his cronies organised the Bierkeller Putsch, a risible attempt to overthrow the Bavarian government that left four policemen and fourteen Nazis dead. Sadly, on this occasion Hitler reneged on a promise to shoot himself should the uprising fail, choosing instead to spend a few months honing his bigotry and paranoia in a suspiciously comfortable prison cell.

Germany might have been in turmoil, but the wartime Allies could at least take comfort from claims that their weapons inspectors had reduced its immense wartime military machine to a lightly armed gendarmerie of 104,000 men, the Reichswehr, and removed the threat of German aggression for the foreseeable future. Yet the reality was that nothing had been done to reorder German society away from Prussian militarism and, worse still, the German High Command, the Reichswehrministerium, had made good use of the hiatus between the 1918 armistice and the arrival of weapons inspectors in January 1920. Train loads of armaments had vanished into the vast German rail network, warplane makers Heinkel and

Junkers had set up plants in Sweden, Dornier had moved across Lake Constance to Altenrhein in Switzerland and Anton Fokker had spirited airframes, engines and equipment into his native Holland. It was also proving a simple matter for the supposedly 104,000-strong Reichswehr to conceal its true numbers with paramilitary organisations like the civil police being used to provide basic military training.

The covertly expanding Reichswehr now needed discreet locations where armaments factories and training facilities could be set up well away from prying Allied eyes and in 1922 there was only one option: Russia. Post-war Germany and Russia had much in common; Germany had bankrolled the 1917 Bolshevik revolution in the hope that Lenin would take Russia out of the war, both countries had been defeated, both had undergone a radical change of government and both were groping towards a foreign policy fit for the post-war world. A rapprochement was clearly in their best interests and in April 1922 the two countries signed a treaty restoring diplomatic ties, waiving war reparations and embarking on a new era of economic cooperation.

The Treaty of Rapallo drove a coach and horses through the fragile post-war European settlement, but worse was to come when secret military codicils initialled a few weeks later in Berlin saw Germany's reactionary right-wing Prussian Junkers making common cause with the hated Bolsheviks. Rearmament could now start in earnest and a flight training school equipped with 50 Dutch-built Fokker fighters began operations at Lipetsk, a bleak Soviet airfield south of Moscow. A tank training school was opened at Kazan in Siberia, a chemical weapons factory was built at Chapayevsk in the Volga valley and German firm Junkers set up an aircraft factory at Fili on the outskirts of the Soviet capital.[25]

It was a start, but successful rearmament must be guided by accurate intelligence on the military amd industrial capabilities of friend and potential foe alike. Banned from any form of military intelligence organisation by the post-war peacemakers, the Reichswehrministerium had only been allowed to maintain a small counter-intelligence cell named Abwehr, an innocuous term that literally translates as 'Defence'. But they did have an established espionage proxy in the Deutscher Überseedienst, an organisation set up by German industrialists during the war to spread propaganda and carry out low level espionage against the Allies. Post-war, and with covert Reichswehr funding, the Überseedienst absorbed talented former officers, among them one Hermann Göring, and expanded its operations into military intelligence.[26]

The British were well aware of what the Germans were up to and had infiltrated an agent, Captain Kenneth Stott, into the Überseedienst. Abandoned into the Tranmere workhouse when his alcoholic Liverpool accountant father attempted suicide by walking into the Mersey in August 1896, Stott had subsequently emigrated to South Africa. There, according to a sternly disapproving MI5, 'he gave information to the Boers about the British and to the British about the Boers', during the Second Boer War. Serving in the King's Liverpool Regiment of the British Army during the First World War, he was wounded and commissioned. His medal card suggests that he cheekily asked for permission to wear the Boer Burger Medal in addition to his British decorations.[27]

Employed by the fanatically anti-communist Sir George Makgill's Industrial Intelligence Bureau, a privately funded right-wing organisation uncannily similar to the Überseedienst and closely linked to both MI5 and MI6, Stott and his young 'secretary', Esther Le Roy, made several visits to Europe and reported that Überseedienst agents were funding left-wing British politicians and trades unions to stir up industrial unrest, thus opening the door to German competitors. Clearly calculating that a touch of melodrama would add weight to his reports, he claimed to have deposited a list of German spies in Britain at his bank with instructions that, should anything untoward happen to him, it was to be passed to MI6.

Makgill passed Stott's reports to MI6 Head of Production Desmond Morton who seems, initially at least, to have taken them seriously. MI5 on the other hand found Stott 'a most dangerous individual', and dismissed his material as 'extraordinarily fantastic . . . valueless . . . entirely erroneous'. And MI5 were right to be sceptical; the Überseedienst's precious few British agents were ludicrously amateurish and none more so than former RAF officer and serial bigamist Vivian Stranders. Recruited by the Überseedienst in 1925 to steal British and French military technology, Stranders had inadvertently engaged a Sûreté de l'État belge agent as an accomplice and, by the time he was arrested in 1926, had unwittingly provided the British, French and Belgians with a more reassuringly accurate picture of Überseedienst activities than the overheated fantasies of Kenneth Stott. The unlamented Überseedienst was wound up in 1928.[28]

Abwehr had meanwhile expanded under the capable leadership of First World War intelligence veteran Major Friedrich Gempp and, despite still limited resources, now comprised two divisions, one looking east and the other west, each of which contained subdivisions Abwehr I (espionage), Abwehr II (signals intelligence) and Abwehr III (counter-espionage). Further expansion and reorganisation came when, in March 1928, just as the Überseedienst was closing down, Abwehr absorbed the small intelligence cell operated by the Reichsmarine, the contemporary name for the German Navy, and was itself transformed into an independent command directly responsible to the Reichswehrministerium.[29]

On paper at least, Abwehr now looked impressive with its three divisions, the Abwehr I espionage division being further divided into Eins Heer (IH) dealing with army espionage, Eins Marine (IM) dealing with naval espionage and Eins Luft (IL) dealing with air espionage. Abwehr II was now responsible for sabotage, Abwehr III retained responsibility for counter-espionage, the Amtsgruppe Ausland (Foreign) division collected largely open source material from overseas sources and the Zentrale (Z) division was responsible for administration and records. There was also an extensive network of Abwehrstellen out-stations (Ast for short) and Nebenstellen sub-stations (Nest for short) scattered across Germany's Wehrkreis military districts, most with their own army, naval and air intelligence desks. Prior to the outbreak of war in 1939 the whole labyrinthine structure was under the control of Oberkommando des Heeres, in other words the Wehrmacht high command as then still distinct from the Nazi Party machine.

There would be further growth, particularly following a 1938 overhaul and the outbreak of war the following year, yet the outcome of this rapid expansion was an organisation with too many roles across both espionage and counter-espionage. Its espionage priorities were muddled, its operations dogged by amateurish methodology and its agent recruitment woefully naïve. Restricted opportunities for promotion made Abwehr an unpopular posting for talented officers so its staff, many of them time-servers or Kaiser-era officers doggedly resistant to change, tended to be intellectually ill-equipped for the work they were doing. Its decentralised structure coupled with a lack of effective oversight meant that the growing network of Abwehrstellen and Nebenstellen were all too often running operations against the same intelligence targets.

In truth, Abwehr's spymasters, like their predecessors in the Überseedienst, were merely building on a tradition of failure set by Germany's First World War military intelligence service Abteilung IIIB, an organisation whose record is exemplified in the short, inglorious career of the Dutch stripper, prostitute and failed double agent Margaretha Zelle, better known as 'Mata Hari'.

As for Christopher Draper's spymaster the mysterious Degenhardt, he may have been Oberst Dr Ludwig Dischler, then a Hamburg-based Abwehr officer responsible for espionage in Britain. Dischler had first come to the notice of MI5 when, on 1 May 1930, he had stepped ashore at Southampton, England, unaware that, thanks to his part in a cack-handed attempt to burgle a French Sûreté safe, he was already on a watch list at British ports of entry. His efforts to appear inconspicuous on this and several subsequent visits to Britain were somewhat stymied by his wooden leg.[30]

Unlike the Master of Sempill and Norman Baillie-Stewart, Christopher Draper was neither obnoxious nor even particularly devious. His poor choice of friends and his flirtation with Nazism suggest naïvety, but he was really just a ham actor and inept con artist out to make a fast buck in the bleak years of the Depression. Vulnerable at a time when homosexuality was illegal, he at least had the sense to call a halt to his idiotic scheme to fleece Abwehr once the risks became clear.

Draper then operated as the first British double agent against the Nazis until, according to MI5, 'nothing of great interest came of this [case] and the matter lapsed completely'. In truth, without the cooperation of the Army, Royal Navy and Royal Air Force, MI5 simply ran out of a sufficiently credible mix of falsehoods and chicken-feed intelligence to keep Abwehr interested. The lessons of the Draper case were not forgotten, and when the British turned captured enemy agents against the Germans during the Second World War, the inter-service Twenty Committee, an unsubtle reference to both the Roman numeral XX for 20 and the expression double-cross, was formed to ensure a ready supply of plausible fabrications.[31]

Christopher Draper must have imagined that his foray into espionage had ended with a last letter from Hamburg in January 1934, but he could hardly have been more wrong. His career as a double agent was only just beginning and he would soon be drawn into an extraordinary international conspiracy that included, amongst others, an infamous New York Nazi, a drug-addicted US Army deserter, a treacherous Scottish hairdresser, a renegade French naval officer and anti-Nazi Hollywood movie stars.

Abwehr might have given up on Major Draper for the present, but now it had two new aviation spies waiting in the wings, one bound for Britain and the other for the United States. Both would become notorious in the months and years ahead, one languishing for years in British and Irish prisons, the other featuring in a best-selling book by a former FBI special agent. But first, Germany would shock the world with a graphic demonstration of the terrible fate that awaited its home-grown traitors.

Chapter 2

Executioner, do your duty!

He was engaged in building Experimental Scout Bombers
Curtiss Nos. 1 and 2 for the United States Navy.

FBI report on Abwehr spy Werner Gudenberg

In October 1933, just as the Draper case appeared to be fizzling out
in Britain, a prolific informant known only as 'Source L' handed
the French embassy in Berlin a copy of the first draft of the secret
German Flugzeug-Beschaffungsprogramm (Aircraft Procurement
Programme). While 'Source L' has never been identified, circumstantial evidence suggests that he or she was probably linked to 'Count'
Jerzy Sosnowski, a Polish spy who, posing as a wealthy aristocrat,
specialised in seducing Reichswehrministerium secretaries, secretly
photographing them in compromising positions, then blackmailing
them into stealing copies of secret Nazi documents. Sosnowski's
haul is believed to have included the aircraft procurement plan
handed to the French.

Betrayed by a Polish turncoat and a jealous lover, the cunning if
decidedly creepy Sosnowski was arrested in February 1934 and
exchanged for two Abwehr agents then being held in Poland. One of
the Polish spy's stooges, Reichswehrministerium secretary Irène von
Iéna, was jailed for life, but the Volksgerichtshof (People's Court) had
a very different fate in mind for his principal accomplice and lover,
glamorous Swiss-born Baroness Benita von Falkenhayn, and her friend,
32-year-old Reichswehrministerium typist Renate von Natzmer.[1]

Her face bleached white by terror, her wrists manacled and the
back of her head crudely shaved, Benita von Falkenhayn was led out

into a freezing courtyard in Berlin's Plötzensee Prison before dawn on 18 February 1935. As the prison bell tolled mournfully, State Prosecutor Paul Jorn intoned the death sentence, then turned to executioner Karl Gröpler and ordered, 'Scharfrichter, führen ihrer pflicht!' (Executioner, do your duty!) Two assistants grabbed the shivering Baroness and stretched her neck over a red-painted block while Gröpler, a bull-necked former horse butcher bizarrely decked out in evening dress, reached for an axe that had been chilled in a bucket of ice to stem the blood flow. Moments later, Benita's severed head lay in a pile of sand. The grisly slaughterhouse ritual was repeated a few minutes later when a terrified Renate von Natzmer was brought out for her date with Gröpler's ice-cold axe.[2]

The stolen Reichswehrministerium documents had cost two women their lives and another her liberty, yet much of what they had revealed came as no surprise to seasoned watchers, not least the British and French intelligence services. Nor had there been any shortage of press stories about Germany's clandestine rearmament, the British *Manchester Guardian* revealing the existence of the Junkers military aircraft factory near Moscow in December 1926, almost a decade before the Berlin beheadings. And what the Germans were up to in Russia was thrown into tragic focus in August 1930 when a young woman passenger threw herself out of a Lufthansa airliner flying over Kilianstädten north of Frankfurt. A farm labourer happened to look up on hearing the aircraft passing overhead and watched in mounting horror as the woman crashed to earth just yards away from him. It transpired that Elfriede Amlinger's husband had been killed in a flying accident at Lipetsk, the secret German training airfield south of Moscow and she had decided to join him in death.[3]

The reality was that, prior to 1933, there was no appetite in London, Paris or Washington for a confrontation with Germany over its flagrant breaches of the 1919 peace settlement. But the Flugzeug-Beschaffungsprogramm was a different matter as it detailed Nazi plans for an air force of 500 modern combat aircraft by October 1935 and more than 10,000 by the end of 1938. The sheer scale of what the Nazis were planning caused an almighty scare when the document reached Paris and the French announced an urgent expansion of their Armée de l'Air. But chronic political instability and the draining of defence budgets to fund the ill-conceived Maginot Line had reduced the Armée de l'Air to a toothless tiger. And, as a perceptive report prepared for the American State Department in 1933 revealed, the sclerotic, strike-ridden, endemically corrupt French aviation industry could never hope to come close to matching the German production figures.[4]

A copy of the Flugzeug-Beschaffungsprogramm was passed to London in the hope that it would spur the British into expanding the Royal Air Force. But the RAF had, like its French counterpart, been allowed to wither on the vine by naïve British politicians who, blithely ignoring the fact that most airliners of the time could be swiftly converted to military use, were suggesting that all military aviation could, and indeed should, be banned. Labour Party leader George Lansbury, a Christian pacifist, made no secret of that, were he to win power, he would close every recruiting station, disband the British Army, the Royal Navy and the Royal Air Force. Other equally well-meaning, albeit less doctrinaire, pacifists were pressuring the RAF to make its air show displays less overtly warlike; nice formation flying and pretty aerobatics were fine, but simulated air combat and pretending to drop bombs should never be shown.

The prevailing mood of pacifism and retrenchment was understandable with memories of the slaughter in Flanders still fresh and a search for financial savings was likewise understandable given the parlous state of the global economy. But both Europe and the Far East were becoming increasingly unstable and an April 1934 Cabinet memorandum laid bare the parlous state of Britain's air defences:

> Our present air strength is admittedly wholly inadequate for the requirements of Imperial security and we are still short of what was as long ago as 1923 regarded as the *minimum* number of squadrons required for home defence . . . we have disarmed to the edge of risk.[5]

The Flugzeug-Beschaffungsprogramm was actually, as RAF chiefs were quick to recognise, more wildly optimistic wish list than firm production plan. Yet it was still a clear statement of Nazi intent to form, in very short order, the world's most powerful air force and, on 26 February 1935, Hitler formally announced the creation of the Luftwaffe. Other sources, not least a senior Luftwaffe officer recruited in 1935 by MI6 Head of Station in Berlin Frank Foley and another officer code-named A.52 recruited in Zurich in 1934 by Czech Military Intelligence, confirmed what the Nazis were up to. Yet, despite the steady flow of top quality intelligence, the British Air Ministry chose to dismiss reports of Luftwaffe expansion with an absurd suggestion that MI6 was ill-qualified to report on technical matters. Later, in 1938, British Ambassador in Berlin Sir Nevile Henderson, a dedicated appeaser, would foolishly order Foley to drop the anti-Nazi Luftwaffe officer source for fear of causing a diplomatic incident.[6]

But the British, like the French, simply had to respond to the Flugzeug-Beschaffungsprogramm and, on 29 November 1933, just weeks after the stolen German document reached London, a Cabinet decision to expand the RAF by ten full squadrons was announced in the House of Commons. Ironically, by helping to stimulate the initially limited RAF expansion schemes that gave birth to the Hurricane and Spitfire fighters, Jerzy Sosnowski and his unfortunate accomplices may deserve some of the credit for helping to make an RAF victory in the 1940 Battle of Britain possible. Ironically, the RAF expansion partly set in train by the Flugzeug-Beschaffungsprogramm also made it a tempting target for German spies and, having given up on its last RAF spy Christopher Draper in January 1934, Abwehr needed a replacement. There was a short hiatus as Hitler had expressly forbidden German espionage in Britain to avoid embarrassment during the negotiations that led to the Anglo-German Naval Agreement of 18 June 1935, but permission was given for limited spying operations thereafter.[7]

A few British airmen, among them Christopher Draper, Oswald Mosley, Alliott Verdon-Roe of warplane builders Avro, and Charles Grey, editor of the influential magazine *The Aeroplane*, were openly pro-Nazi. An intensely narcissistic elite, these 'air-minded' men saw the birth of aviation as having ushered in a new machine age in which airmen, latter-day Nietzschean Übermenschen, would be dominant. Intense patriots first and Nazi fellow travellers second, few if any of these men would ever have considered treachery. Only the profoundly unsavoury Master of Sempill, promoter of Draper's *Aces of the Air* tour, Japanese spy and variously chairman and president of the Royal Aeronautical Society, was actively hawking British aviation technology to Junkers AB Flygindustri, a Swedish firm that he well knew was a front for the eponymous German warplane builder.[8]

So for their next aviation spy in Britain, Abwehr and the Luftwaffe would have to fall back on a suitably qualified German, ideally an experienced aviator who knew his way around the country. Yet, as Abwehr spymaster Kapitanleutnant Erich Pfeiffer would later recall, finding a suitably qualified agent was not going to be easy:

> The placing of agents in Britain itself was extremely difficult. The British were in a position to exercise a far more efficient system of supervision over all foreigners entering their island than is possible in the case of a country with a land frontier . . . The average Briton, too, views all foreigners with a measure of distrust, however polite he may be to them in his normal daily intercourse.[9]

Cometh the hour, though, cometh the man in the form of 44-year-old Hamburg lawyer and German air force veteran Hermann Görtz. Riding a small Zündapp motorcycle with his teenage girlfriend, Marianne Emig, perched on the pillion seat, Görtz landed at Southampton on the morning of 19 July 1935, a month after the spying ban in Britain was partially lifted. Telling immigration officers that he was a writer, that Marianne was his niece and secretary, he claimed that they would be staying at Queen Anne's Mansions, a large block of serviced apartments in central London. Görtz was lying; the pair had no intention of travelling to London, at least not yet. Instead they drove just a quarter of a mile into Southampton where they took a room at the Alliance Hotel, the first stop on a tour of southern England to spy on the Royal Air Force.[10]

Not exactly dedicated to their task, Görtz and Marianne whiled away the next two weeks swimming and sunbathing at Freshwater Bay on the Isle of Wight and Slapton in Devon. The weather that summer was perfect and it was, as Marianne would wistfully recall, 'a lovely trip'. The only espionage the pair had undertaken by the time they left Slapton on 8 August had been two pleasure boat trips, one to surreptitiously photograph the RAF flying boat base at Lee-on-Solent and the other to photograph the flying boat base at Mount Batten in Plymouth harbour.

Urgently needing something more substantial to show for their travels, Görtz and Marianne were taking a roundabout route across Dartmoor to RAF Westonzoyland in Somerset when a road accident necessitated an unwelcome visit to the police station at Launceston in Cornwall and a week-long delay while both the motorcycle and Görtz' teeth were repaired. Ironically, given what was to come, they chose to spend three nights of this enforced hiatus at the isolated Dartmoor village of Princetown, within sight of the grim walls of Dartmoor Prison.[11]

Expenditure on motorcycle repairs and dental treatment had made a sizeable dent in the cash that Görtz and Marianne were given before leaving Germany. So it was with a real sense of urgency that they left Launceston on 16 August. They visited Westonzoyland, stopped overnight at Shaftesbury in Dorset and crossed England to the Lion Hotel at Buckden in Cambridgeshire, a tiring journey of over 300 miles on a small, uncomfortable motorcycle. They snooped around RAF Wyton the next morning, then travelled on to Suffolk, took a room at the Bull Inn in Barton Mills and spent the next three days photographing and mapping the new RAF airfield at nearby Mildenhall.

Marianne was then installed in The Limes, a Mildenhall guest house, while Görtz set off alone to catch a ferry from Harwich to Rotterdam. Whether the sketches and 54 enlargements of photographs that Görtz handed over two days later in Berlin had any real intelligence value is debatable, but he returned to Mildenhall on 29 August armed with a letter of credit for £100, collected Marianne and set about fixing the positions of the RAF airfields at Duxford, Feltwell, Hunstanton and Bircham Newton by measuring distances from nearby towns.[12]

Travelling south to London, they bought the *Air Force List* at the Air Ministry bookshop on 5 September, cashed the letter of credit at Barclays Bank in Fenchurch Street later that same day and took a room for two nights at the Brent Bridge Hotel in Hendon. They photographed RAF Hendon on 6 September, watched the King's Cup air race at the De Havilland aircraft factory in Hatfield on Saturday, 7 September, and then, on 10 September, snooped around RAF Martlesham Heath, another expansion scheme airfield near Ipswich. Crossing south of the Thames to the Kent coast resort of Broadstairs on Wednesday, 11 September, Görtz and Marianne appeared at the office of letting agents Cockett Henderson, identified themselves as Dr Görtz of Mildenhall and his daughter, and asked about furnished houses to let in the area.[13]

Its beach packed with summer holidaymakers, Punch and Judy shows, donkey rides and ice-cream sellers, Broadstairs was well used to colourful visitors. Yet the motorcycling Germans in their leather coats, riding breeches and white flying helmets still managed to stand out like sore thumbs from the moment they arrived. Cockett Henderson clerk Percy Shelvey would later claim that he was immediately suspicious of the pair, telling a reporter that Görtz, who was 44 years old, reminded him of the recently deceased 85-year-old German President Paul von Hindenburg. 'He was tall and spoke in slightly broken English. I could tell immediately he was a German – there was a touch of Hindenburg about his appearance, though he was in plus-fours at the time. He was a man of aristocratic bearing.' Chief Clerk William Porter also thought Görtz and Marianne decidedly odd, but arranged for them to view a house in the town the following morning.

As 55-year-old Mrs Florence Johnson showed her prospective tenants round her neat bungalow, named 'Havelock' after one Victorian imperial hero, at 6 Stanley Road, a leafy street named after another, she too thought the German 'novelist' and his 'niece' rather strange. Perhaps she did notice Görtz' careless slip in introducing Marianne as his niece after telling Porter the previous day that she was his daughter, but she had been left in straitened circumstances by the death of her husband, Arthur, a former journalist and the town's entertainments manager, in August 1933. And the German motorcyclists were welcome late season tenants who, when all said and done, paid six weeks' rent in cash, in advance.

Görtz and Marianne had moved their operations from Mildenhall to Broadstairs so they could visit front-line fighter bases like Hornchurch, Hawkinge, Biggin Hill and Eastchurch that would, five years later, become synonymous with the Battle of Britain. Görtz would later recall an afternoon early in October when he and Marianne visited RAF Manston, five miles from Broadstairs and then one of the five most important military airfields in Britain. They crossed the airfield by the public road and drew up next to a bus stop at Pouce's Farm crossroads:

There were two or three of the smaller machines on the aerodrome, they were starting and landing. The hangar which is situated near the crossroads was open. When we reached the crossroads, one or two machines were just brought into this hangar. There was only one machine in the air. As this machine was strongly banking, I was fond of watching it . . . Having watched for a little while the flying, I felt a little uneasy as some airmen were looking at me and Miss Emig, so I went with her to the airmen on duty on the fire car and said, according to the best of my recollection, 'I am a German,' or, 'I am a foreigner. Am I allowed to stay here and watch the flying?' The airman answered (I cannot recollect the exact words) 'Stay on the road.' Then I asked again, 'I am a sort of journalist. May I make some notes?' and he answered that on the road I could do what I liked. After this answer I went back to my bicycle on the road and made a provisional sketch. Whilst I was doing this, the last plane came down, run to the hangar and the pilot stepped out. It was an officer according to my recollection, a tall blonde [sic] man, he might have been a little over 20, he had one ring on his sleeve and long trousers . . . A few days after I had made the sketch I improved it at home.[14]

The German pair were actually watching some of the last silver-winged biplanes in RAF service, Hawker Audax light bombers of No. 2 Squadron. Beautiful but hopelessly obsolete, the Audax was nevertheless a winged greyhound when compared to the ancient and utterly useless Vickers Virginia biplane bombers of 500 Squadron lined up on the other side of the airfield. Indicative only of the woeful state of the RAF's front line strength in 1935, the Audax and the Virginia were, thanks in part to the Flugzeug-Beschaffungsprogramm, destined for the scrapheap.

Yet, as Görtz got busy with his sketch pad that autumn afternoon, secure in the knowledge that the lovely Marianne would distract any curious airmen, the spying game must have seemed thoroughly enjoyable. Here he was on an all-expenses-paid holiday with his teenage mistress and, unlike in Germany where anyone caught sketching a military airfield would have found themselves on the wrong end of a most unfriendly Gestapo interrogation, spying on airfields in Britain seemed simplicity itself. Little did he know that, as Marianne drove him back to Broadstairs that evening, his nemesis was already at hand. And she would turn out to be that most thoroughly British institution, a nosey seaside landlady.[15]

* * *

Görtz and Marianne might have been wasting both their time, and Abwehr's cash, spying on rusting relics at a British airfield about which the Luftwaffe already knew all it needed to know, but in Germany the Nazis were discovering that there is much more to creating an air force than simply ordering large numbers of aircraft. Even coming close to meeting the ambitious targets set out in the Flugzeug-Beschaffungsprogramm was going to involve recruiting and training thousands of personnel, building dozens of new airfields and radically overhauling their small aviation industry. It would also involve obtaining, by fair means or foul, the latest aviation technology from the country with the world's most advanced aviation industry.

Most British and French passenger aircraft were still canvas-covered biplanes, but American stunt pilots were barnstorming from state to state, air racing was fast becoming a national sport, crop dusters were transforming agriculture and a line of aviation beacons stretched for 2,000 miles along the mail-plane route from Chicago to Salt Lake City. More importantly, while American military aviation was weak and chronically under-resourced, the latest Boeing and Douglas civil airliners were fast, all-metal monoplanes with retractable undercarriages, precisely the technology that the new Luftwaffe needed. It was also ripe for the picking as spies would easily merge into the vast German-American diaspora and wartime German air veterans who had migrated to work in American aviation would, Abwehr reasoned, be only too eager to become informants. Better still, security in American aircraft factories was all but non-existent.

Towards the end of 1934, Oberst Friedrich Busch of Abwehr's Abw.1 air intelligence division asked Kapitänleutnant Erich Pfeiffer at Abwehr's Wilhemshaven Nebenstelle out-station if a courier Pfeiffer was running aboard a transatlantic liner could collect material from an agent who was about to leave on a mission to spy on American aviation. This came as a surprise as Pfeiffer had only recently been barred from infiltrating agents into the United States for fear of causing diplomatic embarrassment. Yet now Busch was assuring him that Berlin was 'vitally interested' in any secrets that their new spy, Wilhelm Lonkowski, could steal from American warplane manufacturers . . . although, of course, the ban on spying in the United States still applied. Absurd double-talk such as this was entirely typical of Abwehr, but Pfeiffer was able to tell Busch that he actually had two suitable couriers; Karl Schlüter, a steward and zealous Ortsgruppenleiter (head of the Nazi Party cell) on the Norddeutsche-Lloyd Atlantic liner *Europa*, and Carl Eitel, a wine waiter on the *Europa's* sister ship, *Bremen*.[16]

Wilhelm Lonkowski must have seemed an ideal recruit to spy on American aviation when he left Hamburg aboard the liner

Deutschland on 10 January 1935. He had served in the German air force during the First World War, he was an ardent Nazi and he had already spent a year working for the Ireland Aircraft Co. at Roosevelt Field, Long Island, in 1929. Landing at New York on 18 January 1935 and posing as a piano tuner, he quickly established himself and his wife, Auguste, in a rented apartment in Hempstead, Long Island, and got to work. Lonkowski was soon a familiar face in bars used by engineers from the nearby aircraft factories who never guessed that the boozy, garrulous aviation enthusiast who gave his name as Willi Lonkis, William Meller or William Sexton was actually a German spy fishing for intelligence.[17]

Pfeiffer's couriers were soon bringing back packages from New York, but Abwehr's new star agent in the United States was also an enthusiastic alcoholic armed with a $500 monthly expense account. Auguste 'Gunny' Lonkowski was every bit as fond of the bottle as her husband and soon befriended German-born Senta Dewanger, the proprietor of the Clinton Wine Shop on the corner of Clinton Street and Van Cott Avenue in Hempstead. When Senta said that she was thinking of moving as her house was far too large for one person living alone, Gunny immediately suggested that she and Willi could rent two of her spare rooms. After all, Gunny continued, they were now such firm friends and her piano tuner husband Willi 'was ill with stomach ulcers and did not have long to live', so it would suit everyone. Stomach ulcers are rarely fatal, even when aggravated by excessive alcohol intake, but Senta agreed and, thinking the couple had little money, let them have the rooms for $20 a month.

One of Lonkowski's favoured ruses was to don a smart suit, rent a room at the Hotel St George in Brooklyn and pose as a businessman interviewing candidates for vague but well-paid jobs in German aviation. Engineer Fred Backhus quickly saw through the scam, realising that the generous salary he was being offered depended on him divulging everything he had learned about automatic pilots while working for Sperry Gyroscope. Backhus made his excuses and left. Others whom Lonkowski attempted to recruit included John Kögel, a foreman with the Kollmorgen Optical Corporation in Brooklyn and Johannes Steuer, a former colleague of Backhus' at Sperry Gyroscope in Brooklyn.

Lonkowski also renewed contact with Otto Voss, an aircraft mechanic he had first met during his earlier spell in the United States. Voss had served as a combat engineer in the German Army and had run a garage business in Hamburg before emigrating to the United States in October 1928 and getting a job alongside Lonkowski at Ireland Aviation. Tall, gaunt, humourless and, despite thinning hair, prone to dandruff, he had drifted through a succession of short-lived jobs until, on 2 January 1935, he started work as a steel fitting mechanic at the Seversky Aircraft factory in Farmingdale, Long Island. For the first three weeks or so, Voss did not impress his new employers; he was a loner and showed little interest in his work. Then his old friend Wilhelm Lonkowski returned from Germany and Voss suddenly started taking blueprints home to work on at night. Delighted Seversky bosses were, of course, unaware that their newly conscientious mechanic was actually taking the drawings to Lonkowski who was photographing them, then passing the negatives to Erich Pfeiffer's couriers.[18]

Werner Gudenberg, another acquaintance from Lonkowski's earlier time in the United States, had emigrated on the same ship as Voss from Hamburg in October 1928 and had found work at Ireland Aviation. Considerably smarter than either Lonkowski or Voss, by 1935 he was a foreman at the Curtiss-Wright aircraft factory in Buffalo and, with a pretty American-born wife, an infant daughter and a colonial style house on Victoria Boulevard. Gudenberg was living the American dream, a dream that would be shattered that August by the arrival of three uninvited guests in the form of Lonkowski, his wife Gunny and her sister, Elizabeth Beck. Lonkowski explained that he was taking his wife and sister-in-law for a short holiday at Elmira, Mark Twain's summer retreat in Chemung County, and that their old friend Otto Voss had given him Gudenberg's address and suggested that he pay a visit. Accepting the offer of a beer, Lonkowski wasted no time in coming to the point; would Gudenberg, as a good German, smuggle aircraft blueprints out of the Curtiss-Wright factory to be photographed?[19]

Nothing, Lonkowski sought to reassure his reluctant host, could possibly go wrong as he would deliver the photographs personally to couriers, stewards named Schlüter and Eitel aboard German liners who took them straight back to Kapitänleutnant Pfeiffer in Bremen. Gudenberg was later at pains to convince the FBI that he had wanted nothing to do with Lonkowski's scheming, but the spy tried to ease his misgivings by claiming that Voss

> had been furnishing him with some information; that he also had a man in Connecticut and another man in Long Island who were furnishing him with information concerning the details of plane construction . . . Lonkowski advised him that Germany has not build [sic] many military planes and was therefore badly in need of information with respect to the type of planes America was building.

Gudenberg's reluctance was gradually worn down as the beer flowed and the questions grew more insistent. How fast could Curtiss warplanes fly? How high could they fly? What armament did they carry? Where were the guns fitted? What was their range? How many were being built? Almost before he knew it, Gudenberg was telling Lonkowski everything he knew about the experimental XSBC-1 and XSBC-2 carrier-based fighters that Curtiss were developing for the US Navy. Then Lonkowski asked what was in a briefcase lying against the living room wall and Gudenberg admitted that it held Curtiss blueprints. Later that night, once everyone else had gone to bed, Lonkowski got busy with his camera. Eager to impress Abwehr with his latest coup, before leaving Buffalo for Elvira the next morning Lonkowski mailed the undeveloped film of Gudenberg's blueprints to Senta Dewanger, his Long Island land-lady, with instructions that she was to deliver it to one Karl Schlüter, a steward on the *Europa*.[20]

Senta had by then realised that her tenants were spending a lot more money than a piano tuner could ever earn, especially one who seemed to do little or no actual piano tuning. They had installed a telephone, they had bought a car, they had set up photographic equipment in a locked upstairs room and they were throwing frequent boozy parties for aviation acquaintances from the nearby Roosevelt and Mitchel fields. And then there were the odd visitors like surly ship's steward Karl Schlüter, gloomy, bespectacled Otto Voss and Lonkowski's oddly dedicated physician, Dr Ignatz Griebl, who insisted on making regular house calls on an ulcer patient perfectly capable of driving to his office. Senta later told the FBI that her curiosity finally got the better of her as she and Auguste were working their way down a bottle of gin one evening before the Lonkowskis left to visit Gudenberg. She asked where all the money was coming from and Gunny drunkenly blurted out that her Wilhelm was no piano tuner. No, she slurred, he was an important man who was being paid by the government. 'Which government?' Senta asked. 'Why,' Gunny replied, 'the German government, of course.'

No worse than her husband's inebriated blabbing to Gudenberg about Abwehr's transatlantic courier system, Gunny's drunken boast was still potentially catastrophic as she had exposed her husband to an American citizen whose discretion could not be counted on. A furious Lonkowski warned Senta of the dire consequences for her family back in Germany should she breathe a word of what his wife had said. From now on, he continued menacingly, if she knew what was good for her she would do whatever he asked, immediately and without question.

Senta was no shrinking violet, but this was just six months after Benita von Falkenhayn and Renate von Natzmer had been beheaded in Berlin, six months in which the press had been printing yet more horrifying accounts of the fate of those, Americans included, who had fallen foul of the Nazi regime. And Lonkowski's threats were still ringing in Senta's ears when the package with the film of Gudenberg's blueprints arrived from Buffalo, so she drove straight to Manhattan, boarded the *Europa* and, on finding that Schlüter was not aboard, left it with the purser who promised to pass it on. Lonkowski flew into a rage when she told him what she had done, but calmed down when Schlüter called to say he had received the package safely.[21]

Early in September 1935, in the same week that Hermann Görtz and Marianne Emig were visiting airfields around London, Wilhelm Lonkowski was busy with his camera, photographing yet more blueprints of the US Navy's XSBC-2 scout bomber smuggled out of the Curtiss factory in Buffalo by Gudenberg. This time, however, he was taking no chances with the handover to Pfeiffer's courier and, late on Friday, 27 September 1935, customs guard Morris Josephs spotted a shifty-looking man with a violin case in conversation with a steward from the *Europa* on Pier 86 in the North River. The steward, actually Karl Schlüter, slipped back aboard the ship as soon as he saw the customs guard approaching, but Josephs was able to intercept the other man and demanded that he hand over the violin case to be searched for what he suspected were smuggled drugs.

The violin case turned out to be empty apart from seven photographic negatives and some letters written mostly in German. Still suspicious, Josephs turned his protesting captive over to his supervisor, John Roberts, who spotted English phrases like 'single strut, fully streamlined landing gear' in the letters and called in Major Stanley Grogan of US Army Intelligence. The two men could get nothing out of their prisoner beyond an endlessly repeated refrain that he was William Lonkowski, an innocent piano tuner from Long Island, who was freelancing a few articles for a German aviation magazine. Unable to make out what was on the negatives and unsure whether there was anything sinister about the letters, Grogan and Roberts decided to let their piano tuner go, though not before they had extracted a promise that he would return for questioning on Monday. Meanwhile, if Mr Lonkowski didn't mind, they would hold on to the negatives and letters.

Hurrying across Manhattan that Saturday morning, Lonkowski knew that Grogan might at any moment realise that the negatives were images of Gudenberg's Curtiss-Wright blueprints, or that the letters were reports from Otto Voss on Seversky seaplane floats, hydraulic pumps, landplane undercarriages and gun sights. Whatever happened, he also knew that not showing up for the Monday interview with Josephs and Grogan would almost certainly lead to a Federal arrest warrant, so he had at best three days to get himself and Auguste out of the country. What he needed now was someone with the right contacts, someone who had arranged this sort of thing before, so he drove straight to Dr Ignatz Griebl's Upper East Side apartment.

A notorious German-American Nazi and one of Lonkowski's regular visitors at Lincoln Boulevard, back in 1933 Griebl had successfully smuggled Nazi agitator Heinz Spanknöbel, a fugitive from a Federal arrest warrant, aboard a German liner. This time, however, Griebl realised that sneaking Lonkowski and his wife aboard the *Europa*, which was due to sail that same evening for Germany, would have risked bumping into Josephs or Roberts again. Otherwise, the nearest safety lay 300 miles away across the Canadian border, but travelling there by rail would mean running the risk of being trapped aboard a train with Federal Agents in hot pursuit. Crossing the border by road – although less risky than travelling by train – would also be fraught with danger, so it seemed that the safest option would be for Lonkowski to bribe one of his Long Island aviation contacts to fly him and Gunny north along one of the booze-smuggling routes used during the Prohibition era. Decision made, Lonkowski called his wife to tell her of the escape plan.

Back at Lincoln Boulevard, Gunny Lonkowski had been sobbing hysterically that her Wilhelm had not returned from visiting a friend aboard the *Europa* and must be in some kind of trouble. Then she took the call from Dr Griebl's office and rushed out of the house telling Senta Dewanger that she had to 'collect some things from the bank'. Returning a short while later and hurriedly packing a case, Gunny offered Senta a wad of cash, which Senta refused to have anything to do with, then left, calling over her shoulder as she hurried away that she was going to her sister's in the Bronx.

A 'very nervous and excited' Lonkowski turned up at the Lincoln Boulevard house about an hour later and, claiming that he had been arrested while trying to get aboard the *Europa* but had managed to talk his way out of trouble, rushed around the house constantly repeating, 'Now I've got to get out of here,' as he destroyed papers, packed another case and drove off in the direction of Roosevelt Field. Senta was at work later that morning when a breathless Lonkowski burst into at the Clinton Wine Shop and asked her to look after $1,000, doubtless cash that his aviation contacts had turned down on smelling the large rat lurking behind the hasty flight plan. The spy then drove away and Senta never saw either of the Lonkowskis again.[22]

Now the only viable escape route was by road, but they dare not try to cross the border in Lonkowski's car and Griebl could hardly drive them to Canada as his well-known involvement in the Spanknöbel episode would make him a prime suspect in any escape plan. What they needed now was a hideout, somewhere well away from New York City where the Lonkowskis could hole up while Griebl made more discreet arrangements. That same night he drove the fugitives two hours north to his holiday retreat, an isolated cottage near the village of Tompkins Corners in Putnam County, then hurried back to New York before dawn lest his absence should excite suspicion.

Late on Sunday, 29 September 1935, after two tense days in which the fugitives had not dared to turn on a light, Griebl associate Ullrich Haussmann collected the pair from Tompkins Corners and sped through the night up Route 9, across the Canadian border at Champlain and on to Montreal. From there, with Erich Pfeiffer's help, they arranged passage home on a German ship. In New York, when Lonkowski failed to turn up for the Monday interview, the negatives and letters that Morris Josephs had found in the violin case were filed away and forgotten. They would resurface three years later as evidence in one of America's first spy trials since the First World War.[23]

Chapter 3

The Bungalow Brunette

Big English aeroplanes are flying around. The English
are flying busily. In a week our work will be finished.
We will then go to Berlin. At present we are writing a
big report. Much depends on it.

Hermann Görtz, 1935

Abwehr's aviation spy in the United States might have managed
to exfiltrate himself in the nick of time, but Hermann Görtz, their
aviation spy in Britain, would not be so fortunate. At first, his
counter-intuitive ruse of gathering aviation intelligence openly with
Marianne Emig as an alluring distraction for the curious seemed
to be working. But on Thursday, 24 October, Görtz' Broadstairs
landlady, Florence Johnson, called round to tend her garden at
'Havelock' and found the house apparently abandoned; the back
door unlocked, the side gate and garden shed left wide open, a set
of overalls lying on the ground outside the shed and a full milk
bottle on the doorstep. Adding to the air of mystery, Görtz had sent
her a telegram that read, 'Two days for Germany. Back Saturday.
Take care of my combination and photo.' What her tenant meant
by 'combination' and 'photo' was not immediately obvious, but a
postcard that arrived the next day from Ostend seemed to make
things a little clearer.

I had on account of news I received to hurry to Germany.
I will be back on Saturday to deliver you your home, clean
and in order. I left my bicycle combination behind the door

of the little house. Please take care of it. Sincerely yours, Hermann Görtz.[1]

Mrs Johnson would later claim that, as she hung the overalls up in the shed, she just happened to notice a small camera in one of the pockets. This, she thought, might explain the 'photo' in Görtz' telegram. But the Zündapp motorcycle she assumed he meant by 'bicycle combination' was nowhere to be seen and, thinking it stolen, she hurried off to tell William Porter, chief clerk at her letting agents Cockett Henderson.

Whether Florence Johnson really did notice the camera accidentally or simply rifled her tenant's pockets is open to question, but Porter had been suspicious of the Germans at 'Havelock' from the moment they arrived. After all, Norman Baillie-Stewart was still generating headlines from Maidstone jail, his girlfriend Marie-Louise was still an enigma, and the terrible fate of Jerzy Sosnowski's accomplices was every bit as fresh in the minds of British newspaper readers as it had been in the mind of Senta Dewanger. And now Mrs Johnson's tale of an abandoned house, a cryptic telegram, a missing motorcycle and a miniature camera seemed to confirm his worst fears. Porter decided to inspect 'Havelock' the following day and asked a policeman friend, Detective Constable Fred Smith, to accompany him. Smith led the way in via the still unlocked back door and

> In the front bedroom I found a cabin trunk, a suitcase, a ladies suitcase and an attaché case. In the drawing room, I found a large number of papers, all written or typewritten in German, in the bureau a German typewriter and a number of books. In the lodge at the back of the house I found a boiler suit in the pocket of which was a small but efficient German camera, and a Royal Air Force stick as carried by air force ratings. Mrs Johnston [sic] informed me that she had found the boiler suit lying in the yard and had placed it in the lodge. I examined the telegram and postcard and found that Görtz referred to the cycle-combination, which

I took to refer to the motorcycle. He also stated on the postcard that he would be returning that day. In consequence of this, I made arrangements with Mrs Johnston to notify me when Görtz returned as I intended to interview him ostensibly in connection with his registration under the aliens order.[2]

An experienced 29-year-old detective with three commendations, Smith's suspicions had been well and truly aroused. And when Görtz and Marianne had still not returned to Broadstairs by the following Wednesday he decided to take a closer look at Mrs Johnson's bungalow.[3]

I visited 'Havelock' on the evening of 30th October 1935 and obtained possession of a number of papers from the attaché case. I showed these papers to Mr Bradley of Alexander House School, Broadstairs. Nothing was found that would indicate any subversive activities on the part of Görtz. It was found, however, that Görtz was an officer in the German Air Force Reserve . . . I made a further search . . . A writing pad was found in which was contained a copy of a letter written by the young woman to an Aircraftsman named Kenneth Lewis who was stationed at the School of Naval Cooperation, Royal Air Force, Lee on Solent. This man's mother, Mrs Lewis, lives at St Nicholas, Carlton Avenue, Broadstairs, only a short distance from 'Havelock'.[4]

Returning to 'Havelock' the next morning, Smith found a hand-drawn map showing RAF airfields across southern England and an unfinished letter in which Görtz told his estranged wife that he was working for the Nachrichtendienst (Intelligence Service). There was also a letter from a Dr Heinrich Röhl in Hamburg telling Görtz that, as his legal practice had collapsed along with his marriage, his licence to practise was about to be withdrawn. If he was to avoid this, Röhl continued, 'It would perhaps be necessary to tell the Faculty of Solicitors the unvarnished truth and inform them about your activities in England.' This, together with the miniature camera and the link to Aircraftsman Kenneth Lewis, was enough to bring MI5 officer Tommy Robertson hurrying to Broadstairs the next morning, Saturday, 2 November.[5]

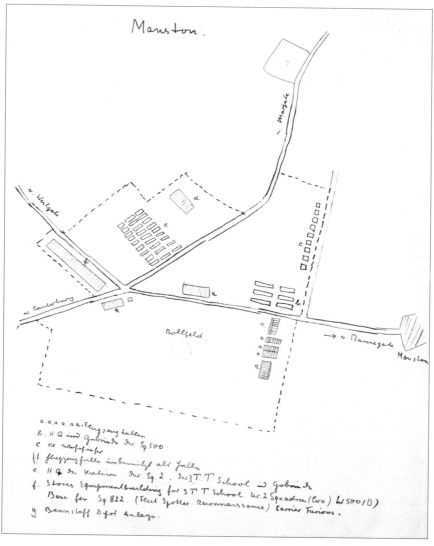

The sketch of RAF Manston found among Hermann Görtz' belongings in the Broadstairs bungalow (National Archives)

Smith and Robertson, a recent MI5 recruit known to colleagues as 'Tar' after his initials, broke open the locked trunk in the front bedroom and found a September 1935 *Air Force List*, an RAF diary, newspaper cuttings about the RAF, a copy of *The Air Pilot, Great Britain and Ireland* and a hand-drawn plan of Manston airfield carefully annotated to show bomb dumps, fuel stores and other vulnerable installations. The Manston plan was the only truly incriminating evidence found thus far, but there was also a sheaf of hotel bills that revealed Görtz' movements around southern England and a letter from the Berlin merchant named Otto Suhr who had transferred the £100 to London for Görtz. Robertson was in no doubt that 'this was undoubtedly a case of espionage and that . . . the case should be submitted to the Director of Public Prosecutions in order to find out whether he was willing to proceed with a charge under the Official Secrets Acts.'[6]

Broadstairs was a small town where, particularly outside the holiday season, everyone knew everyone else's business and the strange goings-on in Stanley Road were soon the subject of feverish local speculation. Some were suggesting that Florence Johnson's German tenants had come to Broadstairs to meet Dr Arthur Tester, a notorious fascist and fraudster who, funded by Nazi propaganda chief Joseph Goebbels, lived in some style in a clifftop mansion north of the town. Others were pointing the finger of suspicion at Josephine Lewis, the half-German divorcée who lived at the top of Carlton Avenue, just yards from the Stanley Road bungalow and whose 21-year-old son Kenneth was the RAF aircraftsman referred to in Constable Smith's report of his findings at 'Havelock'. So it was an understandably furious Josephine Lewis who confronted Florence Johnson in the street outside 'Havelock' on Wednesday, 6 November, four days after Robertson's visit, and loudly accused her of introducing her son to a German spy. Waving a letter from Kenneth and a postcard from Marianne in Mrs Johnson's face, Josephine yelled that she had written to her son that very morning warning him to steer clear of Marianne as she was a spy.[7]

Rapidly becoming accustomed to the role of housewife-spy-catcher, Florence Johnson snatched Kenneth's letter and Marianne's postcard from Josephine's hand and, assuring her that she would return it later, scurried off into 'Havelock'. Slamming the door in a speechless Josephine's face, she handed the letter to Constable Robert Clayton who was on duty in the house in case Görtz and Marianne sidestepped the arrest warrants waiting for them at British ports and airports. Reading that Kenneth was promising to send Marianne 'tons of photographs of aeroplanes and the camp', Clayton, a 26-year-old former Royal Marine, realised this was vital evidence that must be photographed before Josephine realised just how incriminating it was and destroyed it. There was no telephone in 'Havelock' so, telling Florence Johnson to let nobody, especially Josephine Lewis, in while he was away, the policeman left unobtrusively by the lane at the back of the house and hurried off to Broadstairs Police Station.

Returning to the Stanley Road kitchen less than an hour later, Clayton discovered that Josephine had beaten him to it, screaming hysterical abuse through the letter box until Florence Johnson simply had to let her in and keep her talking until the policeman arrived with the letter and postcard. It turned out that Josephine had been reduced to tears by a neighbour, retired army officer Captain John Rogers, who was putting it about that the Broadstairs drama was another Baillie-Stewart case with Marianne in the Marie-Louise role and 'that German woman's' son Kenneth as the traitor. 'My son has sent photographs,' Josephine wailed, 'and my gentleman lodger has said he was a silly boy to do so and has advised me to write and tell Kenneth to cease correspondence with them.' Wrapped up in her self-pity, Josephine failed to notice Clayton surreptitiously passing Kenneth's newly photographed letter to Florence Johnson who, again thinking on her feet, went into another room then reappeared with it in her hand as though it had been in there all the time.

As the drama played out in the kitchen at Stanley Road, back at Broadstairs Police Station Superintendent James Stuchfield was reading Kenneth Lewis' letter over the phone to Edward Hinchley Cooke at MI5 and passing on the information that, in a letter posted that very morning, Josephine had told her son to avoid Marianne as she was a spy. If MI5 wanted Görtz and Marianne to return so they could be arrested, Stuchfield pointed out, the last thing they needed was for the German pair to be tipped off by a lovesick Kenneth Lewis. Hinchley Cooke acted fast and Josephine's letter was intercepted that same evening at a sorting office in Redhill, Surrey.[8]

Aircraftsman Kenneth Lewis remained blissfully unaware of the storm brewing around him until he was frogmarched into the guardroom at RAF Lee-on-Solent the following morning and confronted by the RAF Provost Marshal, Squadron Leader Frederic Stammers, and a Major Hinchley Cooke who had a vague job in the War Office. Informed that his girlfriend was a German spy and invited to make a statement, a deeply shocked Lewis told Hinchley Cooke 'that he was perfectly prepared to tell us all he knew . . . he was quite prepared to assist in any way he could and if necessary to write letters to Emig under our instructions until she returns to this country'. Handing over two letters that Marianne had sent him and a photograph of her seated on the Zündapp motorcycle, he then launched into his tale.

It had started, he claimed, one Saturday afternoon towards the end of September 1935. He was home on leave and tinkering with his broken-down motorcycle near the bottom of Crow Hill in Broadstairs when a beautiful girl motorcyclist stopped and, in an intriguing foreign accent, offered to help. He was instantly smitten by this vision of loveliness dressed in brown leather boots, yellow breeches, green pullover, white scarf and white flying helmet astride one of the latest Zündapp machines, and

> After some conversation about the motorcycle, she said, 'I have seen you before. You live at the top of Carlton Avenue.' She told me she lived at Havelock bungalow. I had to push my motorcycle up the hill and, although her engine was going, she also pushed her machine up the hill by my side . . . at her gate she asked that I meet her again the following evening, Sunday. I agreed to this.
>
> I met her by appointment the following evening as arranged by the Clocktower on the Front at Broadstairs. We went for a walk, I was in mufti [civilian clothes] and she was

in female attire. The conversation [was] about motorcycles. I met her about eight o'clock when it was dark. I saw her nearly every day, but always in the evening after dark. During that week, she did not mention Air Force matters at all.

And it was during one of these nocturnal seaside strolls, Lewis claimed, that Marianne had invited to him to tea at 'Havelock' on his next weekend leave. He had duly arrived at the house at 5.30 pm on Saturday, 19 October, and

A man who I was given to understand was her uncle met me at the door, he was very friendly and very gushing. We sat down and started tea, within ten minutes he was talking very freely about the German Air Force and his experience as a German war pilot, working the conversation round to the Royal Air Force. He told me that he had been attached to Captain Goering's squadron. He told me that they had wireless controlled airplanes in Germany similar to our Queen Bee. During the conversation Miss Emig told me that they had been out in a motor boat on the Solent from the Isle of Wight, while they were staying at Ryde, and had watched the flying boats.

It was during this conversation at tea time that she first mentioned Manston, showing great interest in the station. I was rather amazed at her knowledge of the station, for instance she told me that there were underground hangars there, this I did not know myself and thought that it was rather a fantastic story. She knew all about Manston, the squadrons that were stationed there, the fact that 500 was an Auxiliary Squadron and that the Drivers Petrol [sic] were trained there. She rather sneered at the Vickers Virginia which she called large night bombers, she thought they were very slow and had too big a wing surface. It was during this conversation that she told me she was a girl glider pilot in Germany and was very much interested in aviation.

During the talk she asked me if I could get another fourteen days leave and go over with her to Hamburg. I told her that I could not afford it and moreover that I should have to mind my 'p's and 'q's over there on account of present conditions in Germany. She told me that possibly she could help me financially . . . She then went on to talk about the Countess and the girls in the German War Office who had been executed for spying, saying they thoroughly deserved their fate. She made me feel very much happier about Germany and said, 'You must remember that in the next war Germany and England will be on the same side.'[9]

His virginal head turned by a tantalising invitation to stay with Marianne when she came over to London for the International Motorcycle Show in November, it never occurred to Lewis that he was being duped, not even when she insisted that he write to her regularly in Germany, but only on RAF headed stationery. He must also, she told him, immediately destroy any letters he might receive from her. Alarm bells still failed to ring when Marianne wrote from Berlin a few days later asking for photographs of RAF Lee-on-Solent and, even as Tommy Robertson and Fred Smith were sifting through his beloved Marianne's luggage at 'Havelock', he dutifully sent off four picture postcards of the base. Later, in a letter that got no further than the mail room at RAF Lee-on-Solent before it was redirected to MI5, he excitedly told his mother that Marianne had offered to pay for him to spend his Christmas leave with her in Germany. 'There is one thing my friend Marianne has impressed,' he wrote, 'that any time I am short of money I have only to let her know and she will forward.'

That same evening, as Hinchley Cooke and Stammers finished their interrogation of Lewis and a police officer waited in the darkened Broadstairs bungalow for the spy and his accomplice to return, Hermann Görtz boarded a North Sea ferry at Rotterdam. Alone this time and unaware of the unfolding drama in Broadstairs, he stepped ashore in Harwich at eight o'clock the next morning, Friday, 8 November, and handed immigration officer Robert McKenna his landing card. Looking over McKenna's shoulder, Special Branch Constable Albert Coleman immediately recognised the name on the card and called over Sergeant Charles Allen who confronted Görtz saying, 'A warrant is in existence and you will be detained pending the arrival of the officers executing the warrant.' Visibly shocked, as he was being led away Görtz could only splutter, 'What is it for? I have done nothing.'[10]

***

MI5 and the police had spent the two weeks since Florence Johnson's discoveries building up a picture of Görtz' and Marianne's activities from documents found in the Broadstairs bungalow, evidence if nothing else of either a staggering level of incompetence or a naïve belief that they could get away with espionage by being open about what they were doing. Of particular interest were four subtly differing versions of Görtz' *lebenslauf*, or curriculum vitae, which revealed that he was the son of a Lübeck lawyer, that he had been born in 1890 and that he had studied international law and languages at Edinburgh, Paris, Heidelberg and Kiel before volunteering for the German Army on the outbreak of war in 1914.

Badly wounded while fighting on the Eastern Front, he had been transferred to less arduous duty as an air photography specialist and had flown on air operations far behind Russian lines, dangerous missions that had earned him an Iron Cross first class. But the strain of long hours over enemy territory had taken its toll and, following another long spell in hospital, he had been posted to the Western Front in 1918 as an intelligence officer responsible for interrogating captured Allied aircrew. Later, he would boast that Allied airmen had been particularly warned to be on their guard should they find themselves being questioned by him:

> The enemy had heard of my methods of interrogation from an American officer who had been interrogated by me but later escaped from a German prison camp. On two American officers who were shot down I found warnings, describing me as an especially dangerous intelligence officer . . . [11]

Post-war, Görtz had served in a right-wing paramilitary unit fighting Bolshevik revolutionaries in Lübeck and worked as a commercial lawyer in Lübeck and Bremen until the collapse of the German economy in the mid-1920s forced a move to the United States. He had practised law in New York and Chicago for two years before returning to his wife, Ellen, and their three children in Hamburg in 1928. He was then retained as junior counsel for the vast Siemens-Halske industrial corporation in a complex legal case being heard in London. The Siemens-Halske case had dragged on for three years only to be lost and the senior counsel with whom he had been working had defrauded Görtz of his 150,000 reichsmark fee, a financial blow that led to the collapse of both his marriage and his legal practice. Determined to stave off bankruptcy, he had even travelled to the Canary Islands in 1933 to track down a witness who could help recover his fees. This proved a wasted journey that only added to his financial woes.[12]

The Broadstairs document cache also revealed that Görtz had been planning an escape from his creditors since the Nazi Party, which he had joined in 1928, had been ushered into power in 1933. Hitler was promising to throw off the shackles imposed on the German military at Versailles and here, Görtz had reasoned, was an ideal opportunity not only to earn a regular salary, but also to relive the halcyon days of his youth by joining a rejuvenated German Air Force. He certainly had the qualifications and experience and, as a long-standing party member, once back in the military he would be able to count on some protection from his creditors. He went to great lengths to prove his Aryan descent and passed a rigorous medical examination, but his application was abruptly rejected in a letter dated 9 June 1935 because, Görtz suspected, the Luftwaffe had realised that his motives had little to do with patriotic zeal.

Yet someone clearly appreciated that a former airman who had studied in Edinburgh and practised law in London, Chicago and New York had potential as an aviation spy. Granted, he had a crackpot theory about a secret bomber force hidden away at remote British airfields, but the well-publicised RAF expansion plans were worthy of investigation and he might just get away with it. Another letter sent just ten days after the rejection letter referred to a meeting with senior Luftwaffe intelligence officers in Berlin.[13]

Potentially incriminating documents found at Broadstairs included a visiting card for Leon Kets, a known Abwehr agent in Belgium, and a sheaf of hotel bills that allowed MI5 to trace the route that Görtz and Marianne had taken across southern England. There were also letters from German industrialist Walter Bartram introducing Görtz to Paul Rykens, Dutch-born chairman of the Anglo-Dutch Unilever conglomerate, and from the Deutsche-Englische Handelskammer Gesellschaft, the Anglo-German Chamber of Commerce in London, that, taken together, pointed to a feeble attempt at giving Görtz commercial cover. And, when arrested at Harwich, he was carrying a notebook with the London address of Hans Thost, the Abwehr talent spotter who had recruited Christopher Draper, a copy of the sketch of RAF Manston, five picture postcards of RAF Lee-on-Solent given to Marianne by Kenneth Lewis and one of the letters Lewis had sent Marianne.

Less incriminating, but still of interest for the light they shone on Görtz' parlous financial position, were letters from some of his most pressing creditors, not least an increasingly irate Maida Vale piano maker, Claude Rahardt, who was owed a sizeable sum from the sale of two properties in Berlin. Half-German on his father's side, Rahardt was furious that the last he had heard from Görtz was a promise in the spring of 1935 to hand over the money when he visited England that summer. The letter did not make it clear how Görtz planned to smuggle the cash past Germany's notoriously strict capital controls. While Rahardt was clearly a knowing party to the cash smuggling scheme, an MI5 intercept on his mail soon confirmed that there was nothing more sinister in his relationship with Görtz.[14]

Precisely who decided that Görtz should take his pretty nineteen-year-old secretary and mistress along on his mission to England is unclear, but the pair were advanced £100 (around £5,000 at 2020 values), considerably more than was allowed out of Germany under Nazi currency regulations, to cover their travel expenses. They bought a second-hand Zündapp K200 motorcycle and a 'Robot' miniature camera which, handily for a spy, was fitted with a lens that gave considerable depth of field and a viewfinder that could be rotated through 90 degrees so that, from a short distance away, the photographer would appear to be facing away from his real subject. The receipt for the camera, found at 'Havelock', was dated 12 July 1935, a week before Görtz and Marianne rode the Zündapp off the Channel ferry at Southampton.

Görtz' carefully crafted *lebenslauf* seems genuine enough at first reading and, despite the marked variations in the four versions found at Broadstairs, historians have hitherto tended to accept them at face value. Yet there are critical passages, in particular on the Siemens-Halske affair, that simply do not ring true. It is inconceivable, for example, that a respected Hamburg-based international barrister with learned articles published in legal journals would spend the three years in London working for an industrial giant like Siemens-Halske while only being paid what Görtz claimed were 'the barest travelling expenses'. And the case was not, as he claimed, lost in the summer of 1931; Mr Justice Maugham, brother of author Somerset Maugham, actually gave his decision in Siemens-Halske AG v Standard Telephones and Cables in February 1932, seven months after Görtz had left London apparently penniless.[15]

Another, and perhaps more plausible, explanation for what happened would come to light after press reports of Görtz' arrest in Dublin in 1941 prompted a British naval officer to come forward with a claim that the German had been somehow implicated in his 1931 divorce. Records of the interrogation of Sub-Lieutenant Stanley McLeish by MI5 officer John Stephenson were weeded from MI5 files in 1959, but other sources suggest that McLeish, a barrister's clerk in civilian life, had befriended Görtz during the Siemens-Halske case and introduced him to his wife, Sylvia, a former dancer in the legendary Anna Pavlova's elite corps de ballet. Sylvia Nicholls, as she was before her marriage, had toured North America, Australia, New Zealand and Europe with Pavlova while still a teenager. But the heady mix of glamour, travel and public adoration had ended when she married McLeish in 1928 and now there were no cheering crowds, just a dull husband and a shabby apartment next to a busy railway line in Fulham, south-west London.

Sylvia had escaped Pavlova's stifling puritanism only to find herself trapped in a boring marriage. But there was one consolation; she was just a short bus ride away from Chelsea Arts Club, a male-dominated haven for west London's eccentric artists and louche bohemians where she was drawn into the orbit of charismatic, half-German painter Rudolf Haybrook. And it would have been through her that her husband Stanley's new friend Hermann Görtz, the lonely German lawyer, was introduced to 'Rudy' Haybrook.[16]

Görtz and Haybrook, who had anglicised his name from Heubach in 1920, became friends. But they shared more than just a common language; they also had an unhealthy interest in girls much younger than themselves and hedonistic Chelsea with its endless round of drug-fuelled parties was the ideal environment in which to indulge their carnal fantasies. Around the time he met Görtz, for example, the 30-year-old Haybrook was wooing Elizabeth Tucker Faithfull, the seventeen-year-old daughter of a failed American businessman. Elizabeth, along with her mother and older sister Starr, paid three lengthy visits to London between 1928 and 1930 and would later claim that she and Haybrook had been practically engaged, a claim that must have come as a surprise to Ethel Haybrook, the artist's wife.

It would likewise have surprised the impressionable Elizabeth to learn that her beloved Rudy was also bedding her sister Starr, a beautiful but tragic wild child who could have come straight from the pages of an F. Scott Fitzgerald novel. Sexually abused as a child by a prominent politician, Starr had been further traumatised by her mother and stepfather accepting large sums in hush money from her abuser, at a stroke reducing themselves to pimps and their daughter to a whore. Starr would spend the rest of her short life increasingly dependent on drugs, sex and alcohol as she tried to suppress a tide of self-loathing that threatened to overwhelm her. On one occasion, she and Haybrook were making so much noise at his Gower Street studio that the landlady had to hammer on the door to get them to quieten down. Starr later confided to her diary that Haybrook had been 'a bit too rough' with her. On another occasion, she appeared stark naked from the ladies lavatory in a Fulham Road bar and sat down on the knee of a doubtless pleasantly surprised army officer. A gun was apparently fired in the ensuing melee.[17]

This would have been the debauched lifestyle that Görtz was drawn into through his friendship with the McLeish couple and Haybrook. And, given that he had a reputation as a ladies' man and would have known Starr Faithfull through Haybrook, it is highly likely that he was one of her many lovers during her visits to London, which just happened to coincide with his. This might explain why, as Starr was notoriously free with other people's cash, Görtz left London without any money. It might explain Edward Hinchley Cooke's laconic margin comments in Görtz' MI5 file referring to the German's 'nocturnal and other activities'. It might explain why the date Görtz gives in his *lebenslauf* for the end of the Siemens-Halske case and his departure from London changes from 1931 to 1932, depending on whom he thinks will read it. And it might point to a direct link between the hapless Starr Faithfull's body mysteriously washing up on a Long Island beach in June 1931 and Görtz' abrupt departure from London that same week, just as the police and press were hot on the heels of the dead woman's friends and lovers in the city.[18]

This version of events is based on circumstantial, albeit compelling, evidence. But it might also explain why Görtz, trapped in a web of his own deceit, had to go through with the charade of suing Siemens-Halske for his ostensibly unpaid fees, an action that he inevitably lost at considerable further cost to himself. And when Heinrich Ehlers, the Berlin-based senior counsel supposedly behind the fraud, made disparaging remarks about Görtz' conduct in London and Görtz sued, it was Görtz who ended up convicted of defamation.

At the end of July 1931, a month after Görtz' hasty departure, Stanley McLeish had his wife followed to the Queens Hotel in Southsea near Portsmouth where she was spending a long weekend with Rudolf Haybrook. Divorce papers citing Haybrook as co-respondent were served on the pair at the artist's Gower Street studio a week later, and the fact that McLeish made his statement to MI5 following Hermann Görtz' arrest in Ireland in 1941 suggests that he had evidence that Sylvia had also been involved with the spy.[19]

* * *

Not a word about events in Broadstairs was allowed to appear in the press for ten days after the arrest in Harwich as it was hoped that Marianne might still turn up. When Fleet Street's finest did eventually descend on Broadstairs, they discovered that Florence Johnson and Josephine Lewis had been sworn to silence. Frustrated reporters had to content themselves with a bland War Office news release and titillating gossip from Stanley Road neighbour Captain John Rogers about the mysterious femme fatale, dubbed 'The Bungalow Brunette' by the *Daily Express*, who had turned the head of a young RAF airman. Rogers went on to describe seeing the two Germans busily drawing and writing at a table in the living room. None of the reporters seem to have noticed that the French windows into the conservatory through which Rogers claimed he had watched Görtz and Marianne were on the opposite side of 'Havelock' from the retired army officer's house.

The *Daily Express* did track Marianne down to her parents' small apartment in Repsoldstrasse, a narrow street next to Hamburg Central railway station, but the 'spy suspect's friend' would say little beyond maintaining that Dr Görtz was entirely innocent. She did admit that she was neither his niece nor his daughter, though she was at pains to point out, somewhat unconvincingly, that there was nothing improper in her relationship with her employer.

Görtz and Marianne were now hot news and a large posse of eager pressmen and photographers representing every British newspaper from *The Times* to the *Broadstairs and St Peters Mail* was waiting when, a handkerchief over his head, Görtz arrived for a remand hearing before Margate Magistrates on 26 November. Smartly dressed in a double-breasted grey suit, grey shirt and red tie, he looked on impassively while the prosecution case was outlined and Florence Johnson detailed her discoveries outside the back door of 'Havelock'. He remained oddly detached from proceedings when Ken Lewis told his tale of the beautiful girl motorcyclist who offered to help when he was tinkering with his broken-down machine and of having seen Marianne every day for the rest of his leave. Indeed his only reaction came when Edward Hinchley Cooke quoted a passage from a letter found at 'Havelock' in which, according to the half-German MI5 officer's translation, he had told his estranged wife, 'I should like to place myself at the disposal of the Secret Service.' At that Görtz leapt to his feet and shouted, 'I protest; this translation is entirely wrong.' The Magistrates ignored Görtz' protest and, during a subsequent hearing on 3 December, committed him for trial at the Old Bailey.

Newspaper accounts of a mysterious code, a miniature camera, a map of an unidentified RAF airfield and a young temptress trying to subvert an RAF serviceman made the Old Bailey trial appear a mere formality. Yet the evidence against Görtz was actually far from robust; none of the documents found at 'Havelock' had been remotely confidential and the picture postcards of RAF Lee-on-Solent that Lewis had sent Marianne were freely on sale to the public. Nor had Görtz ever knowingly strayed on to RAF property. In the case of RAF Manston, for example, witnesses confirmed that he had asked permission to watch the flying and had confined himself to the public road that crossed the airfield, a favourite spot for countless camera-wielding aviation enthusiasts.

Further weakening the prosecution case, in a letter to Görtz that was intercepted and copied to MI5 and the Director of Public Prosecutions a few days after the hearing in Margate, Marianne dismissed Kenneth Lewis' version of events as nonsense. 'How is it possible,' she wondered, 'that he can tell such a lie-story . . . I would never have believed that he is such a coward.' By way of confirmation, she was showing British reporters two letters from Lewis that, she claimed, 'put right all questions'. Critical was a letter sent on 30 September 1935 to 'Miss Zundapp' at 'Havelock' in which Lewis refers to himself as 'an utter stranger' and writes that he had admired her motorcycle while home on leave in Broadstairs the previous week. Making no reference to a meeting on Crow Hill, he continued, 'I am a very keen motorcyclist and have always wanted to have a lady motorcyclist as a pen-friend.'[20]

Clearly, if the letter that Marianne was showing journalists in Hamburg was genuine, and the draft reply found in 'Havelock' suggested that it was, Lewis' story was nothing but a fevered adolescent fantasy dreamt up to win bragging rights in the airmens' mess. Josephine Lewis was certainly coming to the conclusion that her son's evidence was nonsense, telling Constable Fred Smith that

> she was very worried that her son had lied about his meeting with the German girl, Miss Emig. She told me that he had at first told her that Mrs Johnson had given the girl his address and that the girl had written to him at the RAF Lee-on-Solent. He later told his mother that this was not true and that he had written a letter to the girl which he addressed 'Miss Zundapp'.[21]

Likewise, MI5 Director General Colonel Sir Vernon Kell was under no illusions about the young aircraftsman's honesty, remarking in a letter to the Director of Public Prosecutions Sir Edward Tindall Atkinson that he was 'undoubtedly an unreliable witness and, if he is any way shaken on a material fact, would crumple up hopelessly under further cross-examination'. This would inevitably lead to the rest of his evidence, in particular his account of the tea party at 'Havelock' and his correspondence with Marianne, being hopelessly compromised and could, Kell feared, even lead to the collapse of the entire prosecution case.[22]

There had, of course, been no meeting over a broken-down motorcycle on Crow Hill, no leisurely stroll up the hill to Stanley Road and no late-night assignations with an exotic girlfriend at the Broadstairs clock tower. What actually happened was that Josephine Lewis and Kenneth, who was home on leave, were at the window of their house in Carlton Avenue when the Zündapp passed by a few days after the Germans arrived, its two-stroke engine rasping in protest as it struggled up the hill under the combined weight of Marianne, who was driving, and Görtz. 'Did you ever see such a get-up as that?' Kenneth, a keen motorcyclist had said, 'They're equipped for flying, not crawling along on a machine of that make.'[23]

Little did Josephine know it then, but her son's offhand remarks masked a rapidly growing interest in the girl on the snarling Zündapp, and, if a letter from Marianne is to be believed, she had spotted him hanging around outside 'Havelock' soon afterwards, possibly even later that same day, ostentatiously examining the parked Zündapp. Lewis had clearly been hoping for a reaction from within and, when this failed to materialise, had asked both Florence Johnson and neighbour Captain John Rogers to make a formal introduction. Both had refused, Rogers even warning the young airman to steer well clear of German girls, so he had written the 'Miss Zundapp' letter on his return to RAF Lee-on-Solent on 30 September. This had led to the invitation to tea at 'Havelock' on 19 October, four days before Marianne and her 'uncle' disappeared.

Contrary to what Lewis had told MI5 and the RAF Provost Marshal, the 'Havelock' tea party on Saturday, 19 October was the only occasion on which he actually met Marianne and the invitation had come on the postcard that Florence Johnson had snatched from Josephine Lewis' hand during their confrontation in the street outside 'Havelock', not during a romantic stroll along the Broadstairs promenade.

Lewis was lying, but was clearly prepared to perjure himself rather than suffer the loss of face that would come with admitting his story was a tissue of lies; after all, Marianne was hardly about to come to London to challenge his evidence under oath. As Vernon Kell seems to be acknowledging in his letter to the Director of Public Prosecutions, Lewis' dishonesty was a welcome boost for the prosecution case in what was little more than a show trial. Referring to the 'Miss Zundapp' letter that Lewis had clearly sent on 30 September and Lewis' 'somewhat foolish' reasons for denying he had done so, he wrote, 'Normally speaking, I would of course like to examine LEWIS on this point with a view to clearing the matter up, but I think you agree with me that there are certain very obvious objections to this course of action.'[24]

The Old Bailey trial duly went ahead in March 1936 with prosecuting counsel, eminent barrister and former Conservative MP James Cassels KC, deftly painting a picture of Görtz as a sinister

Nazi master spy and wisely concentrating on his intention to spy rather than on any actual damage that he might or, more to the point, might not have done to British national security. Homing in on the sketch map of RAF Manston and the notebook in which he had meticulously recorded his visits to other RAF airfields, Cassels also pointed to Görtz having had the London address and telephone number of Hans Thost, the Nazi 'journalist' and, though he could not reveal it in open court, Abwehr talent spotter who had recruited Christopher Draper two years before.[25]

In his defence, Görtz maintained an air of faintly bewildered detachment, stuck doggedly to his story about being a novelist on a research trip with his secretary and claimed, with some justification, that he had stolen no secrets and broken no laws. Yet few doubted Görtz' intention to gather information, secret or otherwise, about the RAF and he was in deep trouble as soon as Cassels began probing the military contacts in Germany found among his papers at 'Havelock'. Damningly, he looked nervous and responded with an evasive, 'I cannot dare answer. It is impossible for me,' when asked about the names of officers found among the papers at 'Havelock'.

Edward Hinchley Cooke then gave the court a rather melodramatic description of a date-based cipher identification indicator found in Görtz' luggage, nimbly skating over the fact that it was actually a cipher system commonly used by German lawyers and considerably less sinister than he made it out to be. He also translated some of the draft letters that had been found at 'Havelock' including one in which Görtz told his former secretary, Gerda Hagemann, 'Outside big English aeroplanes are flying around. The English are flying busily. In a week our work will be finished. We will then go to Berlin . . . At present we are writing a big report. Much depends on it.' There was also a rather sad, unfinished letter to his estranged wife Ellen in which Görtz lamented the breakdown of their marriage and referred to his work for the 'Nachrichtendienst' (Intelligence Service), and there was his Luftwaffe application form in which he had claimed to be 'particularly suited for employment in the intelligence service'.

Quite why Görtz, an international lawyer who should have

known a great deal better, had trailed so much potentially incriminating evidence around with him is unclear. Indeed, observers at the Old Bailey found it hard to pin down the enigmatic character in the dock, a man who seemed at once strangely self-assured and obsessive about the minutiae of Hinchley Cooke's translations, yet oddly careless for having left the documents there in the first place. While it was true that he had only been apprehended thanks to the curiosity of Florence Johnson and the intuition of Constable Fred Smith, had he really seen himself as an international master spy able to outwit the British security services? Or, if he really was just the eccentric Hamburg lawyer and aeronautical novelist that he claimed to be, why had he and Marianne left Broadstairs in such a tearing hurry and why, for that matter, had Marianne not returned to Britain with him in November? Had she had a change of heart about her espionage adventure; had she been having pangs of conscience brought on by her deception of Kenneth Lewis; or had she simply tired of her middle-aged and impecunious sugar daddy?

The prosecution case was, even with the dubious benefit of Lewis' tainted evidence, still decidedly thin. Yet, curiously for a highly experienced barrister, Görtz' defending counsel, Reginald Croom-Johnson MP, played what should have been a strong hand very badly, at one stage pointlessly debating whether 'Nachrichtendienst' translated as 'Secret Service' or 'Intelligence Service'. He then made a feeble attempt to discredit Constable Fred Smith by asking whether he had found 'masks, false beards, a cloak or a hat to pull low over the eyes' at 'Havelock'. And, while he could scarcely have been unaware of the existence of the 'Miss Zundapp' letter, not least because Marianne had sent a copy to Görtz at Maidstone Prison, he seems to have been oddly reluctant to do what any halfway competent defence lawyer ought to have done, that is expose Kenneth Lewis for the liar that he all too obviously was.[26]

Görtz probably still believed that, having not apparently broken any laws and having only gathered information that was publicly available, he would eventually be found innocent. This would certainly account for his apparent complacency in court as his defence team appeared to flounder. Yet, in his anxiety to please his new

Luftwaffe air intelligence and Abwehr masters, he had failed to take into account the catch-all terms of the British Official Secrets Acts. Nor had he reckoned with the ruthless duplicity that the British state was prepared to employ in pursuit of a preferred outcome in a trial that, like Baillie-Stewart's three years before, would both send a clear 'keep off the grass' message to Berlin and warn British servicemen against cooperating, even unwittingly, with foreign agents. After six months of trial by media, the Old Bailey jury's verdict was never in doubt and they took less than an hour to reach a guilty verdict.

On 9 March 1936, Hermann Görtz was jailed for four years, a sentence that even the Director of Public Prosecutions acknowledged was unduly harsh. A Reuters correspondent who telephoned the spy's elderly mother in Lübeck to get her reaction heard her reply, 'Oh, mein Gott!', and the sound of the telephone crashing to the floor. After a few moments' silence, a maid came on the line and said that Frau Görtz was 'recovering from the shock. She is weeping and does not want to say anything more.' Marianne was meanwhile posing winsomely for photographers in a Hamburg café and still insisting that Görtz was innocent. Playing her part to perfection, she gazed demurely at the cameras from under a wide-brimmed hat and simpered, 'I am sorry that this has happened. I thought your England was such a lovely place and I was so happy there. The people were all so kind to me. Now my memory of it is all spoiled.'[27]

* * *

As Hermann Görtz cooled his heels in Maidstone Prison, penning romantic fiction to pass the time, deliberately misleading leaks to the British news media suggested that he had been under close surveillance by an all-seeing MI5 for months prior to his arrest. Yet the reality was that this most inept of spies had only been caught because he and Marianne had stayed too long in Broadstairs and attracted far too much attention to themselves. Even then he might have got away with it but for a small error in his otherwise excellent English; the 'bicycle combination' he had mentioned in the telegram and postcard to Florence Johnson had been his one-piece motorcycling suit, not the motorcycle itself which, if fitted with a sidecar, could have been referred to in English as a motorcycle combination. All he had done was anglicise the German *kombination* for overall, thus inadvertently starting the chain of events that led to his arrest. Had he and Marianne simply packed up and handed back the 'Havelock' keys, they would have got clean away.[28]

Getting caught was, for Görtz at least, unfortunate. But it was not even as though the scraps of information, almost immediately out of date at a time of rapid rearmament, that he and Marianne had been able to gather had been worth all the effort, risk and expense. Postcards on sale in the Manston village shop included revealing images of the airfield and, if the Luftwaffe really were that desperate for intelligence on RAF Mildenhall, they could have simply, and quite legally, joined the thousands of spectators who crowded on to the newly opened base for the start of the MacRobertson Air Race to Australia in October 1934. Or they could have paid the admission charge and freely photographed 356 of the RAF's latest aircraft when both Mildenhall and nearby RAF Duxford were thrown open for the Royal Review of the RAF on 6 July 1935, two weeks before Görtz and Marianne landed at Southampton.

The Lonkowski operation in the United States had been another idiotic fool's errand. Auguste's inebriated crowing to Senta Dewanger about her husband being in the pay of the German government had been a potentially disastrous blunder, but she was not alone in her alcohol-sodden indiscretions. Her husband, whom Bremen spymaster Erich Pfeiffer would later dismiss as 'something of a dipsomaniac', had identified Pfeiffer and his Atlantic couriers, Schlüter and Eitel, during that first boozy night at Gudenberg's. During another drinking session in a Manhattan bar, Lonkowski had bragged to Carl Eitel that he was living at the Hempstead home of a woman named Senta and that he had been the cause of 'some jealousy between his wife and that woman'. During yet another drinking session with Eitel, he had slurred that his Abwehr code name was 'Sex' and that he threw lavish parties at the Hempstead house during which aviation workers were plied with alcohol and encouraged into inebriated disclosures about their work. Eitel would later ruefully admit that he was somewhat put out that he had never been invited.[29]

Worse still, as with Görtz, the intelligence Lonkowski's informants had stolen was simply not worth all the effort and expense. Gudenberg's Curtiss-Wright blueprints were quite useless, the XSBC-2 biplane having proved a backward step long before it entered US Navy service in 1937, and the experimental Seversky designs stolen by Voss were either worthless before they left the drawing board, or discarded soon afterwards. Lonkowski did once boast to Gudenberg that he had informants in Connecticut and Seattle, by which he probably meant to imply Pratt & Whitney's Hartford aero-engine plant and the giant Boeing factory, but he was far more likely to have been referring to bar-room buddies who knew someone who worked in Pratt & Whitney or Boeing.

More detailed and up-to-date aviation technology than Lonkowski's contacts could ever have stolen was, in any case, readily available on the open market or from German subsidiaries of American aviation companies. Pratt & Whitney, whose industrial giant parent company Du Pont was among several American corporations bankrolling the Nazis, had licensed production of their aero engines to BMW months before Lonkowski arrived in New York. The Senate Munitions Committee would reveal that Pratt & Whitney had sold $1,455,000 ($56,000,000 at 2022 values) worth of aircraft parts and machine tools to the Nazis in the first six months of 1934 alone. Standard Oil were meanwhile building refineries in Germany that would supply the Luftwaffe with 100 octane aviation fuel.[30]

Salesmen from Curtiss-Wright, Bendix and other American aviation firms were openly competing for German orders for everything from complete aircraft to engines, gun sights and hydraulics. Bendix alone would supply Germany with aircraft construction data as late as 1940, circumventing the wartime British blockade to do so. Even the attempt to recruit engineer Fred Backus had been a waste of time as Sperry had licensed production of its auto-pilots and gyro-compasses to Askaniawerke AG of Berlin in 1934. And the Americans were by no means alone; De Havilland, Handley Page and Rolls-Royce were among the British aviation firms peddling their wares in Nazi Germany. There were, in truth, few real secrets in aviation and the Luftwaffe only had to buy an air show ticket, pick up a magazine or get out their cheque book if they wanted the latest American or British aviation technology.[31]

All that Abwehr had achieved with the Lonkowskis was to add to a growing list of espionage disasters by sending two garrulous drunks on a risky yet pointless mission to spy on a rising super-power the Nazis could ill afford to antagonise. That they had got away with it was down to the open and polyglot nature of American society coupled with the inexperience of customs supervisor John Roberts and US Army Intelligence officer Major Stanley Grogan, not the skill of their agent. Likewise, all that Abwehr had achieved with Görtz, who did not get away with it, was to reinforce the growing British perception of the Nazis as aggressive militarists.

The Görtz trial, like that of Norman Baillie-Stewart, was largely played out in the public domain, the clear intention on both occasions being to send an unmistakable message to Berlin. Yet that message, if it was received at all, does not appear to have made much of an impression and other contemporary cases that MI5 kept under wraps included that of army officer Geoffrey Pye-Smith who reported an oddly worded invitation to meet an Austrian acquaintance in Duisberg for 'a talk'. Travelling to Germany in June 1935 as an MI5 agent, Pye-Smith met a 'Herr Eschaus' at the Café Reichard in Cologne and was given a questionnaire, 100 Dutch florins and two 'Umschlagstellen' mail relay addresses which he handed over to MI5 on his return to London.

Abwehr courier Elisabeth Fischer came ashore at Harwich on 15 August and, watched by Special Branch, caught a train to London where she collected the questionnaire, complete with innocuous answers concocted by MI5, and handed Pye-Smith £15 in return. (Pye-Smith should have been paid £25, but a hard-up Abwehr officer had creamed off £10 for himself.) Three further Abwehr couriers visited Pye-Smith with questionnaires, money and secret ink while civil servant's wife Nina Bromley of Powis Square in Notting Hill was recruited as another London Umschlagstelle. The case was eventually terminated when MI5 discovered that Pye-Smith had not declared all of the money Abwehr had sent him and was deliberately trying to drag the case out as a source of added income.[32]

Abwehr's balance sheet from the Pye-Smith episode alone could hardly have been worse, yet nowhere was the litany of Abwehr failure more apparent than in France where the so-called Apostles of Peace, a group of Abwehr agents smuggling Nazi propaganda into France, had been infiltrated by a journalist, Armand Avronsart. Cultivating one of the leading Apostles, an urbane former Austrian cavalry officer named Edward Bernhuber, Avronsart deliberately left the Austrian alone with drawings of a new French aircraft that he was writing a magazine article on. Bernhuber was calmly smoking a cigarette when Avronsart went back into the room, but the drawings had been moved.

Avronsart took his suspicions to the Sûreté only to discover that they too were watching Bernhuber but had as yet insufficient evidence for a prosecution. At least they didn't until, on 10 March 1935, Bernhuber met Avronsart at the Hôtel Continental and, in a deserted ballroom overlooking the Tuileries, handed the journalist an Abwehr questionnaire which Avronsart, a fluent German speaker, pretended to be unable to read. He needed Bernhuber to incriminate himself, so he asked for a French translation which the Austrian obligingly wrote out on hotel notepaper.[33]

Three days later, using his code name Trocadero, Bernhuber telephoned to ask for the completed questionnaire. Avronsart, with one eye on the lucrative exclusive he was about to sell to the popular magazine *Miroir du Monde*, kept a careful, verbatim note of the conversation:

> Allo! Allo! Ici Trocadero. Avez-vous faites le nécessaire?
> *Hello! Hello! This is Trocadero. Have you got the goods?*
>
> Oui.
> *Yes*
>
> Vous avez tout?
> *You have everything?*

Tout.
Everything.

Il faut que je vous voie d'urgence.
I need to see you right away.

Entendu. Où?
I understand. Where?

Si vous êtes libre de suite, retrouvez-moi entre onze heures et onze heures quinze chez Cuvillier.
If you're free right now, meet me between eleven and eleven fifteen at Cuvillier's.

Cuvillier? Je ne connais pas.
Cuvillier's? I don't know it.

C'est un magasin de fruits au coin de l'avenue des Champs-Elysées et de la rue Lincoln. La cave sert de bar, et c'est très discret. Nous pourrons nous entretenir en toute tranquillité.
It's a fruit shop at the corner of Champs Elysées and rue Lincoln. There's a bar in the cellar that is very discreet. We can talk there in complete secrecy.

Bien. A tout à l'heure.
Good. I will see you then.

Alerted by a tap on Bernhuber's telephone, Sûreté officers were waiting when he left his rue Franqueville apartment a few minutes later. A car leapt forward into his path, doors were thrown open and Commissaire Fernand Linas said quietly, 'Montez donc, je vous prie, Monsieur Bernhuber,' then turned to the driver and gave the order to drive to Sûreté headquarters, saying tersely, 'A la rue des Saussaies.'[34]

News of Bernhuber's arrest broke two weeks later with reports that a search of his apartment had yielded another Abwehr questionnaire, an automatic pistol and a tear gas pistol disguised as a propelling pencil. The press also discovered that he had enjoyed 'une collaboration sentimentale' with Italian lingerie model and Folies Bergère dancer Dina Saronni. Obligingly posing for photographs in silk pyjamas and full make up, Dina claimed that the first she knew that her beloved 'Eddy' was a spy was when Sûreté officers turned up at her Paris apartment. 'When the police arrived to search my flat,' she simpered, 'I hid under the bedclothes for more than an hour. Nobody seemed to notice.' Asked about a young American dancer who was claiming that Bernhuber had invited her to join him in a champagne bath, Dina, clearly irritated by this allegation of somewhat sticky infidelity, replied, 'I loved Edward . . . Anyway, love is blind.' Bernhuber was sent to cool his heels and his overactive libido in jail for five years.[35]

Yet more incompetent Abwehr agents were being caught spying on the Maginot Line, France's northern defences against German invasion. Typical was the case of army NCO Charles Cridlig based in Metz who was selling Abwehr blueprints of anti-aircraft guns installed in the the fortifications. Cridlig's flighty beauty queen wife, whose expensive tastes had driven him to espionage, wasted no time in giving evidence against him in return for her freedom, then returned to her family in Morocco and sued for divorce. Mme Cridlig had not, however, bargained for her husband's jailed Abwehr handlers, Phillipp Altmayer and an associate named Hussinger, giving fresh evidence of her complicity and she was arrested as she went on stage at a beauty contest in Casablanca. Released on bail, she became deeply depressed at the prospect of a lengthy prison sentence and, on 29 August 1936, a boy playing on the beach at Rabat in Morocco watched a young woman place her hat, shoes and handbag neatly on a rock, swim out to sea, raise her arms and disappear. Gendarmes searching the handbag found a small automatic pistol and a driving licence in the name of France-Marguerite Cridlig. There was no suicide note.[36]

Elsewhere in that summer of spies, a Luxembourg horse butcher was caught spying to feed a cocaine habit, a Brussels taxi driver was arrested while trying to smuggle a machine gun into Germany and a German was caught sketching Dutch border fortifications while an accomplice posing as a missionary distracted guards by offering them religious tracts. Travelling salesman Joseph Primadzula's tyre pump was found to conceal an ingenious miniature camera after his bicycle proved oddly prone to punctures when he passed Belgian border defences and glamorous 24-year-old Anna Deinel seduced a Czechoslovak Army doctor, then asked for military secrets in return for her favours. When arrested in Prague, Anna had three Abwehr questionnaires stuffed into her bra. In Morocco, snake dancer Irenè von Zivers was caught offering Foreign Legionnaires of German extraction 1,000 francs each to desert and join the Wehrmacht. Irenè was arrested at her Casablanca apartment . . . once, that is, the large and rather unfriendly snakes she used in her act had been subdued.

As 1935 drew to a close, it seemed that Abwehr had scored yet another spectacular own goal when Sûreté belge officers dragged electrician René Defauwes and three accomplices out of a Liège café on 21 December. The Belgians had been tipped off about Defauwes by the British after MI6 linked him to a Belgian Nazi and to Henri Havard, a suspected German agent who had run brothels in London during the First World War. By then, however, the Defauwes gang had smuggled a treasure trove of military secrets into Germany, often pinned to the underside of railway carriage seats. In particular, they had sold Abwehr the secrets of Fort Eben Emael, a vast fortress defending the River Meuse and Albert Canal crossings north of Liège.

The cost of Defauwes' treachery would only become apparent when 62 glider-borne Wehrmacht engineers equipped with charges specially designed to cut through Eben Emael's armour plate, samples of which had been supplied by the Belgian, neutralised the fortress in two hours on 10 May 1940. Most of the bridges it was built to defend fell into German hands undamaged and the British Expeditionary Force and French 1st Army, surging into Belgium to meet the apparent challenge, drove straight into a German trap. The shattered remnants of the Allied force were evacuated from Dunkirk three weeks later.[37]

* * *

With Defauwes, Abwehr had achieved one of the few truly game-changing German intelligence coups of the interwar years, albeit one that would pale into insignificance when compared with the Franco-Polish-British exchange of Enigma cryptography secrets in the last weeks of peace, yet nothing could conceal the scale of the existential problems that it was facing at the end of 1935. Ambitious Nazi apparatchiks Heinrich Himmler, head of the Gestapo, and Reinhard Heydrich, head of the Nazi Party security service Sicherheitsdienst, were muscling in on Abwehr territory with their own brand of useless agents and sinister thugs. In the Gestapo's case, this often involved the kidnap and murder of anti-Nazi exiles like Jewish journalist Berthold Jacob Salomon who was lured to the aptly named Crooked Corner café in Basel, Switzerland, drugged and bundled into a car which then crashed through a Swiss border post into Germany.[38]

Another Jewish exile, Josef Lampersberger, was duped into going to the Czech-German border to meet relatives ostensibly arriving from Germany by train. The border runs through the middle of Železná Ruda-Alžbětín station and, when the train drew in, two Gestapo heavies leapt out, ran along the platform on to Czech soil, beat up a Czech border guard and dragged Lampersberger back on to the German side. Salomon and Lampersberger were released after months of diplomatic pressure, but opposing intelligence services, not to mention the newspaper-reading public, tended to lump such ham-fisted dirty tricks together with Abwehr's bungled operations.[39]

Abwehr chief Conrad Patzig had read the runes and resigned at the end of 1934, soon after his immediate predecessor was murdered by Nazi thugs. Patzig's replacement, Kapitän zur See Wilhelm Canaris, took up his post on 1 January 1935 and, initially at least, appeared to embrace the Nazi regime. He purged Abwehr officers with a history of involvement in leftist or republican politics and contributed to the culture of fear that sustained the Nazi regime by greatly expanding Abw.III, the Abwehr division responsible for counter-espionage. And, as the hapless Benita von Falkenhayn and Renate von Natzmer spent their fear-filled last days in Plötzensee Prison, he speedily concluded a jurisdictional agreement with Himmler and

Heydrich, then secured a fresh remit to monitor British, French, Czech, Polish and Spanish reaction to German rearmament.[40]

His personal position secure for the present, Canaris embarked on a round of inspections. Visiting the under-performing Nebenstelle at Wilhelmshaven naval base on 25 March 1935 he found, as Kapitänleutnant Erich Pfeiffer had discovered on being posted there in 1933:

> The station, for all practical purposes, had neither agents nor any channels of communication. Originally the Wilhelmshaven station's sole task was the organisation in Holland and Belgium of a network of informers able to bring information in the event of any crisis or mobilisation in any other country, and particularly France and Great Britain. Spade work of this kind is hardly ever the most satisfying sort of employment; the potential informers enlisted in case of need remain devoid of any training, and when a crisis occurs, they usually fail to accomplish the task allotted to them.[41]

It was, Pfeiffer had concluded ruefully 'a somewhat forlorn picture'. Canaris agreed and, having concluded that a closed naval dockyard was the wrong place from which to operate networks of civilian informants, he ordered an immediate move to the port city of Bremen. When Stelleleiter Kapitänleutnant Ludolf von Hohnhorst objected to losing his comfortable sinecure:

> Canaris . . . coldly told von Hohnhorst that since he was not in agreement with the plan, it would be entrusted to Pfeiffer [and] the latter must be ready to move out of Wilhelmshaven to a new office in Bremen by 1 October 1935.[42]

That, at least, was Pfeiffer's version of events. Less flattering accounts, given by former Abwehr personnel to Allied interrogators in 1945, have an intensely ambitious Pfeiffer lobbying Canaris for promotion behind the backs of senior colleagues. Quite why Canaris should favour Pfeiffer, a pleasure-loving 43-year-old naval veteran who had only been working in Abwehr for ten months, over more experienced intelligence officers is not clear. Perhaps he was taking the opportunity to clear out dead wood, perhaps it was because Pfeiffer had an economics degree and had recently worked as an industrial statistician, or perhaps it was because Pfeiffer was, like the new Abwehr chief, a former U-boat officer.

Whatever Canaris' reasoning, even allowing for Abwehr's shallow pool of talent, Pfeiffer's promotion was conspicuously rapid for an officer with little experience of intelligence work. And this lack of experience was never more apparent than in his handling of Henry Addicks, a salesman for the Bremen Exporters Association he recruited in the spring of 1935 to spy on French coastal defences. A German-born South African, Addicks had no military experience and would have been hard pushed to tell a machine gun from a rifle, so Pfeiffer agreed that he could enlist the help of a friend, Eric Newman-Hall, a former British Territorial Army officer who, unbeknown to Addicks, had a smattering of German. No traitor, Newman-Hall reported the approach to an army acquaintance, Captain John Nicholson, who, in typically British fashion, briefed an MI6 officer friend over lunch at the Guards Club in Mayfair.[43]

Now a British double agent and pretending that he could not speak German, Newman-Hall accompanied Addicks to a meeting with a 'Dr Spielmann' in Wilhelmshaven on 5 June 1935 and was decidedly put out when he overheard Spielmann agree with Addicks that 'der Englander' would be a convenient scapegoat should the espionage mission in France go wrong. At another meeting in a Bremen restaurant two days later, Newman-Hall, who had been allocated the agent or Vertrauensmann number R2502 and the code name Baron, overheard a naval officer greet Spielmann as Kapitänleutnant Pfeiffer. Indeed, so indiscreet were Pfeiffer's colleagues, Newman-Hall was able to tell John Nicholson on his return that the Bremen spymaster was a naval gunnery specialist who had served aboard a German battleship at the 1916 Battle of Jutland.[44]

Thus far, unlike their counterparts in Abwehr, British intelligence officers had kept Newman-Hall at arm's length, using John Nicholson as go-between. But now, with the Abwehr mission to France imminent, MI5 case officer Edward Hinchley Cooke arranged a rendezvous with Newman-Hall in London's Victoria Station. In a delightfully arcane touch, Newman-Hall was to go to the ticket barrier on platform thirteen and identify himself to Hinchley Cooke by holding a packet of Craven A cigarettes prominently in his left hand. Sadly, this plan fell through and the two met a week later over lunch at the Junior United Services Club where Newman-Hall was told to carry out the Abwehr mission exactly as required by Pfeiffer.

On his return, and with MI5 approval, Newman-Hall sent Pfeiffer a report claiming that he and Addicks had

> Left London 11.00 p.m. on the 10th July. Booked in at hotel – 'Au filet du Sole' at Malo les Bains. After luncheon 'A' [Addicks] to bed – drunk – I went to Dunkerque ostensibly to get in touch with somebody useful.
>
> This happened two or three times – 'A' always being either too drunk or too shaky to accompany me. I managed to produce one ex-Gunner NCO and one constructional engineer from whom I might reasonably be expected to procure some of the information required. It was impressed on 'A' that he must on no account try to pump them himself. I also found a French NCO of Artillery and told 'A' that I had got something from him – but that no notes must be made until we reached England.
>
> At no time did 'A' make any effort to do any work – pleading nerves due to over-drinking. I was also drinking heavily – but managed to avoid suffering for it – and duly left him at reasonable times.
>
> The French had an air-attack exercise on the harbour which gave me the location of some of their A.A. batteries and also of their heavy oil stores. I produced a plan of the harbour on which to mark points of interest.
>
> On the 16th, in the afternoon, I took 'A' into Dunkerque

and made him walk with me round the entire dock area that is not closed just to scare into him some sense of what was going on.

On our return – on the date given – I held up our report to Wilhelmshaven as long as I could without arousing suspicion. It was finally completed and sent off on Friday July 19th together with some details of the 'Dunkerque' which was launched on the 18th.[45]

Pfeiffer was less than impressed with the report, acknowledging it with a bland three-word telegram, 'Report nineteen received', sent to Addicks, Poste Restante, at Charing Cross Post Office. ('Nineteen' refers to the date on which the report had been despatched from London.) What Newman-Hall did not know was that the Sûreté, acting on a tip-off from MI6 Deputy Director General Colonel Stewart Menzies, had kept a close watch on the two 'spies' during their stay in Dunkerque, even searching their belongings while they were away from their hotel. The French had found that there was not

the slightest indication that either of them were [sic] engaged in espionage of any kind. Newman-Hall's statement as to having located some of the French anti-aircraft batteries etc., etc., is, according to the French, completely false. Neither he nor Addicks was ever found in the proximity of defensive points. 'The two musketeers' spent their time in drinking *abondament*, sleeping, eating and bathing in the sea.[46]

Already suspecting that Addicks and Newman-Hall were thoroughly incompetent agents, Pfeiffer lost interest when two of his couriers reported in the autumn of 1935 that Addicks, a hopelessly indiscreet alcoholic, was leaving for South Africa to escape mounting debts and a preposterously tangled love life, and that Newman-Hall was another drunken fantasist. By then, Hinchley Cooke had also concluded that Newman-Hall was also 'an inveterate liar and a drunkard' and he was quietly dropped, though not before, desperate for money, he tried to double-cross MI5 by making direct contact with Pfeiffer on his own behalf.

In Addicks, Pfeiffer had recruited one wholly unsuitable agent, then allowed that agent to recruit another even more unsuitable accomplice, if such a thing were possible, in Newman-Hall. He had let both men get far too close to him and his garrulous staff and he had been glacially slow to realise that the pair were utterly useless. As a result, MI5 was able to form a comprehensive picture of the new Bremen Nebenstelle even before it officially began operations on 1 October 1935, a brass plate beside the Rövekamp 12 entrance to the Haus des Reichs indiscreetly identifying the tenants of ground floor offices as 'N. Spielmann, Import & Export'. That same night Pfeiffer had to burn the midnight oil while he arranged passage home from Canada for Wilhelm and Auguste Lonkowski following their dramatic escape from the United States.

* * *

Of the surviving members of the Lonkowski ring, only Otto Voss would continue handing over material on the Seversky P-35 fighter in development for the US Army Air Corps at meetings with courier Herbert Jänichen in the Hotel Astor lobby throughout 1936 and early 1937. But it was worthless intelligence as the P-35 proved inferior to both Germany's Messerschmitt 109 and Britain's Supermarine Spitfire. Spying on the P-35 was, in any case, a complete waste of time as Seversky would mount an aggressive and unsuccessful marketing campaign to sell the aircraft to the RAF and the Luftwaffe during which all of its 'secrets' were on open display.[47]

Voss then reduced what little value he had as a spy to zero by resigning from Seversky in July 1937 and taking a long holiday in Germany. Intriguingly, however, he did have two meetings with Erich Pfeiffer during his holiday and was asked to spy on the US Navy's new aircraft carriers *Yorktown* and *Enterprise*, then nearing completion at Newport News in Virginia.

The Kriegsmarine had first seriously considered an aircraft carrier programme in 1929 with the initial proposals being for modest

vessels primarily for operations in the Baltic. The operational envelope grew to include the Atlantic following the Nazi accession to
power in 1933 and, partly also in recognition that modern aircraft
would need longer flight decks, the consequent size of the three pro-
jected ships increased to 45,000 tons. But these were still little more
than ill-defined concepts, not least because the Kriegsmarine had
no experience of carrier operations and open source information
gathered from technical publications was of little help. The German
Naval Attaché in Britain, Kapitän zur See Erwin Wassner, was
tasked with getting information on Royal Navy carriers, but found
his hands tied as Berlin was concerned that the British would almost
certainly require reciprocal scrutiny of Germany's treaty violating
naval expansion.

Heinz Ohlerich, a senior member of the German design team,
did manage to join a public tour of the carrier HMS *Furious* during
Portsmouth Navy Day in August 1935 and other informants did
manage a close look at her sister HMS *Courageous* when she visited
Copenhagen in 1936. The Japanese, whose naval aviation arm had
ironically been developed with the assistance of a British mission led
by Japanese spy Lord Sempill, who had succeeded to the title on the
death of his father in February 1934, gave German officers limited
access to the carrier *Akagi*, but little in the way of useful information
was gained. As a result of this lack of intelligence, along with woeful
under-resourcing of the Kriegsmarine design team allocated to the
project, numerous detailed design questions remained unanswered
when, in November 1935, orders were placed for three 33,500-ton
ships similar in many respects to the American carrier *Saratoga*.
Most of these questions would remain unresolved when work finally
began on *Flugzeugträger A* at Kiel a year later. Voss had to admit to
Pfeiffer that he knew nothing whatsoever about warships, far less
aircraft carriers, so the Bremen spymaster turned to his New York
City agent, Ignatz Griebl.[48]

Yet barely a month was passing without Griebl's activities, not to
mention his over-active libido, featuring in the American press and
any halfway competent spymaster would have avoided this greedy,
preening, loud-mouthed, Nazi zealot like the plague. And Griebl had

other things on his mind in 1936, not least a burgeoning affair with his latest conquest, German-born nurse, retirement home owner and divorcee Kay Moog. He was also dabbling in domestic politics, campaigning for pro-Nazi Christian Party candidate William Dudley Pelley who was running against President Roosevelt in the 1936 presidential election. The deranged Pelley only managed to get on the ballot in Washington State where, despite Griebl's intervention, he won a grand total of just 1,598 votes.

Yet, when Griebl and Otto Voss boarded the liner *Bremen* in New York early in December 1935 and handed Abwehr courier Carl Eitel a letter for Erich Pfeiffer offering to restart the flow of intelligence interrupted two months before by the Lonkowski escape, the Bremen spymaster had delightedly dashed off a reply welcoming the two mens' 'cooperative spirit' and asking for 'information about destroyers then building in US Navy yards and all possible aircraft construction data'.[49]

Pfeiffer had no knowledge of Griebl beyond what his couriers Carl Eitel and Karl Schlüter had been able to tell him, so what could possibly have induced him to encourage this most unsuitable agent to step into the role recently vacated by Lonkowski? There was no doubting Griebl's Nazi credentials, frequently validated by fellow party zealot Schlüter, yet ideological purity is unlikely to have been a reason because, as MI5 would conclude following a lengthy post-war interrogation, Pfeiffer 'was never a Nazi'. Perhaps it was over-eagerness to justify his recent promotion or perhaps, as with Addicks, it was just that having any agent in the field, no matter how dubious, brought job security and access to expense accounts. Perhaps the ambitious Pfeiffer believed that, by recruiting Griebl, he would take control of Abwehr's New York spy ring from his new Bremen Nebenstelle, or perhaps this most naïve and inept of spymasters realised that there was little danger of even the most ham-fisted German spy being detected in the United States.

* * *

In the last week of June 1937, as Otto Voss was packing for his German holiday and Ignatz Griebl was preparing to spy on the US

Navy's latest aircraft carriers, a middle-aged blonde woman could be seen walking slowly along Queens Avenue in Aldershot, a British garrison town. Any casual observer would have taken her for the mother of one of the young soldiers in the nearby barracks. Yet she was moving slowly and with an oddly measured gait because that was precisely what she was doing; she was pacing out the size of barrack blocks, counting the number of floors and identifying nearby landmarks. Every now and then she would stop, nervously check that nobody was watching and scribble some notes on a piece of paper or make careful annotations on a picture postcard. Her name was Jessie Jordan and she was an Abwehr spy on a mission to identify targets for Luftwaffe air raids. She and Ignatz Griebl would never meet, but their destinies would collide in a post office in Dundee, Scotland.

Chapter 4

An Agent of the Hamburg Service

There is no doubt whatever that JORDAN is a member of the German espionage organisation.

MI5, 12 January 1938

Mary Curran sensed immediately that there was something not right about the fashionably dressed woman with a marked German accent who called at her tenement home in Church Street, Dundee, on Friday, 30 July 1937. Mary's brother-in-law, James, had advertised his hairdressing and tobacconist business in nearby Kinloch Street for sale and her visitor, who introduced herself as Mrs Jessie Jordan, had come to enquire about taking it over. But why, Mary wondered, was this woman who claimed to have owned three hairdressing salons in Hamburg interested in a shabby, back-street business in a working-class area of Dundee?

Once a small medieval port on the east coast of Scotland, Dundee had expanded rapidly during the nineteenth century thanks to a booming textile industry, in particular the processing of raw jute fibre imported from the Indian subcontinent. A lucky few made vast fortunes, but the city's low-paid and predominantly female workforce was crammed into cheaply built tenements where disease was endemic and infant mortality was the highest in Scotland. By the time Jessie Jordan arrived in 1937, the staple jute industry was in decline and the Hilltown area north of the city centre, which included the Kinloch Street business, was one of its most deprived.

Jessie Jordan took over at Kinloch Street on Monday, 6 September 1937. Mary, who had worked part-time for her brother-in-law in addition to her regular job as a cleaner at Green's Playhouse cinema in Dundee, was kept on and the more she saw of Jessie, the more suspicious she became. Money, it seemed, was no object as new water heaters, sinks, lights and mirrors were fitted, decorators gave the premises a smart new look and, at the end of September, Jessie disappeared to Germany to buy the latest hairdressing appliances. Where was all the cash coming from, Mary wondered; why was so much being invested in what would never be anything other than a very modest business; and why had Jessie insisted that she tell nobody, not even her husband, about Jessie's trip to Germany? Could it be that Jessie Jordan was really a Nazi spy?[1]

Mary's concerns about Jessie Jordan were entirely understandable as, like Britain's other housewife spycatcher Florence Johnson, she had lived for two decades under the long shadow of the First World War. She was also from a cinema-going generation whose attitudes were being shaped by movies like Hitchcock's 1935 masterpiece *The 39 Steps* with its dashing hero Richard Hannay battling sinister German agents across Scottish moorland. And the real world was fast becoming a more menacing place than even that portrayed in movie fiction like Alexander Korda's 1936 picture *Things To Come* with its dystopian vision of air raids and chemical warfare. Recent news stories had included the blitzing of the Spanish city of Guernica, fascist Italy and Nazi Germany moving towards an alliance, Japan's brutal invasion of China, blackshirts marching in London and Hitler presenting colours to SS guards from a concentration camp near the Bavarian town of Dachau.

Her suspicions thoroughly aroused and with her employer still away in Germany, on 2 October Mary found a scrap of paper on which Jessie Jordan had written the word 'Zeppelin', a term that conjured up frightening images of First World War air raids. She showed this to her husband, John, a Dundee tram conductor, but he thought the very idea of a German spy in the city ridiculous. Patrick Robbins, John's boss in the Dundee Tramway garage, agreed and suggested that Mary was just letting her imagination run away with her. Mary put the paper back where she had found it before Jessie Jordan returned from Germany the following day, but kept her eyes open and happened across another suspicious piece of paper a few days later. Hidden between the pages of a child's 'jotter' exercise book that had been left on a shelf under the counter, this one had the word 'Zeppelin' along with a row of 24 numerals.

Mary could not hope to copy this without being seen by Jessie who had returned from Germany and was busy about the salon. But she had a plan. Hurrying home at lunchtime, she told John to call at Kinloch Street that afternoon on the pretext that they were going to the cinema when she finished work. John arrived as instructed and, as Mary recalled:

> Standing behind the counter I pretended to read a book . . . and Mr Curran, standing on the other side of the counter also 'reading' a book, copied the letters on to a piece of paper he had brought from home. I put Mrs Jordan's paper back in the jotter. Mrs Jordan was very careless. Maybe she thought we knew nothing and would know nothing. When I looked a day or two later to see if Mrs Jordan's paper with the letter on it was still there, it was gone.[2]

The row of numerals did look as though they might be some form of cipher, but the idea of a Nazi spy in Dundee still appeared so far-fetched that, even now, neither John nor Pat Robbins was convinced. It seemed to Mary that nobody was willing to take her seriously, yet she was a woman on a mission now and what she found at Kinloch Street on Wednesday, 17 November 1937, would bring vindication. Dusting under the counter a good deal more thoroughly than was really necessary that morning, she came across a hand-drawn sketch plan of an unidentified coastal installation showing railways, a pier, factory buildings and some scribbled notes in both German and English. She was never going to be able to copy this without being seen, even with John's help, so she stuffed it down the front of her dress and hurried home. This time Pat Robbins needed no convincing and took the sketch straight to Detective Lieutenant John Carstairs of Dundee Police, a former Scots Guardsman who immediately realised its significance and showed it to his boss, Chief Constable

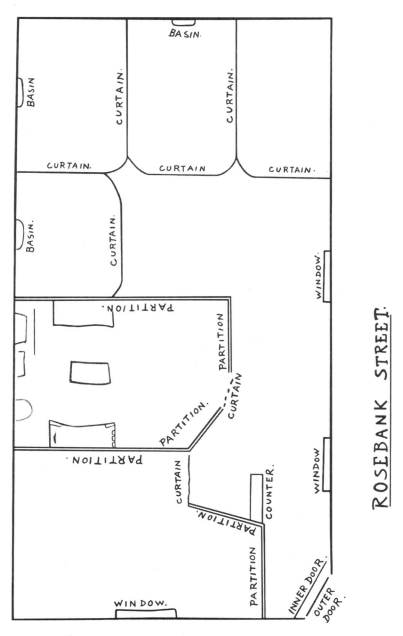

ROSEBANK STREET.

KINLOCH STREET.

A contemporary plan, prepared for Dundee Police, of Jessie Jordan's
Kinloch Street hairdressing salon (Author's collection)

Joe Neilans. The sketch was photographed then, rather than return the original to Kinloch Street, for some unrecorded reason Neilans handed it to Carstairs and told him to take the overnight sleeper to London.[3]

Dundee's housewife spycatcher was now being taken very seriously indeed. And there would be yet more drama later that afternoon when Jessie announced that she would be travelling to England by train at the end of the week. Convinced that Jessie's destination was actually Germany, Mary and John hurried round to Pat Robbins' Corso Street home with the news and Robbins, who had taken on the role of intermediary, passed this on to the police. Sent to Kinloch Street the next morning to check on Mary's information by asking for an appointment for a perm, Constable Annie Ross was offered an appointment the following day, Friday, 19 November, but then not for another ten days as Jessie was 'fully booked'. The appointments book was, as the police already knew from Mary, empty.[4]

Friday began with John Carstairs' arrival at MI5's B Division offices on the top floor of Thames House in Millbank, London. Shown the mysterious sketch and told that it had been discovered in a shop run by a Mrs Jessie Jordan at 1 Kinloch Street, Dundee, Edward Hinchley Cooke produced an MI5 case file marked with Jessie's name and surprised Carstairs by saying, 'Oh, that will be Mrs Jordan of 16 Breadalbane Terrace in Perth.' Told by Carstairs that Mrs Jordan was leaving Dundee that same evening and that Mary Curran suspected she was going to Germany, Hinchley Cooke requested that Jessie should be followed to her port of embarkation.[5]

Mary's suspicions about Jessie's travel plans were confirmed that same afternoon when John Curran called at Kinloch Street to collect Mary after work and Jessie asked him, 'Would you like to go on a big ship with me tonight?' With all the innocence she could muster, Mary asked why Jessie was going by sea when she had earlier said that she would be travelling by train. 'I don't want anyone to know I am going to Germany,' came the reply, 'but I'm leaving tonight at 9 o'clock.' John Curran slipped away to telephone Pat Robbins and, at 8.45 p.m., Detective Inspector Tom Nicholson followed in an unmarked police car as Jessie, Mary and John left the Kinloch Street salon and boarded a bus into the city.

Camperdown Dock was in darkness apart from the dim glow of a few quayside gas lamps and the swaying deck lights of the Currie Line steamer *Courland* as Jessie, Mary and John hurried along a rain-swept Dock Street and, watched by Inspector Nicholson, went aboard the ship. The Currans came ashore about 20 minutes later and, intercepted by Nicholson as they made their weary way homewards, John told the detective that the *Courland* would not now be sailing until the following afternoon. Mary added that she had asked Jessie if she had enough money for her trip. 'Don't worry about me,' had come the enigmatic reply, 'I'll get plenty of money where I'm going.'[6]

* * *

So who was Jessie Jordan, what was her connection with Perth and how was it that MI5 knew so much about her before John Carstairs arrived in London? Her birth certificate shows that she was born in Glasgow on 23 December 1887, the illegitimate daughter of Elizabeth 'Lizzie' Wallace, a nineteen-year-old, Irish-born housemaid.[7] That aside, what little we know of Jessie's early life comes from a series of ghost-written articles that appeared in the Scottish *Sunday Mail* newspaper in 1938 and three MI5 interrogations that she underwent between 1938 and 1940. As she was a prolific if inept liar, these accounts must all be treated with caution.

It seems that Jessie Wallace was brought up by her maternal grandmother until she was five years old, then reclaimed by her mother who had meanwhile married John Haddow, a twice-widowed railwayman twelve years her senior, and set about producing another sixteen children. Unsurprisingly, it was a miserable childhood and Jessie left a grossly overcrowded family home aged sixteen to follow her mother into service. She packed more than her fair share of misadventures into the years that followed, not least a narrow escape from a pimp who wanted to put her on the streets and a serious fall while working in a Manchester hotel that put her in hospital for several weeks. The chance meeting that would dramatically change her life took place in a Dundee hotel in the second week of April 1908, not 1907 as she would later recall it.

> One day, going into the Royal Hotel for food, I met a man coming downstairs, crying. My heart pounded against my ribs. Did I have a premonition that this man, apparently unhappy like myself, was to give me many years of happiness – and then disillusionment? I don't know. I only know that I had met my fate and it was my own unhappiness that wound a golden cord round us both in those fateful few moments on the main stairway of a Dundee Hotel . . .
>
> Out of my sympathy I spoke to the man. 'What is the matter? Can I do anything for you?' I asked. Then I saw that he had a telegram in his hand. He was reading and re-reading it through his tears. He looked up at me, holding the telegram out. In broken English, which I could scarcely understand, he said, 'It says my brother has been killed in an accident in England.' Out of my own sorrow I tried to comfort him. As we talked, I learned that his name was Frederick Jordan, and that he was a waiter at the hotel, but had only been two days in Dundee.[8]

Three decades after the event Jessie can be forgiven for getting the date of this encounter wrong, but it is stretching credulity to suggest that a young housemaid would be dining in Dundee's Royal Hotel which had one of the city's most expensive restaurants. Indeed, another version of the story told years later by her daughter has Jessie actually working in the hotel. Whatever the truth of it, Jessie Wallace made sure that her grieving waiter caught the right train to London and, that September, was invited to spend a month with the Jordan family in Germany. She ended up staying with the Jordans for a year, then took a job as companion to an unmarried but pregnant German girl whose family was packing her off to German East Africa to avoid a scandal.[9]

Friedrich 'Fritz' Jordan was working in Paris when Jessie returned from Africa in 1910 and his parents were keen that he and Jessie should get engaged. 'Obediently,' she recalled later, 'he sent me a ring.' The couple were married in Hamburg's Michaelis Church on 20 August 1912 and a daughter christened Margarethe 'Marga' Wilhelmine Jordan was born on 18 May 1914, six weeks before the First World War broke out. Fritz was one of the first to be called up and survived almost four years in the trenches only to die in July 1918, an early victim of the post-war influenza pandemic.[10]

After spending the war trapped as an enemy alien in Germany and, ironically, shunned by many of her friends who suspected that she was a British spy, Jessie had a brief and unhappy reunion with her family in Scotland. Returning to Hamburg, she married Fritz' cousin Wilhelm Baumgarten and adopted Werner Tillkes, the son of a friend whose merchant seaman husband had deserted her. By 1925 she had opened a hairdressing salon, Damen Friseur Jessie Jordan, in Hartungstrasse, an elegant street in Hamburg's wealthy Rotherbaum district. Astute and hard-working she offered the latest bobbed and marcel-waved *femme moderne* styles inspired by fashion designers like Coco Chanel and Elsa Schiaparelli. The business prospered but her marriage to Baumgarten failed after she discovered he was having an affair with one of the assistants in the salon and the couple divorced in 1926.[11]

On a happier note, in 1931 Jessie's daughter, Marga, gave up a promising stage career to marry salesman Hermann Wobrock and, two years later, give birth to a baby girl christened Jessie after her doting grandmother. Jessie Jordan was now, in 1933, a successful, independent businesswoman who had come a long way from her humble origins in Scotland and, despite her betrayal by Baumgarten, life was good. Yet this was also when the cracks started to appear. First, Hermann Wobrock caught Marga in bed with a Greek hypnotist brought in to treat her post-natal depression and threw her out. Marga then tried to revive her stage career only to find that her mother's illegitimacy meant she could not satisfy the new Nazi racial purity laws. As if this was not bad enough, the cuckolded Wobrock got his revenge when his business collapsed and Jessie was forced to sell her business to repay loans that she had guaranteed for him.

Jessie had lost everything that she had worked so hard for and, through no fault of her own, both she and Marga had been reduced to unemployable non-Aryan citizens by the Nazis. She was at a particularly low ebb at the end of 1936 when a letter arrived from Willie Haddow, her half-brother in Scotland, to say that his wife had died and he needed someone to help look after his four-year-old son Billy. Willie Haddow had been thinking of Marga when he wrote the letter, but she was not keen on a move from the bright lights of Hamburg to a small town in Scotland. As Jessie was at a loose end she agreed to go in her daughter's place as, if nothing else, this would give her an opportunity to trace her father's family in Scotland, prove her Aryan descent and rescue Marga's stage career.

At this point Jessie's account, as given in the *Sunday Mail*, veers off into well-rehearsed but rather obvious fiction. She contends that she booked her passage from Hamburg to Leith in the first week of February 1937, but found that her sailing had been delayed for 24 hours. An unidentified friend who just happened to meet her in the street on the way to the docks and decided to come to see her off, offered to put her up for the night. Returning to the docks the following day, they found that the ship had sailed without her, so she stayed with her accommodating friend for another eight days during which

> Certain requests were made to me to render services to Germany and these I ultimately did render. I was approached and, as a friend, asked to verify certain information that was already in the hands of the Germans . . .
>
> I knew very well what I was doing. It was the old love of change and excitement which made me do it. I was about to become a spy – in reality this time, and not in the imagination of my customers and neighbours. And on their behalf. Not against them. No one knows anything about it except my employers. I shall tell no one. But, by this time, I was a spy, eager for excitement. I awaited orders. They came. I was ordered to go to Scotland and be a spy against my native country . . .

> Maybe I had better say here and now that I did not take this step because I bore Britain any ill-will or had become pro-German. Nothing is further from the Truth. I only did it to oblige friends in Germany and because I felt it would afford some excitement. Excitement and change, as I have already shown, were life's blood to me.[12]

None of this rings true as the recruitment process would have been more prolonged than the eight days Jessie suggests. But she was telling this tale from her prison cell in 1938 at a time when she could still expect repatriation at the end of her sentence and would have been keenly aware that indiscretions could have unpleasant repercussions on her return. There also had to be more to Jessie's decision to become a Nazi spy than mere thrill-seeking. Nothing she said or did suggested that she was a dedicated Nazi and it is far more likely that her Abwehr recruiter played somehow on her weak spot, namely her daughter and granddaughter.

Marga would later tell a *Daily Express* reporter that her mother's recruitment had been down to a Herr Ostjes of Hamburg:

> He is a member of the Gestapo, the German Secret Police. It was Herr Ostjes who made the suggestion to my mother that she should confirm information of military importance when she came to Scotland.

Jessie would later identify the female friend who had put her up when she supposedly missed her sailing to Scotland as Dora Ontjes of Isesstrasse 30, Hamburg. Ontjes and Marga's 'Ostjes' are one and the same, the discrepancy perhaps down to an error in the transcription of a *Daily Express* reporter's shorthand. Dora was married to Abwehrstelle Hamburg counter-intelligence officer Hauptmann Conrad Ontjes and Marga's claim that Conrad belonged to the Gestapo is understandable as she was unlikely to have heard of Abwehr, but would have been only too well aware of the former organisation.[13]

The most likely scenario is that Dora Ontjes told her husband of her friend Jessie's plans to return to Scotland and, as a spycatcher rather than an agent runner, Conrad Ontjes passed this on to his Abwehrstelle Hamburg colleague Hilmar Dierks. A veteran of Germany's First World War military intelligence service Abteilung IIIB and a man so addicted to the spying game that he had even offered his services to MI6 in 1925, Dierks had run a second-hand car dealership before returning to espionage at Abwehrstelle Hamburg in 1935. Recalled by a colleague as an individualist who was allowed to work with a minimum of interference, that lack of oversight would lead to Dierks being allowed to reactivate double agent Christopher Draper in February 1936 with a letter asking if he would be willing to supply 'air mail stamps' for his 'old acquaintances in Hamburg'. Should Draper be ready to restart his career as a Nazi spy, he was to reply to a Herr L. Sanders, P.O. Box 629, Hamburg.[14]

Draper, whom any competent Nazi spymaster would have written off as blown after his earlier brush with Abwehr, reported the approach and MI5 added P.O. Box 629 to their intercept list, partly to keep an eye on Draper whom they did not trust, but principally to see where it led. And it led first to Arthur Owens, a devious and unpleasant British businessman recruited by MI6 in January 1936 to report on German naval developments. Returning from his first trip to Germany as a British spy, the Welsh-born Owens reported that he had also been recruited by Abwehr. Given the code name Snow, a none too subtle partial anagram of his surname, Owens was run as a British double agent for nine months until, in September 1936, MI5's P.O. Box 629 intercept revealed, greatly to MI6's chagrin, that he was playing both sides to maximise access to the money and uncommonly obliging women provided by Dierks and his Abwehr colleagues.[15]

The P.O. Box 629 intercept also revealed that Dierks alias Sanders was replying with vague offers of employment to retired British officers advertising in the Situations Wanted columns of *The Times*. Typical was the case of Captain Jack Battye of the Royal Artillery who, thinking of retiring from the army in October 1936, advertised for a job. This brought an offer of a post as an 'agent of a news agency' from Herr Sanders of P.O. Box 629. Invited to a meeting in Germany and sent £11 to cover his expenses, the innocent Battye decided against retiring, returned the money and rejoined his regiment in India. Still Dierks would not give up, pestering Battye for 'essays of special interest' on the British colony. Another case involved commercial traveller Sidney Gray who advertised for a job in *The Times* and, sent £10 to cover his expenses by Herr Sanders, met Dierks in an Amsterdam hotel on 29 October 1936 and was asked to spy on British and French military airfields. Gray called off the arrangement and later told MI5 that he had only been interested in conning the Germans out of money.[16]

For Dierks, Jessie Jordan would have been another promising recruit. Granted she knew nothing whatsoever about the military, but she could pass for a native in Britain and, with Marga and young Jessie still living in Hamburg, she had a ready-made excuse for frequent trips back to Germany. On 26 June 1937, five months after Jessie had stepped ashore at Leith in Scotland, the MI5 intercept on P.O. Box 629 picked up a letter that had been posted at the village of Talgarth in Brecon, Wales. The envelope held postcards of Aldershot annotated to show prominent landmarks including the Royal Engineers Officers' Mess, a neighbouring parade ground and the prominent spire of the Garrison Church of All Saints. There was also a sheet of notes in German that read:

Officers' Mess. 25 windows. 2 stories.

Tattoo ½ hour of [illegible].

Avenue to Officers' Mess. 1000 paces. It is in the middle.

Long side except G. 1000 paces [illegible].

Have been in the barrack square from back entrance and have watched the horse parade. 9 a.m.. Further by word of mouth.[17]

That a German spy would be interested in a garrison town like Aldershot came as no surprise, but there was nothing to identify the sender until another P.O. Box 629 letter, clearly from the same person and this time postmarked at Broughty Ferry near Dundee, was intercepted three weeks later. This held a folded envelope on which there was a partially erased address that MI5 were able to reconstruct to read Mrs ------, c/o Haddow, 16 Breadalb--- Terrace, Perth, Scotland. The folded envelope held an invitation to a Mrs Jordan to attend a meeting in Holland at the end of July. Further enquiries by the police revealed that a Mrs Jessie Jordan was indeed living with her half-brother Willie Haddow, a railwayman, at 16 Breadalbane Terrace in Perth. The Perth address was immediately added to the MI5 intercept list.[18]

What Jessie had been doing in a remote Welsh village remained a mystery until an intercepted letter from her half-sister Mary revealed that, early in June, she had taken her five-year-old nephew Billy Haddow to visit her aunt who ran a convalescent home at Felin Newydd in Brecon. The primary purpose behind the visit had been to borrow money to start a business, but she also had some spying to do, so she had travelled on alone to Southampton where she bought postcards of the docks, then took a train to Aldershot. As she recalled later:

> Staying the night in a local hotel, I spent the next morning taking a look round. I walked round the barracks, quite slowly, and reached the back. There I saw an open gate and looked through. For a moment or two I stood undecided. Then I boldly entered. After all, I was just a visitor.[19]

An Ordnance Survey map from a nearby stationery shop would have yielded more accurate intelligence, yet this British-born woman could have been under no illusions about the malign intent behind her mission. Just as Hermann Görtz and Marianne Emig had been doing two years before, she was pinpointing targets for Luftwaffe bombs, bombs that would, if dropped, kill or maim many of the soldiers and civilians she could see around her. Her conscience evidently untroubled by this inconvenient truth, Jessie returned to Perth with the promise of a £300 loan from her aunt and started looking for somewhere she could start a hairdressing business. On

27 July 1937 a *Dundee Courier* classified advertisement caught her eye and led her, three days later, to that first meeting with Mary Curran.[20]

> **L**ADIES' and gents' hairdressing saloons, stationer and tobacconist (combined), for sale. Cheap for quick disposal. 36 Advertiser. 8629

The intercept on Jessie's mail in Perth yielded nothing else of interest for the next three months, the same three months during which Mary Curran was trying to get her evidence of Jessie's duplicity taken seriously in Dundee, the same three months that only ended on that dramatic Friday in November 1937 when John Carstairs arrived at MI5 with the sketch Mary had taken from Kinloch Street and, back in Dundee, Mary and John escorted Jessie through the darkened docks to the SS *Courland*.

* * *

Jessie was no longer able to look after Willie Haddow's children now that she was running a business in Dundee, so Marga and her daughter had come over from Germany and moved into the Perth flat while Jessie took a rented room in a Stirling Street tenement close to the Kinloch Street salon. And it was there one bitterly cold morning early in December 1937 that Jessie slipped as she left for work and sprained her ankle. Mary was left to open up at Kinloch Street and discovered that Jessie had left her attaché case in the staff cubicle. Hurriedly rifling through it, she found a road map of Scotland complete with pencil markings in Jessie's handwriting. Opposite the RAF airfield at Montrose was the word Barracks, the coast defence battery at Broughty Ferry was marked with the letters BB and landmarks lining the approaches to the Royal Navy base at Rosyth in the Firth of Forth were highlighted with crosses.

The police obviously had to see this and, once again, the resourceful Mary Curran had a plan. Closing up that evening, she went round to Stirling Street to double-check that her employer was still bed-ridden and unable to walk, then she returned to Kinloch

Street, shoved the map down the front of her dress and hurried home. Detective Lieutenant Carstairs was tracked down to the Dundee Police Christmas dance in the Palais Dance Hall and the map was photographed in time for Mary to replace it later that night.[21]

MI5 had put a mail intercept in place on the Kinloch Street salon immediately after John Carstairs' visit to London and, on 9 December, two days after Mary found the map, Dundee Post Office supervisor Alexander Jack held an envelope addressed to Jessie Jordan in the jet of steam from a boiling kettle just long enough to soften the glue. He then eased open the flap with a sharp knife, drew out the contents and reached for his camera. Resealing the letter and replacing in the system for delivery, he packaged the film and sent it off on the night mail train to the Post Office Investigations Branch at Mount Pleasant Sorting Office in London.

When prints of Alexander Jack's photographs reached MI5 the next morning they revealed a letter, neatly typed in German and posted in New York on 1 December, that Jessie was to forward to a 'Herr S' in Hamburg. Translated by Edward Hinchley Cooke, it said little of consequence beyond an oblique reference to Kinloch Street as 'the English address', the geographic error a reflection of the American habit of referring to the whole United Kingdom as England. But it did include a reference to another mailbox address belonging to Herr S in 'Gneis. Strasse' that MI5 rightly took to be short for a Hamburg street called Gneisenaustrasse. Herr S was clearly Sanders and Hinchley Cooke's margin note in Jessie Jordan's MI5 file confirms that he made the connection with the case of German-born Else Duncombe, another of Sanders' mailbox agents under MI5 surveillance in London, who had begun using a Gneisenaustrasse cut-out address just the previous month.

The only other letter of interest to be intercepted before the end of 1937 was one posted at Groningen in the Netherlands on 28 December that held a compliments slip from a Dutch bank and a single £5 note, Jessie's monthly retainer from Abwehr. Perhaps it was with this that Jessie bought the bottle of whisky she had with her when she joined the Currans for the traditional Scottish Hogmanay celebration to welcome in 1938. Mary recalled that she was 'very merry, chaffing other visitors and singing', though she did become increasingly morose as the evening wore on and her whisky bottle steadily emptied. Another war with Germany was inevitable, she told Mary, and Britain was pushing Germany into it. Perhaps with her own, albeit meagre, efforts on behalf of the Luftwaffe in mind, Jessie even suggested to a shaken Mary that she and her children would be well advised to get out of Britain while they still could.[22]

Jessie was then still unaware that she was under surveillance. The clumsy resealing of one intercepted letter had led her to suspect that her mail was being tampered with, but Mary was able to reassure her that that sort of thing just never happened in Dundee. Another four letters from the New York agent, who was now using the code name Crown, were intercepted in Dundee towards the end of January. The first two were of little interest and the third, picked up on 27 January, outlined Agent Crown's bizarre scheme to use forged White House stationery to steal the plans of the new US Navy aircraft carriers *Yorktown* and *Enterprise*. The scheme was so palpably ludicrous that, rather than lose Jessie's mail as a useful source on Abwehr networks by revealing the case to the Americans, MI5 decided to keep a watching brief to see where it led. That would change the very next day, Friday, 28 January 1938, when the letter that would transform the case into an international counter-espionage investigation was steamed open in Dundee Post Office.

Alexander Jack's photographs of this latest Agent Crown letter arrived at MI5 the next morning and they revealed a plot to lure a US Army officer to a bogus staff meeting in a New York hotel and forcibly relieve him of secret defence plans for the east coast of the United States:

> You have probably heard in the meantime that I am con-
> templating a little coup for the latter part of this month.
> It is a question of obtaining details of coast defence oper-
> ations and bases on the Atlantic coast. These records are
> in the hands of Colonel Eglin, the post commander at Fort
> Totten, N.Y. I shall order the gentleman to appear before

a supposed Emergency Staff Meeting to be held in the Hotel McAlpin in New York on Monday, January 31st or Tuesday, Feb. 1st . . . Upon his arrival at the Hotel I shall ascertain his condition regarding possible companions and shall then take him to a room for which arrangements have previously been made. There we shall attempt to overpower him and remove papers that he will have been ordered to fetch along. I shall make every effort to leave clues that would point to communistic perpetrators. The matter will probably stir up a little dirt, but I believe it will work out all right.[23]

If waiting to see where some correspondence from an apparently low-grade Abwehr agent in New York might lead had seemed sound policy hitherto, this was different. A man's life could be in imminent danger, perhaps even within the next 48 hours, so MI5 Director General Sir Vernon Kell and Edward Hinchley Cooke met with US Military Attaché Colonel Raymond Lee that same afternoon and handed the American a memorandum carefully worded to conceal the source of MI5's information. It read:

We have strong grounds for believing that a serious attempt is to be made, either on Monday, 31st January, or Tuesday, 1st February, to obtain by force from Colonel Eglin, the Post Commander, Fort Totten, New York, information regarding coast defence operations and bases on the Atlantic coast.

Colonel Eglin will receive a bogus message purporting to come from the Aide-de-Camp of the Second Corps area in G.I. ordering him to appear before a supposed emergency staff meeting to be held in the McAlpin Hotel, New York, on one or other of the above dates in question . . .

The actual perpetrator is a German espionage agent (he may be of any nationality: he has a good knowledge of the English language) whose identity is unknown, but concerning him the following facts are available:-

He is, or has been, a pilot, and has been asked to submit

an application for reappointment to the Air Corps, and has done so. In this application in the space provided for 'choice of station' he is alleged to have named in this order:-
    No. 1 Mitchel Field, Long Island, New York.
    No. 2 Barksdale Field, Louisiana.
    No. 3 Albrook Field, Canal Zone.
    It is further believed that he chose Mitchel Field as No. 1 because it is the Headquarters of the Eastern Division of G.H.Q.A.F., where he has comrades and will consequently have access to code books, maps, etc.
    It is of the utmost importance that in any action which is taken on this information, no indication whatever should be given of the fact that it was obtained in Great Britain.

Colonel Lee passed MI5's information on to Washington by enciphered telegram that same evening. But MI5 had not told Lee the whole story; they had not revealed another letter intercepted in Dundee, a letter that would have led the Americans straight to Agent Crown and his accomplices. It was also a letter that would, within weeks, take the investigation in a new and wholly unexpected direction.[24]

Chapter 5

Heil President Roosevelt!

Go ahead, investigate the hell out of these cocksuckers!

U.S. Secretary of State Cordell Hull

Colonel Lee's telegram clattered off a teleprinter in the headquarters of US Army military intelligence at 5.33 p.m. Washington time on that Saturday evening, 29 January 1938. At 2 p.m. on the Sunday, two days after Jessie Jordan's letter was steamed open in Scotland, Lieutenant Colonel Charles Busbee of the US Army General Staff and Major Joe Dalton, the Assistant Chief of Staff, US Army Intelligence (G2), arrived at the FBI Field Office in Foley Square, New York City, their mission to brief the G-men on the plot to lure Colonel Eglin to the Hotel McAlpin. Colonel Eglin was warned to be on his guard and FBI agents kept watch on the lobby of the McAlpin for the next two days, but saw nothing suspicious.[1]

Two weeks later, on Monday, 14 February, Ira Hoyt of the State Department Passport Division in New York received a very peculiar phone call. The caller identified himself as Secretary of State Cordell Hull, claimed he was in New York incognito and instructed Hoyt to send 35 blank American passport application forms to the Taft Hotel in a package marked for the attention of Edward Weston. Hoyt was immediately suspicious and, having checked that Cordell Hull was actually in Washington, called in State Department Special Agent Thomas Fitch who arranged for a dummy package to be sent to the Taft that afternoon. A Mr Weston had meanwhile telephoned the Western Union office in Grand Central Station and asked them to collect his package from the Taft. Unaware that his package was now bait in a carefully laid trap, 'Weston' called Western Union again the following day and was told by a member of staff, who had been briefed by Fitch, that they were now holding his package. 'Weston' gave instructions for the package to be forwarded to the Varick Street Western Union office, then called the Varick Street office and told them to deliver it to the Kings Castle Tavern in nearby Hudson Street.

Watched by a dark-haired man from a soda fountain across Varick Street, a messenger boy left the Western Union office later that afternoon and headed along King Street towards the Kings Castle Tavern. Hurrying along a parallel route on Hudson Street, the dark-haired man arrived opposite the bar just in time to see the messenger disappear inside. The man followed, ordered a beer and carefully checked for any sign that the place was being watched. Nothing seemed out of the ordinary, so he went back outside, handed another boy who just happened to be passing two dollars and asked him to go into the bar and collect Mr Weston's package. The boy did as he was told and was arguing with the man about the size of his tip when New York Police Department detectives John Murray and Arthur Silk pounced and frogmarched the dark-haired man off to the State Department office in the Post Office building on 8th Avenue.[2]

Questioned by Detective Murray, the man gave his name as Günther Rumrich and claimed that he had been drinking at the Steuben Tavern in Times Square when he met an Edward Weston who said he was a member of a syndicate gathering information on the United States military. Weston had asked Rumrich to get the blank passport forms and was due to call him the following day at the Varick Street offices of the Denver Chemical Manufacturing Company where he worked as a translator.

Searching the briefcase that Rumrich had been carrying when he was arrested, State Department Special Agent Clifford Tubbs found, stuffed in among a sheaf of Army and Naval registers and maps, a copy of a message summoning Colonel Henry Eglin, the commanding officer at Fort Totten, to a meeting at the Hotel McAlpin. The message read:

A secret emergency staff meeting is scheduled to be held at the McAlpin Hotel NY on Friday, January 28, 1938. Your attendance is requested and you are called upon to observe the following details:

1. You will not divulge the nature or the circumstances of the meeting to anyone.
2. You will appear in civilian clothes and arrive and leave unattended.
3. You will time your departure so as to arrive at the Hotel McAlpin at 12.20 P.M. on Friday, 28 January 1938.
4. You will sit yourself in the main lobby of the hotel and await being paged as Mr Thomas W. Conway. After identifying yourself as such, you will be escorted to the meeting rooms.
5. You will bring with you all mobilization and coast defence plans in your possession, also pertinent maps and charts and a notebook for entries at the meeting.
6. It is repeated that the utmost discretion is expected of you in regard to this matter, as no one is informed except those directly concerned.
7. You will acknowledge receipt of this memorandum by repeating the same to the officer phoning you this message.

Signed: Malin Craig

Major General, U.S. Army, Chief of Staff.[3]

Tubbs called in Major Joe Dalton from Governors Island who immediately made the connection between the Eglin message and Colonel Lee's telegram from London. Dalton was then still unaware that the information from MI5 had originated in mail intercepted on its way to Jessie Jordan's hairdressing salon in Scotland, a mail intercept that had only been put in place thanks to the efforts of housewife spycatcher Mary Curran. But he did insist that, as the FBI was already investigating the Eglin plot, Rumrich should be handed over to them as soon as possible.

Rumrich spent the next day with detectives Murray and Silk, waiting in his office for a call that never came from the non-existent Mr Weston. Having put the otherwise boring day to good use working out a strategy, he asked that evening if he could expect leniency in return for revealing everything he knew about German spies in the United States, then brazenly handed Special Agent Tom Fitch and Assistant US Attorney Lester Dunigan a list of conditions to be met if he was to cooperate:

1. Personal safety for myself, my wife and children.
2. No press or other kind of publicity to be given in this matter until all persons were in custody.
3. Quashing of all charges against me by the United States Army or any other authority.
4. Aid to wipe out personal indebtedness.
5. Permission to move freely after I have lived up to my side of the bargain.
6. Permission to change my name.
7. No deportation.

Fitch put a call through to Chief Special Agent Robert Bannerman at the State Department in Washington and was firmly told that Rumrich's demands were unacceptable. But Fitch was keen to encourage his prisoner to talk, so he lied and told his prisoner that every effort would be made to meet his conditions. With that, Rumrich launched into his life story saying that he had been born in December 1911 in Chicago where his father, Alfons, was Secretary at the Austro-Hungarian legation. He had spent the war years with his family in Germany before settling in reduced circumstances at Teplitz-Schönau, modern-day Teplice in the Czech Republic. Restless and entitled to American citizenship by accident of birth, he had sailed for New York in September 1929 with just $100 in his pocket, but could scarcely have picked a worse time to emigrate as he arrived just three weeks before Black Thursday ushered in the Wall Street Crash and the Great Depression. Reduced to living in poverty at the Bowery branch of the Y.M.C.A., he had been lucky to find work as a warehouseman, then a carpenter's mate, that saw him through until, on 25 January 1930, he was able to enlist in the US Army.[4]

Rumrich's military career had been, he had to admit, short and undistinguished. Averse to taking orders, he had deserted his post in the Surgeon's Office at Governors Island in New York after just five months and hitch-hiked west as far as Pittsburgh before he ran out of money and had to give himself up. Returning to duty after four months in detention, he was promoted to sergeant in 1932 and posted first to the Panama Canal Zone, then, early in 1935, to Fort Missoula in Montana. It must have seemed that Sergeant Rumrich had turned his life around, but this young man had a considerable talent for getting himself into trouble and, just four months after arriving in Montana, he was forced to marry his pregnant girlfriend, sixteen-year-old Guri Bloomquist. He then did the only other thing he was any good at: he ran away.

With $50 stolen from the Fort Missoula base hospital fund, he made his way to New York, where he found work as a dishwasher in a Manhattan restaurant. He did eventually find a better paid job as a translator at the Denver Chemical Manufacturing Company and, in what must have come as a considerable culture shock after the wide open spaces of Montana, installed his wife and son in a three-roomed apartment in the Bronx. Otherwise, he stuck doggedly to his story about meeting the supposed German spy in the Steuben Bar and being offered money in return for the blank passport forms.

Late editions of the next morning's New York newspapers were found to be running a story about a spy who had been arrested while trying to steal actual passports, not the passport application forms that Rumrich had tried to get. Meanwhile, as furious accusations flew back and forth between State and the NYPD about the press leak, Major Dalton was trying to convince his superiors in US Army Intelligence that this was a far more important case than the theft of a few passport application forms. But State were still refusing to hand Rumrich over to the FBI as, should the Bureau charge him under the Federal Impersonation Statute, Cordell Hull would be called to appear as a witness in court. And Secretary

Hull had made it crystal clear that, sooner than allow that to happen, he would order the passport forms case to be dropped. Rumrich would then be handed over to the military as a deserter.[5]

The bickering between State and Justice continued into the Friday afternoon with FBI Director Hoover now reluctant to take the case on as the newspaper leak meant that others involved in the conspiracy would have been warned off and a Bureau investigation would lead nowhere. Hoover had a point and when detectives Murray and Silk accompanied Rumrich on a visit to see his wife and baby son, he assured his weeping wife that he had been arrested on a minor charge and would be home soon. But Joe Dalton's persistence did finally pay off and, at 10 a.m. the following morning, Saturday, 19 February, Special Agent Fitch delivered his loudly complaining prisoner to the FBI Field Office. State were still far from happy and, as FBI Assistant Director Ed Tamm recorded in a memo for Director Hoover:

> Sometime later in the afternoon of February 19, Mr Fitch telephonically communicated with the Bureau and advised that he had received instructions from the State Department to the effect that he should communicate immediately with the New York office and inform the Bureau that the Secretary of State does not desire that the Bureau prosecute Rumrich under the Impersonation Statute, and suggested that Rumrich be turned over to the military authorities, inasmuch as the latter had admitted that he, in 1935, deserted from the US Army while stationed at Fort Missoula, Montana. Several times during the day Mr Fitch telephoned the New York office and stated that he was being pressed by the State Department for confirmation that the Bureau had turned Rumrich over to the military authorities.[6]

New York Special Agent in Charge Reed Vetterli delegated Rumrich's interrogation to his multi-lingual colleague Leon Turrou. A fascinating if controversial character much given to self-promotion, Turrou inspired one recent author to pithily observe that his many and varied accounts of his early life were 'erratic to the point of invention'. Born Leon Turovsky in September 1895 at Kobryn in what was then Russian-occupied Poland and is now Belarus, he was supposedly orphaned before his first birthday and adopted by a wealthy merchant who sent him to school in Berlin and London. He would later claim that he had emigrated to the United States aged eighteen and worked as a translator for the *New York Times*. His accounts of military service during the First World War are, to say the least, wildly inconsistent. One version had him serving in the Imperial Russian Army on the Eastern Front until the 1917 revolution, then a Polish unit attached to the French Foreign Legion on the Western Front. Another version had him injured while serving with the US Marines at the Battle of Château-Thierry in July 1918 and yet another had him wounded while serving in the French Army in 1916 and falling in love with nurse Teresa Zakrewski in a Paris hospital. The war over, he supposedly followed Teresa to China and married her there.[7]

If this reads like romantic fiction, that is because much of it is just that, pure fiction. Applying for an emergency US passport in Warsaw in July 1922, Teresa Zakrewski produced documents showing that she had married Leon Turovsky at the Mother of God Catholic Church in Vladivostok, Russia, on 19 October 1917, four days after her seventeenth birthday and just as the Bolshevik October Revolution was getting under way in far-off Moscow and Petrograd (St Petersburg). Their first son, Edward, was born in Siberia in November 1918 and their second son, Victor, was born, also in Siberia, in December 1919. Given Leon's necessary procreative role in these events, meeting his supposed military commitments on the Western Front would have made him a most unusually well-travelled soldier. And his presence in Vladivostok and Siberia at this time suggests that he was somehow caught up in the Allied military intervention in the civil war that followed the Bolshevik Revolution.

Private Turovsky actually enlisted in the Marine Corps in France in March 1920, sixteen months after the end of the war in Europe and just as the Soviet-backed Far Eastern Republic was established in the wake of the collapse of the ill-conceived Allied intervention in Siberia. By then he had supposedly been told that Teresa and the children had been killed in the Russian Civil War and, boarding a troopship at Antwerp for New York in November 1920, gave Rebecca Turovsky of 603 Dumont Avenue, Brooklyn, as his mother and emergency contact. This hardly squares with his claim that he had been orphaned more than two decades earlier when his mother had died in childbirth.[8]

Discharged from the Marines on medical grounds in May 1921, Turovsky applied for US citizenship, changed his surname to Turrou and joined the American Relief Agency in post-revolutionary Russia. While in Moscow he was able to trace Teresa and the children and extract them from Siberia, the family reaching New York on 24 March 1923 and eventually setting up home in Westbury, Long Island. Turrou was then involved in a dubious business venture to import dried mushrooms that, if his travels in 1923 are anything to go by, probably had more to do with smuggling valuables into and out of the Soviet Union. The L. &. N. Mushroom Company soon failed and Turrou worked for the Post Office until campaigning for Herbert Hoover, the Republican candidate in the 1928 presidential election and his old boss in the American Relief Agency, earned him a post initially as an interpreter for what was then still the Bureau of Investigation. He might not have had the law degree that J. Edgar Hoover had stipulated as a minimum qualification for a Special Agent, but he was fluent in seven languages, a very useful asset in America's polyglot society. Promoted rapidly, by the time he began the interrogation of Günther Rumrich, Turrou had been involved in several high-profile cases including the still-controversial investigation into the kidnap and murder of the baby son of aviation pioneer Charles Lindbergh.[9]

Questioned by Turrou, Rumrich initially stuck to the statement he had given the State Department agents about meeting a mysterious spy named Weston who had asked him to get the blank passport forms. This was obvious nonsense and Turrou decided the fastest way to the truth was to appeal to his prisoner's very obvious vanity. He wrote later that he began by saying:

'Now look here, Rumrich,' I said suddenly. 'Why did you fool those officers?'

He stiffened, but immediately relaxed further than at
any moment since he had entered the room. Of course, he
hadn't fooled them at all, but he liked the idea.

'Fool them, Sir?' he repeated, 'What do you mean?'

'This statement here,' I said, picking it up. 'Listen to it.'
I read snatches. 'You're not the childish dupe this makes
you out to be. This makes you out a nitwit. The dumbest
jury would laugh in your face!'[10]

According to Turrou, Rumrich appeared lost in thought for a
few moments, then agreed to talk, though only after he had first
spoken to his wife. A call was put through to a grocery store near
the family's apartment in the Bronx and a tearful and heavily pregnant Guri Rumrich duly arrived at Foley Square that afternoon with
her son Gerry only to be told to return to her family in Montana.
Having thus discarded his wife and child, and ended his marriage,
in a matter of minutes, Rumrich did indeed talk at great length, an
exhausted Turrou having to call a halt to that first session in the
early hours of the Sunday morning. But the extraordinary story that
emerged would throw American naïvety about the threat posed by
Nazi espionage and subversion into sharp focus.[11]

* * *

The American counter-intelligence services that had proved so
effective against the Kaiser's spies and saboteurs during the First
World War had been all but closed down. And Secretary of State
Henry Stimson had famously withdrawn funding for the US Army's
Black Chamber cryptanalysis operation in 1929, piously claiming
that 'Gentlemen do not read each other's mail'. The high-minded
Stimson's seemingly naïve, moralist stance was actually cover for
an internal reorganisation driven in part by the US Army Signal
Corps' wish to reorganise its cryptanalysis operations and be rid of
the Black Chamber's erratically brilliant head, Herbert O. Yardley.
But it was soon overtaken by events, not least the October 1929
Wall Street Crash which brought mass unemployment and opened
the door to extremists with seductively simple answers to complex

problems. One such was eccentric press baron William Randolph Hearst who took to extolling Hitler's every deed in print, and another was Catholic priest and anti-Semitic demagogue Father Charles Coughlin who was peddling his race hate on radio, the new mass media.

Hearst and Coughlin were at least openly fascist, but in 1934 a sinister cabal of businessmen was found to have been secretly plotting a Nazi-style *coup d'état* to replace the newly elected President Roosevelt with a fascist dictator. Leading figures in the 'Business Plot' included Singer sewing machine heir Robert Clark, banker Prescott Bush, the grandfather of President George W. Bush, and Du Pont Industries head Irénée du Pont. Clearly unhinged, du Pont once suggested to a group of businessmen that the United States should be run by supermen, a corruption of the Nietzschean Übermenschen concept, who were to be given performance-enhancing drugs soon after birth. The boys to benefit from this treatment would, of course, be selected on the basis of their racial purity. Du Pont also invested heavily in I. G. Farben and General Motors subsidiary Opel, fully aware that both German companies were substantial financial backers of the Nazi Party. Unwisely, however, the business plotters had chosen as their figurehead General Smedley Butler, a Marine Corps hero known for being no lover of bankers and war profiteers. Butler exposed the plot but, aside from an FBI raid on J. P. Morgan banker Grayson Murphy's office, the scandal was covered up to avoid having many of the United States' most prominent businessmen exposed as deranged traitors.[12]

The 'Business Plot' might have failed, but American fascist groups were not slow in seizing the opportunities afforded by the Depression to stir up trouble among German-American communities in Los Angeles, New York, Chicago, Milwaukee and Detroit. Nazi propaganda was being smuggled into New York, American Nazis were drilling with rifles 'borrowed' from the New York National Guard and German-American children were belting out the *Horst-Wessel-Lied* at Nazi camps in Long Island and New Jersey organised by the Friends of the New Germany. Leading American anti-Nazis were receiving death threats and the German vice-consul in Los Angeles was being linked to the Silver Shirts, a pro-Hitler gang with, at its peak, 15,000 members drawn mainly from western states. Led by the half-mad Hollywood scriptwriter, William Dudley Pelley, the Silver Shirts were planning to march on San Diego City Hall and lynch the Under-Sheriff, a Jew.[13]

Seen from Berlin, *New York Times* stories that 20,000 'racial comrades' were giving Nazi salutes and cheering Hitler at swastika-bedecked Madison Square Garden rallies must have suggested to some that the German-American diaspora was at least receptive to the National Socialist message. Yet the vast majority of the 5 million ethnic Germans in the United States were second or third gener-ation Americans, often of German-Jewish stock, who cared little for Germany and still less for Nazism. Indeed, the vast majority of German-Americans were repelled by the likes of Griebl and his associate Raymond Healey, an Irish-American fascist and self-styled American Hitler, who told Un-American Activities Committee co-chairman Sam Dickstein, a Lithuanian-born Jew, that American streets would soon run red with Jewish blood.[14]

In Germany, meanwhile, Nazi Party thugs were adding injury to insult with a string of unprovoked attacks on American visitors. New York furrier Philip Zuckerman and his wife, tourist Rolf Kaltenborn and his sixteen-year-old son, businessman Roland Velz and his wife, Brooklyn doctor Daniel Mulvihill and student Sam Bossard were all beaten up when they ignored Nazi parades. Medical student Walter Orloff was dragged from his bed in Greifswald University and badly beaten, New York student Helen Lyster was interrogated by the Gestapo simply because she had a camera slung over her shoulder while watching Stormtroopers drilling at Munich airport and Chicago teacher Richard Roiderer was jailed for four months in Munich because he had 'suspicious entries' in a notebook. Elsa Sittell from New York spent ten days in prison after she suggested to a German customs officer, rather unwisely, that Hitler was a Jew.

One particularly high-profile case involved merchant seaman Lawrence Simpson from Seattle who was arrested aboard his ship, the SS *Manhattan*, in Cuxhaven harbour on 28 June 1935. The Gestapo clearly knew what they were looking for when they found what was described as 'communist literature' in Simpson's cabin and the young seaman spent fifteen gruelling months in Hamburg's infamous Fuhlsbüttel concentration camp before appearing in court on 28 September 1936. Sentenced to three more years in prison and by then in poor health, Simpson was quietly released and deported back to the United States the following month.

Perhaps the most notorious case involved Isabel Steele, a Canadian-born Los Angeles violinist studying in Berlin. Arrested in the round-up of those linked to Polish spy Jerzy Sosnowski and Baroness Benita von Berg, the garrulous and indiscreet Isabel had not helped her case by voicing strong anti-Nazi sentiments to her seventeen-year-old sister Marian's Nazi zealot boyfriend. The 23-year-old Isabel was no spy, but she was imprisoned for four months before being bundled aboard an American liner at Hamburg in December 1934. Her lurid tales of exhausting interrogations, of being repeatedly told that she was to be executed and of being forced to lure a friend, anti-Nazi film star Brigitte Helm, the hauntingly beautiful star of Fritz Lang's masterpiece *Metropolis*, into a Gestapo trap were syndicated across the United States soon after her return. And all this took place as horrified Americans living in Germany learned that they could be forcibly sterilised if they had what the Nazis deemed were hereditary diseases.[15]

The reality was that those attracted to American Nazi organisations tended to be a small minority of 412,000 post-war immigrants who, like Ignatz Griebl, had been embittered by Germany's 1918 defeat and the chaos that followed. Like all fanatics, they squandered much of their time and energy bickering amongst themselves, but it was all too easy in the febrile atmosphere of the Depression for them to be seen as a viable threat and there was still no federal agency with the power to investigate and prosecute subversion or espionage. President Roosevelt was sufficiently alarmed to summon J. Edgar Hoover, by then Director of the Federal Bureau of Investigation, to the White House in May 1934 and authorise him to conduct a 'very careful and searching investigation' into the Nazi movement in America including 'any possible connection with official representatives of the German government'.

The FBI's new remit was, as one Hoover biographer writes, 'a departure from the 1924 edict of Attorney General Harlan Fiske Stone that the activities of the Bureau "be limited strictly to violations of the law"'. It was also arguably unconstitutional and the White House was careful not to commit it to paper. But the Bureau still had no power to arrest or prosecute spies; this would only change after Office of Naval Intelligence cryptanalyst Agnes Driscoll decrypted a Japanese diplomatic telegram in which the letters TO-MI-MU-RA appeared to identify an intelligence source in the US Navy. Told by a Japanese language specialist that 'mura' could mean 'son', Driscoll realised the telegram referred to a Japanese spy named Tomison, or more likely Thompson. The spy turned out to be former US Navy clerk Harry Thompson who, wearing his old signals yeoman's uniform, had simply walked aboard warships in San Diego naval base, helped himself to documents left lying around and marched ashore again, still unchallenged. On 2 July 1936, Thompson was sentenced to fifteen years at the McNeil Island Corrections Center, the first spy to be convicted in the United States since 1918.[16]

Driscoll's breakthrough led the US Navy to another bungling Japanese spy, alcoholic former naval officer John Farnsworth. Yet the detection of Thompson and Farnsworth had only come about as an accidental by-product of American military espionage, not counter-espionage. The days of innocence were over and the State Department, Secret Service, even the Post Office Department were all vying to take on a counter-espionage role. But it was J. Edgar Hoover who went to the White House at the end of August 1936, a month after Farnsworth's arrest, and was granted what he would interpret as sweeping new powers to investigate both Communists and Nazis. 'Go ahead,' Secretary of State Cordell Hull is said to have told a delighted Hoover, 'investigate the hell out of these cocksuckers!'[17]

* * *

Rumrich, as Turrou rightly observed, 'did some lying about his own complicity' under interrogation but did admit to having decided to become a spy after reading the memoirs of Germany's First World

War spymaster Colonel Walter Nicolai in the New York Public Library. Unsure of how to make contact with the right people in Germany, in January 1936 he hit upon the idea of writing to the Nazi Party newspaper *Völkischer Beobachter* enclosing a letter that he asked the paper to forward to Nicolai. Should Nicolai be interested in his services, he was to place an advertisement in the Public Notices section of the *New York Times* addressed to Theodor Koerner.

Nicolai was then a long-retired faux academic rewriting German history in the Nazi idiom, so Rumrich's letter had been passed to Hilmar Dierks at Abwehrstelle Hamburg and the advertisement that appeared in the *New York Times* on 6 April 1936 carried Dierks' alias Sanders and, in yet another tradecraft lapse, the same P.O. Box 629 address he had used on many other occasions including both the Draper and Jordan cases.

THEODOR KOERNER — LETTER RE-
ceived. please send reply and address to
Sanders, Hamburg 1. Postbox 629, Germany.

Dashing off a reply giving Sanders, in reality Dierks, an exaggerated account of his military service, Rumrich was then asked for details of units stationed in the Panama Canal Zone, a test assignment he was able to complete from memory as he had served there as recently as November 1935. This brought a payment of $40 along with a request for intelligence on US Navy movements off the Atlantic coast of the United States, information that Rumrich had to admit that he could not supply. Asking a former non-commissioned soldier barely able to tell the difference between a destroyer and a cruiser for accurate intelligence on naval movements was only inviting misinformation. This was, in any case, another pointless exercise as daily reports of US Navy movements were published in the *New York Times*.[18]

More than a year had then passed with Rumrich passing on chicken feed and getting nothing in return. It seemed his plan to become a master spy was going nowhere until, in September 1937, he was summoned to a meeting in New York's Café Hindenburg with Abwehr courier Karl Schlüter, the same Karl Schlüter who had worked with Wilhelm Lonkowski two years before. Meetings with Schlüter and other couriers including Theodor Schütz, a steward on the Hamburg-Amerika liner *New York*, had taken place roughly every two weeks and among the schemes Rumrich boasted about to Turrou there was the time he had called the Station Hospital at Fort Hamilton and identified himself as a Major Milton who needed statistics on the incidence of venereal disease at the fort for a lecture. The statistics, which Rumrich knew from his own service included the total strength at the fort, had been delivered by messenger to 'Major Milton' on the corner of East 86th Street and Park Avenue in New York City and passed on to Schlüter at their next meeting. There was the plan to bribe junior officers for information on the new aircraft carriers *Yorktown* and *Enterprise* and there was the plot to lure Colonel Eglin to the bogus staff meeting at the Taft Hotel and relieve him of defence plans. He even claimed to Turrou that an Abwehr courier he only knew as 'Schmidt' would be hiding behind the door armed with a gas gun to help him overpower Colonel Eglin.

At one of their meetings Schlüter had asked Rumrich to trace Senta Dewanger, Wilhelm Lonkowski's former landlady. This was a simple matter that involved looking her up in the Nassau County phone directory before taking a trip out to the Clinton Wine Shop in Hempstead to get a good look at her. He then called her and, posing as a Herr Friedrich von Klotz from Berlin, said that he had a message from her family in Germany that he was unwilling to pass on over the phone. They arranged to meet in the lobby at the Hotel McAlpin a few days later but, having kept a worried Senta waiting for over an hour, 'Herr Klotz' did not show up. Senta was right to be concerned; a post-war investigation by the American Office of Strategic Services (OSS) found evidence that an unidentified Abwehr source had suggested to the Gestapo that they should track down Senta's relatives in Germany, 'who should be punished as hostages'.[19]

Under pressure to justify the $50 monthly stipend he was being paid by Abwehr, Rumrich had invented sub-agents serving in the US Army, among them a soldier improbably named Hestery stationed at Governors Island who was trying to steal a new handgun. Another unnamed and equally imaginary recruit would, if suitably rewarded, be prepared to steal air photographs of American military bases. Pressed by Turrou on his contacts with other German agents and how he communicated with his spymasters, Rumrich revealed that, during one meeting in November 1937, Schlüter had told him that any letters he wished to send to Sanders in Hamburg should be written in English, signed with the code name 'Crown' and addressed to a Mrs Jessie Jordan, 1 Kinloch Street, Dundee, Scotland.[20]

* * *

By the afternoon of Tuesday, 22 February 1938, eight days after his arrest, Rumrich's morale was visibly sinking. He had been expecting that a lawyer would show up to defend him, or that somebody would arrive with bail or even some money for his wife and child. Yet he had heard nothing and any residual loyalty he might have felt for his Abwehr paymasters was waning fast. As Turrou wrote later, when he played on his prisoner's growing sense of isolation and insecurity, he found that Rumrich had saved the best till last:

'Well Rumrich,' I taunted, 'it looks as if your fine-feathered Nazi pals have deserted you.'

His eyes were bitter as he replied, 'Yes it does, Mr Turrou.' He swore quietly for a moment. 'That's why I want to help you smash them.'

'You're not helping us very much,' I said, 'How about your friend Schlüter?'

I really didn't dare hope it would work – but it did. Rumrich continued swearing to himself for almost a full minute; then suddenly he halted, set his small jaw, and declared: 'All right, I'll tell you. Schlüter and his assistant – the red headed Jenni Hofmann – are due in to New York on the next trip of the *Europa*.'[21]

If this exchange really did take place along the lines recorded by Turrou, it does seem odd that he had been unable to work out for himself that couriers Karl Schlüter and Johanna 'Jenni' Hofmann, whom Rumrich had told him were crew aboard *Europa*, would return with the next sailing. But whatever actually happened, Turrou and his team boarded the *Europa* when the liner reached quarantine two days later, on Thursday, 24 February. Posing as immigration officials carrying out a passport check, they found that Schlüter had not sailed but were able to identify Hofmann, easy to spot with her distinctive auburn hair and white uniform. Picked up when she stepped ashore that evening at Pier 86 in the North River and driven to Foley Square, Hofmann admitted that she did indeed know Karl Schlüter, a steward, but that he had not sailed on this trip as he was on holiday. Speaking in German as she had little English, she denied that she had ever met a Günther Rumrich, far less visited his apartment. Then, at a signal from Turrou, Rumrich was brought in and said simply, 'Hallo, Jenni.'[22]

Visibly shocked, Hofmann immediately realised the game was up and confessed that she had first met Schlüter while working on the Norddeutscher Lloyd liner *Gneisenau* and had transferred with him to the *Europa* in February 1936. Having agreed to become Schlüter's courier, she had gone ashore with him when the *Europa* docked in New York on 14 January 1938 and had called on Griebl to discuss espionage targets. They had then visited Martin Schade, a retired German marine engineer whom Schlüter was trying without success to recruit as a spy. Their final call had been on Rumrich who had promised action on getting the aircraft carrier drawings and the blank American passports. They had followed the same routine on their next visit to New York on 4 February, collecting from Rumrich the VD statistics from Fort Hamilton along with typed pages of data copied from the Army and Navy Registers. An Agent Crown letter, posted the next day in New York and intercepted in Dundee, referred to the previous day's visit by 'the gentleman and the lady' who had arrived aboard the *Europa*, and had been given 'several things I have had at my disposal for some time . . . also a letter giving all details about my activity and plans'.

Two weeks later, as the *Europa* was preparing to sail from Bremerhaven on her next run to New York, Schlüter had appeared on board and, after handing her four letters for delivery in New York, told Hofmann that he would not be sailing as he was taking three weeks' holiday. The letters, Hofmann told Turrou, were still in a brown leather bag under her bunk aboard the *Europa* and, on being retrieved from the ship, were found to be addressed to Rumrich, Ignatz Griebl, Kay Moog and Martin Schade. Rumrich's letter was in a simple substitution cipher that would have been a simple matter to decrypt had not Jenni made it even easier for herself, and anyone else for that matter, by stupidly putting the cipher key in the same bag. Decrypted by Hofmann, the letter read:

Dear Friend,

1. I am sending you through Jenni $70 for the code. Kindly give $40 to the one who got the code for you and $30 is for you.
2. How is it with the plans of the aircraft carriers? (Yorktown and Enterprise?) We will pay for all the plans $1,000. If you can get them for $300, then the $700 is for you. So, dear friend, talk about the whole matter with Jenni and tell her how the matter with the plans will be handled. You need not be afraid. So far as the money is concerned, you will see that I take care of everything promptly.
3. What about the pistol matter which we discussed?
4. How is it about the American passports? Please give attention to Jenni. Please inform Jenni of the price.
5. Can you, dear friend, get me various pictures of Army and Navy? I would be very grateful for such. You must state the price to me.
6. How about the anti-aircraft gun? Can you get me something along that line?
7. Addresses of American engineers who worked abroad and did not return.

8. Key procedure.
9. Everything that is known at the Consulate regarding Russian orders from American industry regarding naval matters.

Turrou had Rumrich brought in and learned that the code referred to in the first paragraph was the list of air traffic control signals that had been copied by a friend, Private Erich Glaser, serving in the Air Corps at Mitchel Field, Long Island. The pistol mentioned in the third paragraph was that supposedly being stolen by one of Rumrich's imaginary sub-agents. The key procedure in paragraph eight was an army cipher that Schlüter had mentioned on one of his visits to New York, but had never followed up. And Rumrich was either unable or unwilling to explain the references to 'the Consulate' and Russian orders from American businesses.

Picked up at Mitchel Field, Erich Glaser was obviously small fry who had been persuaded by Rumrich to join the Army Air Corps and steal intelligence on the latest aircraft radios. Always a reluctant spy, Glaser had achieved nothing beyond copying the worthless list of air traffic control signals. Schade also turned out to be of no interest as he had firmly rebuffed Schlüter's attempts at recruitment. But Ignatz Griebl was a different matter entirely, particularly after FBI agents spent much of 25 February, the day after Hofmann's arrest, looking into the doctor's activities, both covert and public, on behalf of the Nazis.

* * *

One of Cordell Hull's principal Nazi 'cocksuckers', Ignatz Theodor Griebl must have appeared the ideal immigrant when he landed at Ellis Island on 10 October 1924. A decorated war veteran and medical student from Würzburg in Bavaria, he told immigration officers that he planned to complete his medical studies and marry his girlfriend, Austrian nurse Maria 'Mizl' Glanz, who had come to the United States two years before. He did indeed marry four days later, took American citizenship in 1927, finished his medical studies at Long Island and Fordham Universities and, after working

Covertly taken by an unknown photographer armed with a concealed camera – probably one of a select few journalists invited to witness the event – this is the only known image of the immensely damaging Abwehr spy Marc Aubert's execution in Toulon. (Nationaal Archief/Collectie Spaarnestad, Den Haag)

'Hitler's replies appeared to be a shrug of the shoulders, given with an air of absolute boredom ...' Christopher Draper (left) in conversation with Hitler at Munich Airport on 15 October 1932.
(From Draper, *The Mad Major*)

Right. Hermann Görtz, German aviation spy. (The National Archives)

Below. A contemporary photograph of the west side of Manston airfield with, in the foreground, the hangar for No. 2 Squadron's Hawker Audax light bombers. The long buildings in the background form part of the RAF's No.3 School of Technical Training. Hermann Görtz and Marianne Emig parked their motorcycle beside the small, white-roofed bus shelter next to Pouce's Farm crossroads and walked around the black-roofed fire station to watch the flying.
(aviationarchives.info)

Above. Broadstairs housewife spycatcher Florence Johnson arriving at the Central Criminal Court in Old Bailey, London, on 4 March 1936 to give evidence against her former tenant, Hermann Görtz. (TopFoto)

Left. Abwehr spy Wilhelm Lonkowski's Long Island landlady Senta Dewanger. (Author's collection)

Above left. Dr Ignatz Griebl arranged Wilhelm Lonkowski's dramatic escape to Canada, then took over his American spy ring. A Nazi zealot and serial philanderer, once arrested by the FBI he would attempt to clear his own name by implicating blameless German-Americans. (Author's collection)

Above right. A characteristically furious Maria Griebl. (Corbis)

Right. Scottish-born hairdresser and Abwehr spy Jessie Jordan. (National Archives)

Dundee housewife spycatcher and Jessie Jordan's resourceful nemesis Mary Curran with her husband, John. (Sharon Gray)

Abwehr spy Günther Rumrich a.k.a. Agent Crown. His indiscreet correspondence, intercepted en route to Jessie Jordan in Scotland, led to the destruction of the Abwehr's New York spy ring. (Author's collection)

In typically coquettish pose, Ignatz Griebl's mistress and co-conspirator Katharina 'Kay' Moog Busch (Author's collection)

Abwehr aviation spies Otto Voss (right) and Erich Glaser pictured during the June 1938 Federal Grand Jury indictment hearing in New York. (Author's collection)

The Prize: Abwehr tasked its American agents with stealing technical information on the new American aircraft carriers USS *Yorktown* and USS *Enterprise*. This intelligence was to be used in the development of the German aircraft carrier *Graf Zeppelin* pictured following her launch at Kiel on 8 December 1938. The Kriegsmarine's unrealistic 'Z' Plan expansion scheme called for the construction of four aircraft carriers by 1947, but only *Graf Zeppelin* was ever launched. Still incomplete when captured by Soviet forces in 1945, the Nazi aircraft carrier was sunk as a practice bombing target in August 1947. (Bundesarchiv)

Left. Former FBI Special Agent Leon Turrou visited France in June 1939 to promote his book *Nazi Spies in America*, later retitled *The Nazi Spy Conspiracy in America*, and the movie *Confessions of a Nazi Spy.*
(Author's collection)

Below. The front page of the Dundee *Evening Telegraph* records Jessie Jordan's arrest. (By kind permission of D.C. Thomson & Co. Ltd)

Above left. MI5 spycatcher Lieutenant Colonel Edward Hinchley Cooke. (*After the Battle* magazine)

Above right. Marc Aubert, Abwehr spy. (Author's collection)

Right. Poster advertising the 1939 movie *Confessions of a Nazi Spy.*

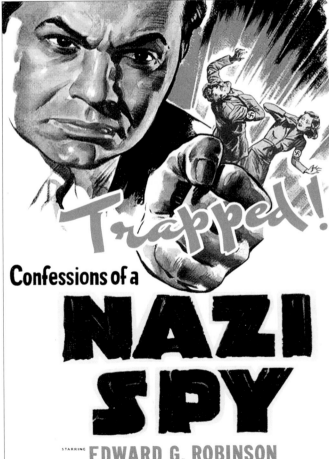

in a practice in Maine, opened his own office amid the German colony in Yorkville, Manhattan, in 1931. The following year he had even demonstrated his apparent loyalty to his adopted homeland with a reserve commission in the US Army Medical Corps.[23]

Yet the FBI researchers soon found that the assiduously cultivated façade of a caring, patriotic American professional was a sham; Griebl was actually an enthusiastic anti-Semite who had joined the nascent Nazi Party during an earlier, failed, attempt to become a doctor in Munich. Arrogant and intensely narcissistic, he now believed that he was the man to lead the Nazification of the United States. Backed by his shrewish wife and a cohort of American Nazi Ordnungsdienst thugs, he began by strong-arming many of New York's German-American cultural organisations into one pro-Nazi umbrella group, the Bund der Freunde des Neuen Deutschland or League of Friends of The New Germany (President Dr I.T. Griebl).

In July 1933, after his heavies had failed to intimidate Victor and Bernard Ridder, Jewish publishers of the popular *New Yorker Staats-Zeitung und Herold*, into toeing the Nazi line, Griebl was named in the *New York Times* as publisher of *Die Brücke*, a weekly newspaper that would 'promote the cause of Hitlerism'. Three months later, during an October 1933 Nazi rally at the Schwabenhalle in Newark, New Jersey, he had just begun a furious rant blaming Jews for communist disorder in Germany when a volley of rocks and stink bombs hurled through the windows started a stampede for the exits. Spilling out into Springfield Avenue, the Newark Nazis were confronted by a hostile mob spearheaded by Jewish boxer Nat Arno, an enforcer for local organised crime boss Abner 'Longy' Zwillman, also a Jew. Two hundred police officers threw a cordon around the Schwabenhalle, but a running battle spread over two blocks. Twenty people were injured and seven were arrested.[24]

The Newark riot gave New York City Mayor John O'Brien a welcome excuse to ban a German Day rally that he had naïvely agreed to address before discovering that he would be confronted by 400 Heil Hitlering Nazis. Griebl moaned that this was merely a ploy to gain the Jewish vote, but Mayor O'Brien was unmoved. 'Alien agitators! Blackguards!' he roared back. 'Neither the long white shirt nor the short brown shirt can spread intolerance in New York City while I am Mayor!' Griebl's wife, Maria, had then made an ill-judged appearance before a Federal Grand Jury investigating the affair, refusing to swear on the Bible as it was 'a Jewish book' or to answer questions from Jewish Attorney William Prager because, 'As an American citizen, I have the right to be questioned by a Gentile.' This, along with the Newark riot and his open racism towards Jewish and black patients while working part-time as a surgeon at Harlem Hospital, had provoked a delegation of Griebl's medical colleagues into marching on City Hall to demand his resignation. Anticipating trouble, the good doctor had beaten them to it by resigning a week earlier.[25]

Usually only too eager to get his latest anti-Semitic diatribe into the press, Griebl was less than amused when confronted by a *New York Evening Post* photographer during a stormy House Un-American Activities Committee hearing into the Friends of the New Germany in May 1934. Leaping to his feet, he yelled, 'You had a helluva nerve to take dat picture . . . Smash dat camera . . . Start a vight . . . Break dat camera!' in, to the delight of reporters, a thick German accent. Officials persuaded the photographer to hand over the glass plate negative, but the next day's newspapers revealed that the wily snapper had switched plates in the commotion, slipping the real one into his pocket and handing over a blank. The press would have another field day in May 1935 when Griebl, a serial philanderer, appeared in the New York Commercial Frauds Court on a charge of grand larceny brought by Antoinette Heim, a 35-year-old 'art dealer' later exposed as a fraudster, who alleged that she had given him $1,500 after he promised to divorce Maria and marry her.[26]

Undaunted, in October that same year Griebl told 20,000 supporters at a German-American rally in Madison Square Garden to demand 'German representation in the American government, so that within ten years all government offices will have Germans in them'. Apparently devoid of any sense of irony, he then called for three Heil Hitlers and, bizarrely, three Heil President Roosevelts, before assuring his wildly cheering audience that he would be cabling the Führer, 'the Great Awakener of the German People', to pledge the loyalty of all present. Clearly his 1928 American citizenship oath, renouncing, 'allegiance and fidelity to any foreign prince, potentate, state or sovereignty, and particularly to the German Reich', had slipped his mind, just as it did a few weeks later when he had the fugitive Lonkowskis spirited across the Canadian border.[27]

On the evening of 25 February, the day after Hofmann's arrest, Special Agents Leon Turrou and Paul Cotter arrived at Griebl's office in a six-storey apartment block at 56 East 87th Street that, ironically, given Griebl's shrill anti-Semitic rants, stands next door to the Park Avenue Synagogue in Manhattan. Brushing a questioning receptionist aside and demanding to see the doctor, they frogmarched him out of the building and took him to Foley Square where he at first flatly denied he had ever met anyone called Karl Schlüter, Johanna Hofmann, Günther Rumrich, Erich Glaser or Martin Schade. To break him Turrou used the same simple ruse that he had employed with Hofmann. Repeatedly asking Griebl if he knew an attractive, auburn-haired girl named Johanna or Jenni Hofmann who had visited his office with Schlüter and getting no for an answer, he gave an agent waiting by the door behind Griebl a discreet signal and Hofmann was brought into the room.

'And yet you don't remember Jenni Hofmann?'
'No, Mr Turrou,' he said solemnly, 'I swear to you that no such girl ever came to my office.'
I looked over his head.
'Jenni!' I snapped. 'Did you ever see this man before?'
'Yes,' came Jenni's voice calmly, 'That is Dr Griebl.'[28]

Having blundered into the same trap as Jenni had done two days before, Griebl now tried to claim that Hofmann and Schlüter had visited his office seeking information on American Jews. In that case, Turrou suggested, he could have no objections to his office being searched. Turrou, Special Agent Paul Cotter and Griebl returned to the doctor's office just before midnight to find that there were indeed numerous files on prominent Americans of full or part Jewish heritage including New York Mayor Fiorello LaGuardia, recently deceased banker Felix Warburg and Secretary of the Treasury Henry Morgenthau. These files, Griebl admitted, had formed the basis of reports that Schlüter had taken to Germany, but they were not evidence of espionage and it seemed the search was going nowhere. Then the phone on Griebl's desk rang; it was Kay Moog who had been told that her lover was being questioned by the FBI. Moog turned up 20 minutes later and, as it was by then very late, Turrou instructed both Griebl and Moog to appear at Foley Square for questioning at 9 a.m. the following morning, Saturday, 26 February 1938.

Then, as now, the FBI and MI5 were very different organisations, the former enjoying a high public profile largely of its own making, the latter so secretive that its existence was not then officially acknowledged. MI5 would have preferred to have left Jessie Jordan in place with her intercepted mail continuing to provide a useful source on Abwehr operations, so there was considerable dismay in London when, even as Griebl's interrogation was getting under way on Saturday, 26 February, the FBI publicity machine issued a news release timed to meet Sunday newspaper deadlines. The *New York Times* led the way with a front-page headline: 'SPY RING IN U.S. ARMY BARED; GERMAN GIRL, TWO SOLDIERS SEIZED AS FOREIGN AGENTS'. The story was also carried in the British Sunday newspapers and, as MI5 Deputy Director Guy Liddell wrote to Valentine Vivian at MI6, 'When we saw in the papers on Sunday, 27 March [this should read February] that the Americans had gone off the deep end, we decided to round up Mrs Jessie JORDAN in Dundee.'[29]

Constable Annie Ross walked into the Kinloch Street salon at 11 a.m. on Wednesday, 2 March. She checked that the premises were empty apart from Jessie and her apprentice, her fourteen-year-old niece Patsy Haddow, went back outside and signalled to a large black police car waiting down the hill in Rosebank Street, just out of sight of the salon. Seated in the back of the car were Colonel Edward Hinchley Cooke, Chief Constable Joseph Neilans and detectives John Carstairs and Tom Nicholson.[30]

Chapter 6

An Interesting Friend from New York

It will get us the Enterprise and Yorktown plans without much expense.

Agent Crown, January 1938

1 Kinloch Street, Dundee, 11 a.m., Wednesday, 2 March 1938

It was almost as though she was expecting them. Jessie Jordan showed no emotion as Chief Constable Joe Neilans read the formal caution: 'Jessie Wallace or Jordan, I am making enquiries as to whether or not you have committed offences under the Official Secrets Acts 1911 and 1920. I have to caution you that you are not obliged to say anything, but anything you do say may be given in evidence.' Mary Curran chose that moment to turn up intent on making arrangements to attend a dance with Jessie the following night and was firmly told to go away by Annie Ross. As Carstairs and Nicholson began searching drawers and cupboards, Jessie went into the staff cubicle and calmly selected a green hat and black coat with a fur collar, then she and a doubtless confused and thoroughly frightened Patsy Haddow were taken away to Police Headquarters.

An unidentified police officer had the unpleasant task of supervising the digging up of the drains, but the only useful evidence found during a thorough search of the Kinloch Street salon was a slip of paper with two Abwehr mailbox addresses that explained why, once she had stopped using P.O. Box 629, MI5 had been unable to intercept Jessie's outgoing mail to Hilmar Dierks in Hamburg. These were Frau Stolp van Straaten, Drogistery, Dusartstraat, Amsterdam, and Otto Moser, Sechslingspforte 14, Hamburg 24. Hinchley Cooke and Neilans next searched the room Jessie had rented in Stirling Street, but found nothing as she had moved out the previous Friday and spent her last four nights of freedom holed up in the salon, living off fish suppers from Mordente's chip shop on the other side of Kinloch Street and sleeping on a bed settee in the staff cubicle. Jessie never explained why she did this: perhaps she had finally realised that her mail was being intercepted. Whatever the reason for moving into the salon, Sunday's press coverage of the arrests in New York would have left her in no doubt that her own arrest was imminent, and she would have known there was no possibility of escape. Even had she been able to slip away unseen, she could hardly make a run for it back to Germany and leave her daughter, Marga, and granddaughter, Jessie, to face the music without her.

Driving on to Perth, Hinchley Cooke and Neilans found a search already under way at Breadalbane Terrace and a shocked Marga turning out her pockets. They then searched Patsy Haddow's home in Coupar Angus before returning to Dundee and sending Patsy home in a police car. At 5.30 p.m. Jessie was brought to Neilans' office and Hinchley Cooke began her first interrogation by handing her a letter that had been delivered to Breadalbane Terrace that morning and asking her to open it. As it had already been intercepted, the MI5 officer was well aware that it held five £1 Bank of England banknotes. Jessie maintained that these were part repayment of a loan to a Captain Weber. She was then shown copies of the postcards and notes on Aldershot garrison that she had posted to Hamburg from Talgarth. 'What makes you send postcards from Aldershot?' asked Hinchley Cooke. 'I was there,' Jessie replied lamely, 'and I sent it.'[1]

Neilans next showed Jessie the sketch that Mary Curran had found hidden under the counter at Kinloch Street and asked, 'Can you tell me anything about it? Are you in the habit of sketching?' Jessie replied, 'Yes,' and when Neilans asked what it was she answered, 'I do not know the name, but I can go to it. He told me to go and find out if there was anything between [there and] Rosyth. I did not know where Rosyth was.' Pressed further, Jessie admitted that she had sent a fair copy of the sketch along with picture postcards of the Forth Bridge and the fortified island of Inchgarvie immediately below it to her friend Captain Weber who also used the names Straaten, Moser and Sanders, the latter alias all too familiar to Hinchley Cooke.[2]

Neilans then asked, 'Do you remember having a map of Scotland and part of England issued by an insurance company on which you made certain marks opposite names?' Jessie tried to pass this off as having been done to settle an argument about whether the coastal fortifications were still manned. Unimpressed, Hinchley Cooke fired back, 'So you discussed the defences of this country when you were in Germany and, to show that it was guarded, you sent this map. Do you think your friend Captain Weber alias Straaten alias Moser would come here to give evidence on your behalf if we were to send him an invitation and pay his fare?' 'No,' Jessie replied weakly, 'I don't think so.' Questioned finally about the mail from New York, all Jessie could offer was the absurd excuse that she thought she was passing on love letters for a married male friend in America.

Jessie had been lying constantly and very obviously throughout the hour-long interrogation, so an exasperated Neilans brought the proceedings to a close saying, 'Well, Mrs Jordan, I am going to charge you. I have to caution you that you are not obliged to say anything in answer to the charge unless you wish to do so, but anything you say will be taken down and may be used in evidence. You are charged with committing an offence under Section 5 of the Official Secrets Act 1920 . . .' Jessie replied, 'I can only admit I have sent them. But I did not know I was doing any harm.' As she was being escorted down to the cells by Annie Ross and Tom Nicholson, Jessie asked if she could see a solicitor. When Nicholson asked if there was anyone in particular that she had in mind, Jessie answered resignedly, 'It doesn't matter. I am going away for a long time anyway.'[3]

Jessie Jordan appeared for less than a minute in Dundee Police Court the following morning. 'A small and full-figured blonde,' according to the *Dundee Courier*, 'she looked pale and anxious as she listened to the proceedings.' Remanded in custody until 10 March, she was taken straight from the court to Neilans' office. The Chief Constable pointed to the sketch of the coastal installation that Mary Curran had found at Kinloch Street and said, 'You remember last night you said you can go to the place where you made this sketch? Are you willing to take us there today?' Jessie answered that she was, but asked, 'Can I have a cup of tea without sugar before we go? The tea I had this morning had sugar in it, and I did not like it.'

Tea was provided, then Hinchley Cooke, Neilans, Ross, Carstairs and Jessie Jordan left Dundee Police Headquarters to catch the 10.30 a.m. ferry over to Fife. Neilans wrote later that the journey passed in strained silence aside from Jessie giving the driver, Sergeant John Wilks, directions to Charlestown, a village on the north shore of the River Forth, and from there to a point about a quarter of a mile beyond the village on West Road that gave an uninterrupted view of the Royal Naval Armaments Depot at Crombie.

Three miles west of Rosyth naval dockyard, RNAD Crombie with its network of underground munitions storage bunkers designed to withstand a direct hit from a 1,000 lb bomb was then, and remains today, one of the Royal Navy's most sensitive sites and the officer in charge of security, Major William Quinlan, confirmed that the sketch was 'a good one'. It had been made, Quinlan said, from a spot known locally as Fiddlers Hall. With that, the party drove back to Dundee and Jessie Jordan was returned to the cells.[4]

That same evening sobering news reached Hinchley Cooke in Dundee that Else Duncombe, another of Dierks' British agents, was dead. Born Else Klara Emma von Boltenstern in Germany in 1888, she had fallen on hard times after a failed first marriage and, having made her living as a housemaid, had acquired British citizenship in 1931 by marrying William Pauncefort Duncombe, an electrical engineer seventeen years her senior. Unsurprisingly given what was to come, Else Dunscombe's MI5 file has not been released to the British National Archives, but a short case summary reveals that she had been first identified as an Abwehr agent in August 1936 and was forwarding mail from other agents in France to the same Gneisenaustrasse, Hamburg, address given to Rumrich in New York. Arrested at her London home towards the end of February 1938, she

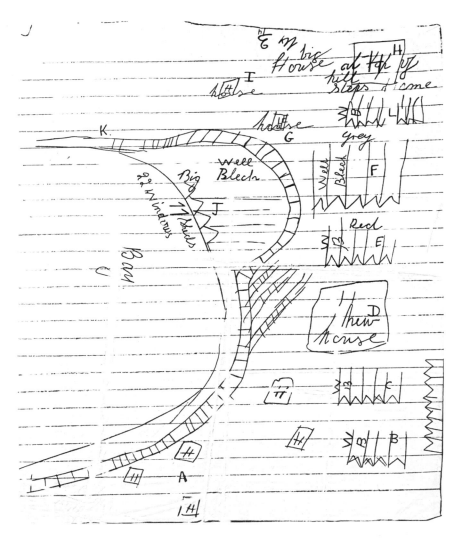

Jessie Jordan's original sketch plan of the Royal Naval Armaments Depot at Crombie in Fife as found hidden under the counter in the Kinloch Street hairdressing salon. MI5 had the difficult task of presenting this useless doodle as somehow useful to an enemy bomber force.
(National Archives)

had somehow managed to swallow a fatal overdose of aspirin tablets while under MI5 interrogation and died in New End Hospital two days later, just as Jessie Jordan was showing Neilans and Hinchley Cooke the place where she had made the sketch of RNAD Crombie.[5]

* * *

As Else Dunscombe lay dying in London and Jessie Jordan was returned to her cell in Dundee, in New York Günther Rumrich was languishing in detention quarters at Governors Island and Johanna Hofmann was locked up at the grim Women's House of Detention in Greenwich Village. At Foley Square the FBI interrogation of Ignatz Griebl was under way and, like Rumrich, he seemed only too eager to talk. He did admit that he had known Wilhelm Lonkowski as a patient being treated for stomach ulcers but reduced his role in the espionage case to that of disinterested observer. He had, he maintained, no further dealings with Germany until he approached a Dr Erich Pfeiffer for help with a real estate deal in Germany and Pfeiffer told him that, as the transaction would also involve a substantial sum being transferred to Griebl's bank in New York in breach of strict Nazi currency laws, he would have to come over to Germany to complete the deal. With Kay Moog in tow, he had sailed aboard the *Europa* on 1 June 1937 and, during the Atlantic passage had happened to make the acquaintance of Karl Schlüter, a steward about whom he had heard much from Lonkowski.

Met by Pfeiffer on landing at Bremerhaven on 6 June, Griebl said that he and Moog had been handed first-class rail tickets to Berlin where accommodation had been booked at the plush Hotel Adlon and meetings had been arranged with top military intelligence officers. Lunching the following day with Kapitänleutnants Udo von Bonin and Hermann Menzel in the Roof Garden restaurant at the Hotel Eden, Griebl had introduced Kay Moog as 'an interesting friend from New York'. Struck by Moog's poise and statuesque beauty, the Abwehr officers had proposed that she rent an apartment in Washington where she could host lavish parties for influential politicians who, plied with alcohol by attractive women like herself, would be encouraged into revealing indiscretions. Indeed, so impressed were the Abwehr officers by Moog, she had later claimed to Griebl that they had both tried, unsuccessfully, 'to see her at the hotel or date her up alone'.

While the party scheme could only go ahead with a substantial input of Abwehr cash that would naturally have to be paid to Griebl himself, both von Bonin and Menzel had made it clear that money would be no object. The Abwehr officers had then asked Griebl if he knew a 'society woman' in Washington named Mrs Driscoll. When Griebl replied that he did not, von Bonin had claimed that Driscoll was among scores of government officials in Washington who were willing to supply Germany with military secrets, in her case a 'device by means of which various codes might be broken up'. This device, von Bonin continued, was particularly valuable to the United States as it had been developed with particular reference to Japan. Germany would therefore be able to sell it to the Japanese in exchange for much needed foreign exchange.[6]

The luncheon over, Griebl and Moog had then spent a few days with relatives before returning to Bremen on 23 June for another meeting, this time with Erich Pfeiffer. Never one to stint on his expense account, Pfeiffer had taken them to the city's famous Astoria nightclub and, while Moog watched the cabaret and danced the night away to Hugo Partsch and his band, bragged to Griebl that he had agents in every important aircraft plant in North America. There was a designer named Emil Zaech in Montreal, Canada, who was sending as many as five rolls of Leica film of blueprints at a time and there were informants in both naval architects Gibbs & Cox in New York and Newport News naval dockyard in Virginia who were being paid $300 each for original blueprints. Karl Schlüter was also working with an aircraft mechanic named Otto Voss, an inspector at the Sperry Gyroscope Company called Johannes Steuer and John Köchel, a foreman at the Hollman Instrument Corporation. Other unnamed Abwehr spies had already betrayed the latest American aircraft automatic pilots, acoustic submarine detection apparatus and plans of the latest US Navy destroyers, ships that Pfeiffer had airily dismissed as 'suicide craft' with hulls so thin that you could shoot through them with an automatic pistol.[7]

Claiming that he was 'the chief of the German Military Intelligence Service with headquarters in Hamburg', Pfeiffer had also enlarged on what von Bonin had said about Agnes Driscoll, saying, 'We got through a Mrs Agnes Driscoll last week a device by means of which various codes may be broken up for $7,000, and I don't understand how the United States Navy Department is hesitating in buying this device. It was invented by a widow of a deceased rear admiral and Mrs Agnes Driscoll.' Pfeiffer said that the device, which would be particularly valuable to Japan, was offered by Mrs Driscoll to the [American] Navy Department for $15,000, but they would not buy it if they knew Germany already had it.

Pfeiffer was also, Griebl claimed, an enthusiastic supporter of the Washington party scheme and had said that he would take every opportunity to attend in person. Before they parted company, the Bremen spymaster had assured Griebl that his efforts in the United States would not go unrewarded, particularly should he and Moog make the right contacts in Washington. He would personally ensure that Griebl got a position as an Air Defence officer should he have to return to Germany and do his utmost to ensure that the doctor's real estate deal in Germany went through without a hitch.[8]

That, at least, was Griebl's version of what had happened in Germany and, delivered with all the panache of a well-practised liar, it was clearly meant to give the impression that he had never even considered espionage until the meetings in Berlin and Bremen. Griebl's statement also matched that being given in another room by Kay Moog in all but a few unimportant details, though this is hardly surprising as they had been given ample time to rehearse after Turrou's visit to Griebl's surgery the previous evening. Indeed, they had probably been preparing for this moment since news of Rumrich's arrest had appeared in the press two weeks before. And Griebl, once he started talking, had wasted no time in attempting to divert any culpability from himself by betraying everyone else who had been involved along with a good many others who had not.

Asked whether he had, like Rumrich, received any letters in cipher from Schlüter, Griebl said no. But he did admit that Schlüter had left him a match book with a handwritten cipher key inside the cover and told him that a Miss Böhm would call to collect it on Friday, 25 February. This just happened to be the same day that the FBI agents came to question him, but she had not turned up by the time they arrived, so Turrou and Cotter took Griebl back to his office, retrieved the match book and confirmed that the cipher key inside the cover was identical to that found in Johanna Hofmann's leather bag. It was also the same cipher used in the letter that Hofmann had been due to deliver to Kay Moog when she was arrested.[9]

So who was the mysterious Miss Böhm? Moog had earlier told the FBI that, at the request of Schlüter, she had arranged to meet a Miss Eleanor Böhm of Elmhurst, Long Island, a 22-year-old American-born Hunter College graduate who had been impressed by the Nazi regime while studying in Germany. Under FBI questioning, Eleanor revealed that she had first encountered Karl Schlüter during a visit to the *Europa* in New York in late 1937 and that Schlüter had subsequently arranged to meet her in Walgreen's Drug Store on the corner of 42nd Street and Times Square in New York City. They had had what she recalled as an 'impersonal conversation' over glasses of Coca-Cola in which she was asked about her education and family background. They had then gone their separate ways.

It had all seemed very odd, particularly when, two weeks later, Eleanor received an unsigned, typewritten letter instructing her to call on a Miss Kate Moog at 276 Riverside Drive in New York City. She duly visited Moog early in January 1938 and, after making rather stilted conversation over coffee, got up to leave. Shaking hands with Moog at the door on her way out, Eleanor felt something being pressed into her hand and, once outside, saw it was a match book with a series of strange hieroglyphics inside the cover. Thoroughly unsettled, she destroyed the match book as soon as she got home. And that was the last Eleanor Böhm heard from Schlüter or Moog until, on being shown the match book found at Griebl's surgery by the FBI, she confirmed that it was identical to the one that Moog had given her.

What role Schlüter had in mind for Eleanor Böhm is unclear, but there was no doubting the role that Griebl had in mind for one Christian Danielsen. During their discussions in Bremen in June

1937, Pfeiffer had instructed Griebl to concentrate his efforts on naval intelligence, particularly the US Navy's new aircraft carriers, *Yorktown* and *Enterprise*. Soon after returning to New York, Griebl sent Pfeiffer a letter stating that the German-born Danielsen, 'a skilled designer of battleships for the United States Navy', was only too keen to reveal all he knew about American warship construction in return for a well-paid job in Germany. Pfeiffer took the bait but would soon discover that the 60-year-old, one-armed Danielsen was only a draftsman at the Bath Iron Works shipyard at Bath, Maine, and had no access to naval secrets of any value, far less any knowledge of aircraft carriers being built over 700 miles away at Newport News in Virginia. Brought up in Germany, Danielsen had lived in the United States since 1900 and had just remarried. He never had any serious intention of moving back to Germany.[10]

Eleanor Böhm might have been a naïve admirer of the Nazis, but she was an American and there is no evidence that she would ever have considered treason. Likewise, Christian Danielsen would appear to have merely been stringing Griebl along to see if there was any money to be made. But Otto Voss was an entirely different matter: he was an active Nazi spy who had been feeding Abwehr's couriers genuine, albeit largely worthless, intelligence on military aircraft being built by the Seversky Aircraft Corporation. He had finally got his old job back at Seversky on 24 February 1938 but, two weeks later, on 9 March, was arrested by the FBI.

Initially, while admitting that he was a dedicated Nazi, Voss refused to confess to any involvement in espionage until Turrou confronted him with diaries that FBI searchers had found at his Floral Park home complete with entries relating to meetings with Wilhelm Lonkowski and Abwehr couriers Carl Eitel and Herbert Jänichen. Voss then agreed to talk, describing his numerous meetings with Lonkowski, Griebl and the Abwehr couriers. He gave the FBI a flavour of the information that he had handed over, but was at pains to make it clear that he had not spied for money; he was an intensely patriotic German and in the three years he had been active had only accepted $75 to cover his travelling expenses to and from meetings with couriers in New York.[11]

The seven negatives that had been taken from Lonkowski's violin case by customs officers while he was attempting to hand them over to Schlüter back in 1935 had by then been tracked down and printed. Werner Gudenberg, Lonkowski's informant at the Curtiss Aeroplane and Motor Company in Buffalo was traced to the Hall Aluminium Aircraft Corporation factory in Bristol, Philadelphia. He admitted that the photographs showed the Curtiss XSB-2 drawings that had been in his home on the first occasion Lonkowski came calling. But he was adamant that there had been no further contact following Lonkowski's second visit, though Voss had subsequently put him under pressure, as a good German, to restart the flow of intelligence. A family man with an American-born wife and two young children, Gudenberg was, despite his earlier complicity which he had already come to regret, no traitor and had not obliged.

Among the others whom Griebl was alleging Pfeiffer had told him were Abwehr informants, Swiss-born Emil Zaech was a Canadian engineer who, until 1936, had sold his inventions to all comers including the British, French, Germans and Russians. In 1936, however, he had been recruited by Abwehr and went to work in a Montreal aircraft factory. Quite how Griebl knew of him is a mystery, but he was watched by the Royal Canadian Mounted Police and interned when war broke out in 1939. German-born Johannes Steuer was, as Griebl claimed, a senior inspector at the Sperry Gyroscope Company in Brooklyn. Questioned at length by the FBI, he vehemently denied any contacts with Nazi agents.

John Kögel, not Kochel as Pfeiffer had supposedly told Griebl, was a foreman working on periscopes for the US Navy at the Kollmorgen Optical Corporation in Brooklyn and not, as Griebl wrongly claimed, the Hollman Instrument Corporation. Brought in for questioning at Foley Square, Kögel revealed that he had been approached to supply information by Lonkowski back in 1935, but had refused. His house was nevertheless searched and his financial affairs investigated, but no evidence of any wrongdoing was found and he was cleared. Adrian van der Schalie, Griebl's supposed informant at naval architects Gibbs & Cox, turned out to be Dutch-born and strongly anti-Nazi. He had, in any case, left Gibbs &

Cox in 1937. There was greater concern about Jacobus Mauritz, a draftsman at Newport News who had worked on the aircraft carriers *Ranger*, *Yorktown* and *Enterprise*, but

> MAURITZ was questioned thoroughly by several agents and steadfastly denied that he had ever participated in espionage activities, stated that he was an American citizen and that as one of his duties of citizenship he would report any contact which a foreign agent would make with him.[12]

At first, the FBI had little option to at least take Griebl's allegations seriously and follow them up. But the doctor's story was unravelling with every supposed Nazi spy who, forced to undergo interrogation and invasion of their privacy, turned out to be completely innocent. And Senta Dewanger, who was able to add much detail to the Lonkowski story, confirmed that Griebl had lied about the spy's escape and that Lonkowski and his wife had actually been exfiltrated to Canada in the doctor's car. She also told of receiving a letter from Lonkowski some time later in which he 'threatened her that she would never see Germany again . . . at this time he could not harm her but that he would wait for a better opportunity'. Lonkowski had apparently sent her this letter because he felt that she had betrayed him to the American authorities, a truly absurd accusation from a man entirely responsible for his own downfall.

Yet more of Griebl's lies were exposed when Turrou had Griebl, who was still being treated as a government witness, set up a meeting with Captain Wilhelm Dreschel, Marine Superintendent in New York for the Hamburg-Amerika Line. The hope was that Dreschel would incriminate himself and identify some of the couriers. Seemingly as eager to please as ever, Griebl reported after the meeting that Dreschel had been forced to assist the New York spy ring and that he had inserted the classified advertisement in the *New York Times* that had started Rumrich's espionage career. Dreschel had also wired a warning to Erich Pfeiffer as soon as he heard of Rumrich's arrest and this had led to a flurry of frantic signals from Germany to the liner *New York* and courier Theodor Schütz, who was on his way to meet Rumrich in New York, being bundled ashore at Havana in Cuba. And Dreschel confirmed that Theodor Schütz was an alias; the courier's real name was Karl Wiegand. What Griebl did not know was that the New York hotel room where the meeting had taken place had been bugged and the FBI already knew that, in his report of the meeting, he had carefully avoided anything that incriminated him. An FBI agent was despatched to Havana in the hope of having Wiegand detained and extradited by the Cuban authorities, but was unsuccessful.[13]

Only in 1945, when Allied interrogators were able to question former Abwehr officers, would the true scale of Griebl's lying become clear. It was, of course, true that he and Moog had travelled to Germany aboard the *Europa* in June 1937, but Udo von Bonin offered a radically different account of that lunch meeting at the Hotel Eden:

> In the year 1936 or 1937 a man, born in Austria, came to Berlin and offered to the Abwehr-Abteilung to work for them in the United States, more especially in Washington. The detainee [von Bonin] had nothing to do with the United States, but he was sent by his group leader, Korvettenkapitän MENZEL, to have two conversations with this person at the Eden Hotel in Berlin.
>
> During these discussions the Austrian proposed that a week-end hotel or club for American civil servants of high rank be opened in Washington, under the management of his girlfriend, who originated from Germany. There, this friend was to listen to the conversations of the leading officials and friends of Roosevelt, and report on it.
>
> The big sum necessary for the realisation of this plan was to be paid to the Austrian by the Abwehr. The detainee advised his group leader to decline this proposal as the Austrian in his opinion was a swindler, and the leader acted accordingly.

Von Bonin, who had no reason to lie about these events in 1945, recalled that he had been infuriated when press reports of Griebl's arrest in 1938 referred to both himself and Menzel as proposers of the Washington apartment scheme. He was adamant that they had 'flatly declined to have anything to do with it'. And decline the Abwehr officers surely did, for nothing was ever done to progress the scheme which was, in any case, just an upmarket version of the boozy parties for Army Air Corps officers Lonkowski had thrown at Senta Dewanger's home back in 1935.[14]

Likewise, when interviewed by Allied interrogators in 1945, Erich Pfeiffer categorically denied that he had met Griebl and Moog when they landed in Bremerhaven from the *Europa* in June 1937. He had not handed them first-class rail tickets to Berlin and he had not booked rooms for them at the Adlon Hotel. He also dismissed Griebl's account of the meeting at the Astoria, an edited version of which had been included in Turrou's book on the case, as 'so naïve, it hardly needs to be dealt with'. He had not invited Griebl to visit Germany, he had never referred to US Navy destroyers as 'suicide craft' and he refuted the nonsense about Abwehr paying $300 for destroyer drawings from Gibbs & Cox. The Washington apartment proposal, which he would never have entertained, was not discussed at the Astoria and he explicitly denied that he told Griebl about Agnes Driscoll supposedly selling the Germans an American cipher machine. Indeed, he had never heard of Driscoll and knew nothing at all about any American decryption machine.[15]

Agnes Meyer Driscoll had, when the FBI interrogated her in 1938, already enjoyed a long and successful career in cryptanalysis with the US Navy which, as we have seen, included the exposure of hapless Japanese spies Harry Thompson and John Farnsworth. Back in 1921, she had put her experience as a code breaker to good use as a cryptographer, working with Commander William Gresham of the Navy's Codes & Signals Section on the development of a mechanical cipher machine rather unimaginatively christened the Communications Machine, or CM for short. Despite being heavy and unwieldy, the CM was standard equipment for secret US Navy communications throughout the 1920s. Commander Gresham had died in August 1935 and his widow, Maud, had petitioned Congress for a payment in lieu of the money her late husband could have earned had the Navy not confiscated the CM machine for its own use, thus preventing him from filing a patent. Critically, however, Agnes Driscoll's name was only added to the Gresham motion on 24 June 1937, so von Bonin simply could not have known of her involvement prior to the Berlin meeting with Griebl on 7 June. Likewise, Pfeiffer could not have been aware of Driscoll when he met Griebl on 23 June, the day before she was added to the Gresham motion.

The very obvious holes in Griebl's allegation that Driscoll was a traitor, not least the discrepancy in dates, seem at first to have escaped the notice of the FBI. Likewise, the Bureau interrogators would appear to have missed the fact that Griebl had confused a cryptography machine that, as in the case of the CM, had been designed to create enciphered text with a cryptanalysis machine designed to break enciphered text. The Navy mounted a global search for surviving CM machines, a quest not helped by the fact that they were long obsolete and many had simply been dumped or scrapped. The Bureau meanwhile, noting with more than a hint of paranoia that Driscoll was of German ancestry and that she 'was employed in one of the most secret offices of the Navy Department', checked her bank accounts for suspicious payments, searched her home and, despite the fact that she was recovering in hospital from serious injuries sustained in a car crash the previous December, interrogated both her and her husband, Michael.[16]

Agnes Driscoll was, of course, wholly innocent and continued her career in cryptanalysis through the Second World War and beyond, only retiring in 1959. Griebl could only have picked up the Gresham motion story from the press after his return from Germany, doubtless when Congress approved it on 11 August 1937, and then, having misunderstood its fundamentals, included it in his statement to Turrou. That the FBI were so credulous of Griebl's nonsense is all the more surprising given that, according to Assistant Director Ed Tamm, Major Joe Dalton had by then confirmed with the New York Field Office that Griebl, who had served as a US Army Reserve medical officer since 1932, 'has been under suspicion as serving as a source of information for the German government, and that he

[Dalton] has a file on him, which he would turn over to the Bureau for examination'.[17]

* * *

Abwehr's entire American venture, from the arrival of the Lonkowskis to the arrest of Rumrich and the questioning of Griebl, had been banal, woefully incompetent and entirely pointless. The Lonkowskis had been useless drunks who achieved nothing of any value. Griebl was a high-profile, loud-mouthed Nazi fanatic, a liar and a conceited fool who was incapable of accepting guidance. Rumrich was another drunk, a drug addict and a diplomatic disaster in the making who had no access to worthwhile intelligence. That he had been recruited in the first place reflects very badly on Hilmar Dierks. That he was so ineptly run reflects equally badly on Erich Pfeiffer's couriers, principally Karl Schlüter who, seemingly having learned nothing from the Lonkowski episode, was just a rather stupid merchant seaman and Nazi fanatic who possessed none of the patience, tact, discretion and management skills required in a successful agent runner.

It is also unclear precisely where Schlüter's loyalties lay. He had been recruited by Bremen Nebenstelle spymaster Erich Pfeiffer in 1934, but Abwehr's labyrinthine structure and lack of oversight meant that he was also receiving instructions from Dierks at Abwehrstelle Hamburg that Pfeiffer knew nothing about. In reality, like his collaborator Griebl, Schlüter was out for himself and evidence of his duplicity surfaced in the form of a letter that was waiting for Rumrich when, soon after his arrest, he was allowed a home visit accompanied by the NYPD detectives. Written on Norddeutscher Lloyd stationery, the letter warned Rumrich against having dealings with other agents and was signed N. Spielmann, one of Pfeiffer's aliases that Schlüter had appropriated, but had no right to use. In 1945 Pfeiffer would tell Allied interrogators that

> Karl SCHLUTER had combined zeal and energy with gross indiscretion; he had, moreover, strayed beyond the fold and was working also for Ast Hamburg as something more than

a loaned courier, as had recently been agreed by Pfeiffer. He had even adopted the latter's covername of SPIELMANN for written communications to agents in America.[18]

Worse still, many of the schemes supposedly dreamt up by Dierks or Pfeiffer were actually ill-formed products of the obsessive minds of Griebl and Schlüter. The passports scheme that led to Rumrich's arrest and the collapse of the New York spy ring is a case in point. It was clearly inspired by the case of Arnold Ikal, an illegal for Soviet military intelligence (GRU) in New York since 1932. Ikal and his Philadelphia-born communist wife, Ruth Boerger, had travelled to the Soviet Union in November 1937 as Donald and Ruth Robinson on false passports issued by the office of Al Marinelli, a corrupt New York County Clerk and close associate of the recently jailed mobster Charles 'Lucky' Luciano.[19]

Griebl could hardly have missed the extensive coverage of the Ikal case in the *New York Times* and is known to have discussed the passports scheme with Schlüter during their meeting on 14 January 1938. Blithely ignoring the fact that the State Department Passport Division would now be alert to fraud, the two men reasoned that Abwehr would pay them a substantial sum for the passport blanks as they could then be used to create false identities for Nazi agents being infiltrated into the Soviet Union, much as the Ikals had been. Neither Griebl nor Schlüter had any intention of running the risk of arrest should their hare-brained plan go awry, but they had the perfect patsy in the form of Rumrich, who confirmed that Schlüter had tasked him with getting blank passports later that same day. But Rumrich, dismissed by Griebl as 'just a dumbbell', seems to have got the wrong idea and, while Schlüter and Griebl were expecting actual blank passports, he only attempted to get blank passport application forms. As for the Ikals, they would have been better advised to stay in New York as they disappeared into grim Butyrskaya Prison within hours of their arrival in Moscow, victims of the paranoid Stalin's purges.[20]

Rumrich had shown some initiative when he secured the VD statistics from Fort Hamilton, though what possible intelligence value lay in the sexual habits of bored peacetime GIs is open to question. Rather less well advised was his ridiculous attempt to produce results on the new aircraft carriers *Yorktown* and *Enterprise* by writing to a US Navy Ensign named William Butler Brown. Rumrich would have seen from the Navy Lists found in his briefcase that Ensign Brown, then serving aboard the old carrier *Saratoga,* was about to transfer to the new *Enterprise*. The letter read:

> There are ways of making money. An enterprising young man can always cash in without much trouble. Why don't you wise up too?
>
> If you are interested, insert an advert in the public notices column of the New York Times. This ad should read, 'Brownie – OK for contact – WB.'
>
> If you pass this on to the intell. services you will suffer dire consequences. If you play the game you will be well taken care of.
>
> Act quickly, we do not like to lose time. We expect to see you before you board the Enterprise.
> Brownie

Ensign Brown promptly handed this bizarre letter over to his commanding officer and the approach led nowhere.[21]

Under intense pressure from Schlüter to act on the carriers, Rumrich may also have dreamt up a scheme revealed by an Agent Crown letter intercepted on its way to Jessie Jordan in Scotland. The letter included a detailed specification for White House stationery that, once reproduced by Abwehr, would be used, along with the forged signature of President Roosevelt, to order the Assistant Secretary of the Navy to send Rumrich a copy of the carrier drawings. 'It will,' Rumrich claimed, 'get us the *Enterprise* and *Yorktown* plans without much expense.' But the very idea that the Assistant Secretary of the Navy's office would be willing to hand over drawings of two of America's latest and most powerful warships to a total stranger without checking first with the White House is simply laughable. And, at a practical level, if Rumrich was planning something like a rerun of the VD statistics delivery by messenger on a New York street corner, he would have been in for a shock; the construction drawings of a complex, 800-foot, 26,000-ton warship are very numerous, very large and very heavy.[22]

Yet none of these mad schemes come anywhere near matching the sheer lunacy of the Colonel Eglin plot, the truly absurd scheme that blew the entire New York spy ring. It had begun, Rumrich told Turrou, when a courier he knew only as 'Schmidt' asked him to get hold of the US Army's coast defence scheme. The two men had come up with the plan to order Colonel Eglin to attend the bogus meeting at the McAlpin and, drawing on his experience as a US Army clerk, Rumrich had drafted the necessary order. He had included a draft of the message for approval by Abwehr in the Agent Crown letter that he had mailed to Jessie Jordan on 17 January 1938. This was the letter that, steamed open in Dundee, led to the emergency meeting between MI5 and Colonel Raymond Lee in London on 29 January and the start of the hunt for Agent Crown. Two weeks later, when Rumrich was arrested while trying to steal passport forms in New York, another copy of this same message in his briefcase had identified him either as Agent Crown or someone close to the plot.

Interrogated in 1945, Erich Pfeiffer was adamant that the Eglin plot had actually been the brainchild of Karl Schlüter. Indeed, the Bremen spymaster had only learned of it when the story broke in the American press and Schlüter had to confess to a furious Pfeiffer that 'he and RUMRICH, an Ast Hamburg agent, had got together and decided, on their own initiative, to show just what good agents they were'. Conscious of possible repercussions should he identify Schlüter with the scheme, Rumrich must have come up with the name Schmidt in an attempt to offload responsibility for the most damning evidence against him on to a courier who did not exist. Whatever happened, Germany was hardly about to launch a transatlantic seaborne invasion of the United States, so why Schlüter was prepared to risk so much for information on the defences of the American east coast remains a mystery.[23]

Even among those agents dredged from Abwehr's extremely shallow pool of talent, Günther Rumrich must rank as one of its most inept recruits. And, thanks to a combination of Hilmar Dierks' incompetent tradecraft and Mary Curran's dogged determination to expose Jessie Jordan's espionage, Rumrich had been a marked man since MI5 started intercepting mail to 1 Kinloch Street, Dundee, in November 1937. All but one of the letters sent between 1 December 1937, when he started using the Dundee address, and his arrest in February 1938, had been stopped and photographed. Indeed every Agent Crown letter had been in the hands of MI5's spycatchers well before Jessie Jordan had forwarded them on to their intended recipient, Hilmar Dierks, in Germany.

As for Jessie Jordan's Crombie sketch found by Mary Curran, that was nothing but a worthless doodle. A German seaman armed with a camera on a coaster bound for the port of Grangemouth could easily have shot far more useful and detailed images of both Crombie and the decaying fortifications on Inchgarvie, not to mention the naval dockyard at Rosyth which was then being used as a scrapyard. That aside, the Crombie sheds, railway sidings and pier, albeit not their purpose, were shown on contemporary Ordnance Survey maps. But, as they had been with Hermann Görz in 1935, MI5 were once again faced with the tricky task of assembling enough evidence to convincingly prove Jessie guilty of espionage while revealing as little as possible about their methods and, in particular, her connection with the case in the United States. So the sketch would form a key part of the prosecution and, as in the Görtz case, a jury with limited or no knowledge of air travel, never mind aerial warfare, could be persuaded that it would have been somehow useful to an enemy bomber. To reinforce the questionable point, Hinchley Cooke and Neilans even took to the air, flying out of RAF Leuchars in Fife on 17 March to take aerial photographs of the Crombie depot.

Likewise, the map found by Mary Curran when she rifled Jessie Jordan's attaché case would be crucial to the prosecution case despite the fact that the information that Jessie had scribbled on it was, to say the very least, dubious. A case in point was her identification of the RAF airfield at Montrose as 'Barracks' while another was her odd description of the coastguard station at Fife Ness as '3 Castels'

[sic]. Nevertheless, Hinchley Cooke and Neilans were back on the road the following day, visiting these and several other locations that Jessie had marked.

In New York meanwhile, the FBI was gathering evidence for a Federal Grand Jury trial of Rumrich, Hofmann, Voss and Glaser, all of whom were safely in custody. Ignatz Griebl was still being treated as a trusted witness and, keen to ingratiate himself with the American authorities, was a frequent visitor to the FBI Field Office with new and increasingly far-fetched allegations about battalions of supposed Nazi agents. He even, along with Hofmann and others, allowed himself to be interrogated while wired up to a polygraph lie-detector machine. The results were inconclusive, but it did not take the latest technology to detect that, with each preposterous statement, the discrepancies in what he was alleging were becoming ever more obvious. With the Grand Jury due to be sworn in on 12 May, he must have known that his position was becoming untenable and, at 7 a.m. on 11 May, an agitated Kay Moog called Leon Turrou with news that her lover had gone missing.

Interviewed later that day, Maria Griebl told Turrou that she had accompanied her husband on a house call to a patient in Greenwich Village the previous evening. He had then driven to the corner of West 48th Street and 2nd Avenue, parked his Buick near Pier 86 where the liner *Bremen* was berthed and, telling Maria that he had to see someone aboard the ship, disappeared up the gangway. He had returned briefly to the car at about 10.15 p.m., then went back aboard, and that was the last she had seen of him. She had waited in the car until after the ship sailed in the early hours of 11 May then, thinking he might have sneaked off to spend the night with his mistress, telephoned Kay Moog and had what she recalled as 'a heated conversation'. As she did not drive, Maria next called the New Niagara Garage at 1832 Second Avenue (still a 24-hour underground parking facility in 2022) and had them send a driver named Jack Hayes to take her home. Hayes would later recall that, as he parked the Buick in East 86th Street, Maria took her husband's medical bag off the back seat and, in a comment that suggested she knew a great deal more about his intentions than she let on to

Turrou, said, 'He won't be using this for some time, he went on an emergency trip.'

The *Bremen*'s log, examined by the FBI when the liner next called at New York, recorded Griebl's discovery:

> This morning at 4.30 a.m. a man who identified himself as Dr Griebl reported to the 4th Officer Krüger when the latter was on an inspection tour through the ship . . . Dr Griebl was locked up in the usual way and kept under guard, and investigation later disclosed that he had no luggage whatsoever except a pistol permit, an automobile license, and money in the amount of 100 American dollars. This money was used by Dr Griebl to purchase a ticket for tourist class passage.[24]

A furious Turrou and Assistant US Attorney Lester Dunigan prepared to fly out by coastguard seaplane and take Griebl off the *Bremen*, but Captain Ahrens refused to stop the ship. The *Bremen*'s log also recorded a failed attempt by the FBI to have the fugitive taken off when the liner called at Cherbourg:

> This morning at 7.00 a.m. the American Consul at Cherbourg and the Commissaire Speciale of the Cherbourg Police appeared on board and informed me that they wanted to arrest and take away a stowaway, Dr I. Griebl, who had paid passage to Bremen and was now a passenger. I explained to the gentlemen that Griebl had paid his passage and should as usual be taken to Bremerhaven and there handed over to the police . . . The gentlemen returned ashore advising me for the purpose of getting in touch with the Embassy in Paris. Shortly before we departed we were informed that they had determined to waive his arrest.[25]

The liner's next port of call was at Southampton and a cable sent from there arrived in the FBI Field Office on 16 May. It read:

> Stop trying to interfere. Will be back in due time. Arrange

passport facilities for return through France with American Consulate Berlin. Griebl.

Kay Moog later told Leon Turrou that Griebl had visited her during the afternoon of 9 May and asked her to marry him once he had secured a divorce from Maria. She had turned him down, whereupon he had stormed out in a foul temper and she had not seen him since. Later Maria Griebl and Kay Moog both received letters in which Griebl apologised for his sudden departure. Writing to Kay, he claimed that a letter from his brother Kurt about the property deal in Germany that he had discussed with Pfeiffer that night in the Astoria had made it, 'imperatif [sic] to sail at once'. Kay, he wrote, could 'rest assured that I am with you when the trial starts. I would not leave you alone in this mess, nor would I want my wife to fight this battle singlehanded.' Bizarrely, he also asked his mistress Kay to 'Please call my wife and console her. She is quite run down physically and needs moral support.' The letter to his wife, 'Dearest Mizl', was just a litany of complaints about his treatment at the hands of Captain Ahrens that ended with a request that she 'Tell Turrou that I will return at the right time'.

US Federal Attorney Lamar Hardy would later tell Guy Liddell of MI5 that Griebl's escape had not been down to negligence on the part of the Department of Justice or the FBI, as he had been assisting the investigation and was not thought likely to run. With the benefit of hindsight, though, it is hard to escape the notion that both State and Justice were secretly rather glad to see the back of him.[26]

* * *

But what of the lucrative real estate deal in Germany that Griebl had been asking Erich Pfeiffer to help usher through in breach of Nazi foreign exchange laws? The deal would involve a Jewish couple, Isidor and Helene Berliner, handing over their home in Alicenstrasse, Giessen, in exchange for the Tompkins Corners cottage in Putnam County where Griebl had hidden the fugitive Lonkowskis in 1935. Nothing less than blatant extortion, it would also involve the desperate Berliners handing over a substantial cash sum that, were Griebl to attempt to transfer to his bank in New York, would indeed fall foul of the Nazi foreign exchange rules. Maria's regular visits to Germany and Griebl's June 1937 trip had really been all about securing Abwehr's help in sidestepping Nazi law and, in return for a little espionage in the United States, ensuring the deal went through regardless.

The Tompkins Corners property was duly signed over to the Berliners for '$1 and other valuable considerations', in July 1937. Then, rightly suspecting that she was being shunted out of the way while her husband carried on his affair with Kay Moog, Maria had been sent to Germany to complete the contract. But she found on arriving in Bremerhaven that neither Abwehr nor Erich Pfeiffer had the slightest interest in pushing her anti-Semitic husband's crooked deal through. Worse still, the Nazi authorities were now demanding 50,000 Reichsmarks ($20,000 in 1937 values and $350,000 in 2022 values) from the already ruined Berliners before they would be allowed to leave Germany.[27]

The Nazi state's demands meant that the Griebls' hopes of being able to profit handsomely from a Jewish family's extreme distress had evaporated. There remained the Berliners' Giessen property and, according to a letter Maria would later show the FBI, due to 'the peculiar circumstances' in this case, a clear reference to Ignatz Griebl's activities in the United States, the Nazi authorities had transferred Alicenstrasse 16 to the Griebls in March 1938. Sadly, while their thirteen-year-old daughter Karla was able to escape to Palestine in 1939 with the help of her older brother, Lothar, this came too late for Isidor and Helene who never reached safety in the United States. Driven from their home by the Griebls and the Nazi state, they were drafted into forced labour, then deported to Treblinka death camp in 1942 and murdered.[28]

Chapter 7

The French Lieutenant's Whore

This intercept has created a tremendous impression in
the Deuxième Bureau and also in French naval circles.

Colonel Valentine Vivian, MI6, 19 October 1938

In January 1938, when MI5 Director General Sir Vernon Kell and
Edward Hinchley Cooke met American Military Attaché Colonel
Raymond Lee in London to pass on the information about Agent
Crown's plan to overpower Colonel Eglin, there was one crucial new
piece of evidence that they did not share with the Americans. This was
a letter, sent to Jessie Jordan from Prague in Czechoslovakia, that had
been steamed open by Alexander Jack in Dundee at the same time as
the Agent Crown letter. Translated from German, it reads in part:

Prague, 24 Jan. 38.

Very esteemed Mr S.

With reference to my brother G. who is active for the cause
in the United States, I beg to offer my services in the same
cause . . . I am studying chemistry at the German University
in Prague and am therefore in the same branch of business
as my brother . . . It has for ever been my wish to serve the
German cause in any possible way. As far as the possibility
exists to carry out such activities in this country I am gladly
prepared to serve you.

Yours,
HANSJORG GUSTAV RUMRICH
PRAGUE 11. ZITNA 3-11.
c/o HOFMAN.

Had MI5 passed this letter, or even an edited version of its content, to Colonel Lee, it would have led the FBI straight to Günther Rumrich alias Agent Crown. But that would have brought the entire case to a swift end and MI5 would have lost Jessie Jordan's intercepted mail as a valuable source on Abwehr operations that the British were keen to nurture, so a degree of reticence was understandable.[1]

The Prague letter would have been delivered to Jessie Jordan at Kinloch Street on 29 January and, forwarded to Hilmar Dierks, would have arrived in Hamburg on or around 3 February. The liner *Europa* arrived in New York early on 4 February and, as Johanna Hofmann recalled for Leon Turrou, she and Karl Schlüter went ashore to call on Ignatz Griebl and Martin Schade. They had then made their way to Rumrich's apartment where, in addition to the venereal disease statistics from Fort Hamilton, they were handed two photographs of Gustav along with his home address in Zeppelinstrasse, Töplitz-Schonau, Czechoslovakia, modern day Kašparova ul in Teplice, and told of his interest in becoming a spy.[2]

According to Erich Pfeiffer's post-war interrogation, on his return to Germany a week later Schlüter told the Bremen spymaster that

> he had a most useful contact in New York, a Sudeten German working for Ast Hamburg. This man, Günther RUMRICH, had a brother in Moravia working in an arms factory, who would be able to supply useful information. Would PFEIFFER allow him to recruit this man? His great friend, Johanna HOFMANN, a hairdresser in the *Europa*, was the mistress of Günther in New York; he (SCHLUTER) would use her to contact Gustav RUMRICH in Czechoslovakia and 'make a proposition' to him.
>
> PFEIFFER indignantly enquired what this HOFMANN woman might know about SCHLUTER's activities. SCHLUTER replied that when he was on leave from the ship he had got Johanna to 'take his stuff'; he had also used her occasionally in New York as he was rather afraid of

Customs. HOFMANN, who would conceal things in her bosom, was less exposed to a search.[3]

Assuming Pfeiffer is correct in his recollection, whether he had worked out that Abwehrstelle Hamburg must have wanted nothing to do with Gustav Rumrich is unclear. Nor is it clear whether he realised that Schlüter was lying about Gustav working in an arms factory and about Johanna being Günther's mistress. Whatever the truth of it, the two men had a testy exchange at the end of which Pfeiffer reluctantly agreed that Schlüter could go on leave and send Hofmann to New York alone on the *Europa*'s next voyage. Meanwhile, Pfeiffer gave Schlüter and Hofmann permission to travel to Czechoslovakia to recruit Gustav Rumrich.

Schlüter and Hofmann arrived in Töplitz-Schonau on 15 February and booked in at the Hotel de Saxe as Herr and Frau Schlüter. They found Gustav Rumrich and his family to be typical of the 3 million ethnic Germans marooned on the Sudetenland western border regions of Czechoslovakia, a state somewhat carelessly created by mapmakers framing the peace settlement that ended the First World War. A rise in German nationalism that mirrored the rise of the Nazi party in neighbouring Germany proved seductive to young Sudeten Germans like 21-year-old Gustav, particularly when Hitler began loudly demanding the reunification of the Sudetenland with Germany. But his eagerness to spy for the Nazis was primarily driven, not by ideology, but by the fact that he was finding it impossible to make ends meet at university.

True to form, Schlüter needlessly told Gustav Rumrich that he and Hofmann worked on the *Europa*, that he was from Bremerhaven, that his 'wife' Jenni was from Dresden and that they were close friends of his brother Günther in New York. He then gave Gustav a copy of the same cipher key that the FBI would find ten days later in Griebl's desk in New York, tasked him with infiltrating the Czech communist party and, as he was about to be called up for compulsory military service, reporting on the Czech Army. Jenni Hofmann would deliver payments and further instructions.[4]

Johanna Hofmann hurried back to Bremerhaven and, unaware that Günther Rumrich was already making his confession to Leon Turrou, boarded the *Europa* for her next voyage to New York, this time without Karl Schlüter. She was arrested as soon as she stepped ashore on 24 February. Jessie Jordan's arrest followed on 2 March and, the Czechs having been tipped off by Harold Gibson, the MI6 Head of Station in Prague, Gustav Rumrich was picked up the following day, 3 March. A week later the *Anschluss*, the Nazi annexation of Austria, sparked a refugee crisis on Czechoslovakia's southern border as thousands of Jews, communists and intellectuals tried to escape. So it was not until 29 April that Harold Gibson was able to pass on a report that the younger Rumrich had 'eventually confessed to having been recruited for the German S.S. [secret service] by Johanna HOFMANN alias Jennie SCHLEUTER'.[5]

The phrase 'eventually confessed' is perhaps a telling reflection of the fact that, given the state of Czechoslovak-German relations in those last weeks before the 1938 Munich Crisis, the interrogation would have been anything but friendly. Gibson's report also included two Abwehr mailbox addresses that Gustav had been given, one being a Mrs Jessie Jordan of 1 Kinloch Street, Dundee, Scotland, and the other a Mrs G. Brandy of 14 Willow Terrace in Dublin, Ireland. Jessie Jordan was by then awaiting trial in Saughton Prison, Edinburgh, but the Dublin address was new and, as much of the Republic of Ireland's mail passed through Britain, an intercept was put in place on 6 May 1938.

Three weeks later, on 27 May, the Dublin intercept turned up an unsigned postcard from the island of Tahiti, a French colony in the South Pacific. The message on the card included the sentence 'J'ai des collections de timbre a vous envoyer', which translates as 'I have stamp collections to send you'. As had been revealed in the Draper case three years before, careless Abwehr spymasters often used the expression 'stamp collections' as shorthand for intelligence. A month later, at midnight on 27 June, Wilfred 'Biffy' Dunderdale, the MI6 head of station in Paris, telephoned Paul Paillole, deputy head of the Service de Centralisation des Renseignements counter-espionage section within the Deuxième Bureau, and asked for an urgent meeting. 'Is it serious?' Paillole asked. 'It's serious,' replied Dunderdale.[6]

Dunderdale arrived at the Deuxième Bureau the following morning accompanied by Edward Hinchley Cooke who told Paillole that MI5 had been watching an address in Dublin at the request of the FBI who had become aware of it during the recent New York spy case. Hinchley Cooke then handed over a still sealed letter that had been postmarked in Paris and was addressed to Mrs Brandy in Dublin. Paillole called in his assistant, André Bonnefous, and the two men steamed open the envelope to reveal four sheets of paper with extensive handwritten notes on dispositions to be made by the French Mediterranean Fleet as tension ratcheted up over the Sudeten region of Czechoslovakia. While these were being photographed Paillole asked if this was the first item of mail that had been intercepted on its way from France to the Dublin mailbox. Presumably referring to the postcard from Tahiti, Hinchley Cooke had to admit that one other letter had been intercepted a month before, but it had said almost nothing and had simply been passed for delivery. After agreeing to pass all future intercepts to Paris without delay, Hinchley Cooke hurried away to catch the next flight from Le Bourget to Croydon airport so that Mrs Brandy's letter could be sent on its way with the minimum of delay.[7]

Assuming Paillole's recollection of the meeting is correct, Hinchley Cooke had been decidedly economical with the truth when he implied that the tip-off about the Dublin address had come from the Americans and made no mention of either the Czechoslovak connection, Gustav Rumrich or Harold Gibson's report from Prague. It is also inconceivable that the sealed envelope Hinchley Cooke handed Paillole had not already been steamed open in London and the contents carefully examined by both MI5 and MI6.

Hinchley Cooke was still in the air over the English Channel when André Bonnefous delivered the photographs of the letter to a shocked Ministère de la Marine in Place de la Concorde. As war was becoming ever more likely in 1938, Britain and France had developed a joint strategy for the defence of the Mediterranean and, particularly in Britain's case, the vital route to Suez, Australia, New

Zealand and its colonies in the Far East. Now this strategy was being comprehensively betrayed by a spy in the Marine Nationale. As Valentine Vivian of MI6 wrote, 'This intercept has created a tremendous impression in the Deuxième Bureau and also in French naval circles.' Indeed, given the serious nature of the content and the danger that the leak posed to both the Marine Nationale and the Royal Navy, Dunderdale's midnight request for an urgent meeting with Paillole is hardly surprising. It was, as Paillole rightly observed, 'une affaire d'une exceptionelle gravité'.[8]

Hinchley Cooke flew back to Paris ten days later with another letter in which the spy, who was using the Abwehr code name 'Charles', asked for a meeting so that he could make an important delivery. This did not give any new information that would help with the identification of Agent Charles, but yet another intercepted letter delivered to Paris in August would provide a vital clue. It had been posted in Antwerp on 16 August and, while André Bonnefous and Jacques Abtey were unable to identify a candidate from a list of naval officers granted permission to travel abroad during August, when they searched through 'several hundred' Antwerp hotel registration cards provided by Sûreté belge, they found what they were looking for. Agent Charles had registered at the Hotel Century under his own name:

Nom: Aubert.
Prénom: Marc.
Profession: Officier.

Bonnefous hurried off to the Ministère de la Marine only to discover that there were several officers with the surname Aubert on the current lists and none of them had the forename Marc. So now the Deuxième Bureau were reduced to comparing the handwriting on Mrs Brandy's intercepted mail with samples from hundreds of Mediterranean Fleet officers, a painstaking task lent immense urgency by fresh intercepts from MI5 that included alert orders to the Marine Nationale during the Munich Crisis. Agent Charles was now a serious threat to French and British naval units operating in the Mediterranean. Yet this was by no means the first time that treachery had struck at the Marine Nationale and the case that inspired Agent Charles to take up espionage had been uncovered in the spring of 1935.

* * *

Lydia Oswald freely admitted that she lived only for money, travel and adventure. And the labels on the suitcases that she and her boyfriend, aristocratic French naval officer Comte Jean de Forceville, loaded into a taxi outside his Brest apartment in Rue d'Aiguillon, Brest, at 5.35 a.m. on 2 March 1935 certainly pointed to someone well travelled. But this was one journey Lydia was destined not to complete and, in Brest railway station a few minutes later, she and de Forceville found themselves surrounded by Commissaire Cadet and a posse of Sûreté officers. Searching the couple's luggage, Sûreté officers discovered 'une certaine quantité d'opium' and an Abwehr questionnaire about French warships.[9]

News that the Comte de Forceville's beautiful girlfriend was a Nazi spy leaked within hours of the arrests. The press were out in force when Lydia was taken to the Palais de Justice the following morning and again that afternoon when an ashen-faced Jean de Forceville returned home, under house arrest, to find his apartment had been ransacked by a Sûreté search team who had found more opium hidden in an empty port bottle. Lydia Oswald was, by then, locked up in a filthy cell in Bouguen prison, a dramatic change of circumstances for a young woman who, only days before, had been the belle of the ball at a glittering Paris society party attended by President Albert Lebrun.

Half-German on her mother's side, Lydia had grown up in St. Gall, a small town in the German-speaking north of Switzerland. Aged just eighteen and bored, she travelled alone to France, Italy, Algeria and Spain, and, along the way, worked as an artist's model in Algiers and had a passionate affair with a journalist in Barcelona. Arriving at Quebec on 29 August 1929 as supposedly the travelling companion of a Welsh fellow passenger, Muriel Lewis-Morgan, she was immediately deported as she had neither passport nor visa.

Arriving in New York three years later, on 18 August 1932, this time with a passport, she travelled on to Hollywood, Colombia, Guatemala and Panama.[10]

Precisely when Lydia was recruited by Abwehr remains a mystery, but it is easy to see why; she was clever, daring, beautiful, sophisticated, multi-lingual and perfectly willing to lie to get her own way. She was almost certainly an Abwehr spy when, posing as a correspondent of the *St Galler Tagblatt* accredited to the League of Nations, she turned up in Geneva in September 1934. An instant hit with homesick diplomats and politicians, she would later claim that the recently widowed French Foreign Minister Louis Barthou 'found great favour in my company . . . Many times he suggested that I should go to Paris, assuring me that I would have an even gayer time than I was having in Geneva.' Whether there is any truth in the story or not, Lydia would follow his advice, though not before Barthou had been accidentally shot and killed during the assassination of King Alexander of Yugoslavia in Marseilles on 9 October 1934.[11]

On 21 January 1935 Lydia and her cocker spaniel named Flow boarded the Brest rapide at Paris Montparnasse station and took a seat next to a young naval officer, enseigne de vaisseau René Guignard. Introducing herself as a journalist whose stupid editor had sent a woman who knew nothing about ships to write about the French Navy, she wondered whether enseigne Guignard might be able to help. And Guignard, a married father of two who still fancied himself as a ladies' man, was only too eager to help his captivating blonde travelling companion, even suggesting that Mademoiselle Oswald might like to start by visiting his ship, the new cruiser *Émile Bertin*. As she booked herself and Flow into an expensive suite at the Hotel Le Continental that evening, Lydia must have hardly been able to believe her luck; *Émile Bertin* was the very ship she had been sent to Brest to spy on and already she had secured an invitation to go aboard. Showing her round a few days later, Guignard obligingly answered all her questions about French torpedo tubes and aircraft catapults, and then entertained her to dinner in the wardroom.[12]

Most days, however, the lovely *journaliste* and her *petit chien* held court in the café at her hotel, surrounded by admiring officers eager to help with her articles. Lydia had also turned the full force of her flirtatious charm on lieutenant Comte Jean de Forceville, a friend of Guignard's serving aboard the cruiser *La Galissonière*. De Forceville was instantly infatuated and on 14 February 1935, just three weeks after she arrived in Brest, took Lydia to an exclusive naval ball in Paris. It was St Valentine's night and, as they waltzed and fox-trotted through the shimmering marble and gold foyers of L'Opera with President Lebrun and the cream of Paris society, Lydia began having delusions about marrying her wealthy, aristocratic sailor and becoming the Comtesse de Forceville. Quite how she expected to get away with it is anyone's guess, but for the next two weeks the couple spent their evenings dining *à deux* at the best restaurants in Brest and making love amid clouds of opium fumes at de Forceville's rue d'Aiguillon apartment. On 1 March 1935 they told friends they were leaving for Paris by train the next morning and that they were planning to get married. The Sûreté were tipped off and were waiting at the station.

Lydia had in fact been under Sûreté surveillance since being betrayed, probably by double agent Stanislas Krauss, in 1934. Her intercepted correspondence had included one letter from an Abwehr contact in Geneva, former naval officer Ernst Haack, with the delightfully enigmatic phrase, 'Merci pour les voeux de la poule d'Emile, mais il s'occupe de tuyaux.' Literally translating as, 'Thank you for the eggs from Emile's chicken, but he looks after tubes,' which was taken to mean, 'Thank you for the information from the *Émile Bertin* officer, but we need more on the torpedo tubes.' The Sûreté were said to be eagerly awaiting the return of *Émile Bertin* and, in particular, her torpedo officer enseigne René Guignard. Enquiries were also under way in St Malo where Lydia and de Forceville had spent the night after visiting an officer friend, and in Britain where she was known to have spent time in 1934.

The case was heard in camera by a military tribunal on 10 September 1935 and Guignard, pale and haggard after six months under close arrest, had to admit that Lydia once told him that she was a spy, but he did not take her seriously. 'How was I to know what to believe,' he protested, 'she told so many lies?' There was an embarrassing moment when Lydia's defence counsel, cross-examining a Sûreté witness, revealed that she had once offered her services to the Deuxième Bureau. And de Forceville had to admit that he had been too besotted with Lydia to heed a discreet Sûreté warning to steer clear of her.

But it was Lydia, elegant and beautiful despite six months in jail, who stole the show. She freely admitted that she had come to Brest as a German spy. 'But,' she said, 'the French officers I met treated me with such dignity, such courtesy, that I soon realised my task was dishonourable. I abandoned it for ever.' With tears filling her large blue eyes, she looked straight at a blushing Jean de Forceville and continued, 'I loved lieutenant de Forceville with all my heart. I love him still. I ask your pardon for the two officers by my side. I had thought to lead them astray, but it is they who saved me. I swear that lieutenant Guignard had no reason to believe I was a spy. I swear that lieutenant de Forceville did not betray his country. Now, gentlemen, do what you will with me.'

It was a bravura performance, and it seems to have worked. De Forceville and Guignard were acquitted and Lydia, dubbed 'The Swiss Mata Hari' by the press, was given a light sentence of just nine months in jail. After a row with prison officers who wanted to keep her fur coat to cover what they termed her expenses, Lydia Oswald was spirited out of Pontaniou jail in Brest in the early hours of 2 December 1935. Counter-intelligence services in Europe, Asia and the United States would soon learn that her sojourn in a French prison had done nothing to dampen her enthusiasm for the spying game.[13]

Spy stories were becoming so routine that they were generally relegated to the inside pages of French newspapers. The exception was when, as in the case of Lydia Oswald, there was a beautiful femme fatale involved. Another case that did make the headlines in 1935 involved naval rating Marcel Rolland who attracted suspicion when he and a glamorous new girlfriend began visiting expensive nightclubs near the French naval base at Toulon. Surveillance revealed that he was peddling secrets to pay for his extravagant lifestyle and he was arrested in the Place des Armes on the evening of 5 May 1935, though not before 'une jeune femme blonde d'une grande beauté', who had been waiting for him in a pearl grey sports car, sped off when she spotted the detectives closing in. The Sûreté were, according to press reports, searching high and low for the mysterious green-eyed blonde and border posts had been alerted to pick her up if she tried to escape to Italy or Switzerland.

* * *

Cases like those involving Lydia Oswald and Marcel Rolland, and there were many of them, were entertaining for French newspaper readers and presented little real risk to national security. But Agent Charles was a different matter entirely; his treachery would strike at the very heart of both the Marine Nationale and the Royal Navy and place the vital sea route to Suez and the Middle East oilfields in jeopardy. Tracking him down was a matter of extreme urgency and the breakthrough came on 22 September 1938, the same day that, during an ill-tempered meeting with British Prime Minister Neville Chamberlain, Adolf Hitler demanded that the Czech Sudetenland be handed over to Germany.

Commissaire Jean Osvald of the Sûreté was at Toulon naval base laboriously comparing the handwriting of Mediterranean Fleet officers with that on Mrs Brandy's intercepted mail and, as Chamberlain and Hitler quarrelled in Bad Godesberg, he called Paul Paillole in Paris to confirm that he had a perfect match. Agent Charles' real name was indeed Marc Aubert, just as André Bonnefous had discovered on the Antwerp hotel registration card, and he was an enseigne aboard the destroyer *Vauquelin*. The Ministère de la Marine had not been able to find his name in the list of Marine Nationale officers because nobody had thought to check the list of the latest graduates from the French naval academy, the École Navale.

The son of a tax inspector, Marc Aubert had been born in Lille in 1912. Joining the Marine Nationale as a seaman and, promoted rapidly, he had entered the École Naval at Lanvéoc near Brest as an officer cadet in October 1935. There he fell into the clutches of Marie-Jeanne Morel, a 25-year-old prostitute from the small town of Pléchâtel south of Rennes, and started having Pygmalionesque delusions about setting her up as a respectable wife of a naval officer. The money-obsessed Morel, on the other hand, saw her latest conquest as just another cash cow and Aubert was soon mired in debt. Inspired by contemporary cases like those of Lydia Oswald and Marcel Rolland, he decided the only source of easy money that he needed was espionage and, encouraged by Morel, wrote to the German military attaché in Paris in the spring of 1936 to offer his services as a spy. The approach was passed to Abwehr headquarters in Berlin who, suspecting a trap, wrote back asking for evidence of Aubert's serious intent. The reply came in the form of a set of current Marine Nationale ciphers that, tested against intercepted signals, were found to work.[14]

The task of running 'this very valuable agent' was delegated to Erich Pfeiffer who arranged a meeting with Aubert in Belgium. Aubert was told to take a room at the Century Hotel next to Antwerp Central Station and, at an agreed time on a particular day early in August 1937, he was to appear in the hotel lobby and identify himself to Pfeiffer by walking with a pronounced limp. Pfeiffer recalled what happened next for his post-war MI5 interrogators:

> [He] waited at the hotel for some time beyond the appointed hour. Eventually he spoke to the porter, who telephoned one of the rooms and assured him that AUBERT was there and would be down in twenty minutes. When still he did not appear PFEIFFER became increasingly nervous, but after several more minutes had passed the lift came down and a man in French naval uniform appeared. He spoke to the porter, PFEIFFER was pointed out to him, and he walked over to introduce himself.
>
> PFEIFFER, 'thought that it was all over,' that this latest indiscretion was unpardonable. He severely rated AUBERT for his tactlessness, then ordered Aubert to return to his room while he went out to think things over.
>
> After careful consideration PFEIFFER, who had weighed up the possibilities of a trap while walking round the block, decided to take 'pot luck'. He advised AUBERT

through the hall porter that he would come up to his room this afternoon.

On arriving there later he was shocked to see a woman with AUBERT who introduced her as his wife. (She was the type of wife to whom the French refer between quotes.)

But he was to have a more severe, if more pleasant, shock. Indicating several suitcases, AUBERT proclaimed that they were filled with very important secret documents stolen from the Brest training establishment; and they were. (When the papers were weighed later in Berlin they turned the scales at 95lb.)

PFEIFFER had a quick look at the material and saw at a glance that it was indeed a valuable haul. In addition to full details of French naval vessels, with blueprints and other documents of incalculable worth, there were papers describing the latest type of remote control mines and torpedoes elaborated by the French, of which the Germans had neither knowledge or suspicion.[15]

The Bremen spymaster handed over a down payment of 500 Reichsmarks with the promise of a sizeable bonus to follow, but getting this much material out of Belgium and into Germany was not going to be easy, particularly as Pfeiffer had another appointment to keep with an agent in the Netherlands. After some discussion the spymaster gave Aubert some money for civilian clothes and instructed him to stay in Antwerp, keeping a low profile, and await another Abwehr officer who would act as courier. Fritz Unterberg crossed into Belgium a few days later and smuggled Aubert's suitcases aboard a German coaster only to be detained by German customs officials on arrival at Hamburg because he was carrying suspicious documents.[16]

Aubert continued sending top-grade material until October 1937 when he sailed on a world cruise aboard the training cruiser *Jeanne d' Arc*, during which he came to the attention of MI5 with his May 1938 postcard sent from Tahiti to Mrs Brandy in Dublin. He and Morel resumed contact with Abwehr after he returned to France in

July 1938 and, as soon as Aubert learned that he was being drafted to the destroyer *Vauquelin* at Toulon, Morel wrote to Pfeiffer using her code name, Charlotte as opposed to his Charles, to propose another meeting in Antwerp on 9 September. Translated from French, her letter reads:

Dear Friend,

Charles will leave for Toulon on 14 Sept. 38 so would like to meet at Antwerp on 9 Sept. 38.

He will arrive at 8.00 a.m. at the Century where he will take a room and will wait for you at the café in the lobby.

He will have to return to Paris the same day at 1900. He will be happy to see you if you can make it.

He has told me that nothing untoward has happened in France and that everything is going well. He will bring some papers, though not a great deal as he has not had much work this year.

Hoping to hear from you soon,

Charlotte

Pfeiffer could not keep the appointment, so little is known about this meeting beyond Aubert's claim that he met a scruffy man of about 50 years old who spoke bad French. But the meeting took place against a background of rapidly rising international tension as Hitler had signed a secret directive, *Fall Grün* (Operation Green), for an invasion of Czechoslovakia to take place not later than 1 October, three weeks later. MI6 had been made aware of the German plans by an anti-Nazi German diplomat in the Hague, Wolfgang zu Putlitz and Generalmajor Wolfgang zu Schweppenburg, the anti-Nazi military attaché in London whose British case officer was Jona 'Klop' Ustinov, the MI5 officer father of the actor Peter Ustinov. German chargé d'affaires Theo Kordt, another courageous anti-Nazi diplomat, was even smuggled into Downing Street to beg Prime Minister Neville Chamberlain to broadcast a statement of support for Czechoslovakia. Kordt's appeal fell on deaf ears and, believing he could dissuade Hitler from war by rational argument, Chamberlain embarked on three weeks of shuttle diplomacy that ended with the infamous Munich Agreement ceding the Sudetenland to Germany without Prague even being consulted and without a shot being fired. A European war had been averted and, infuriated by the British Prime Minister's direct appeals to the German people for peace, Hitler reputedly referred to Chamberlain behind his back as an 'arschloch' [arsehole].[17]

In Toulon, careful plans were then being laid for the arrest of Marc Aubert. It had been decided that André Bonnefous would take on the role of Agent Charles after Aubert's arrest and feed his German spymasters deliberately misleading intelligence, but for this to succeed the arrest had to be made in total secrecy. Posing as civilian visitors, Bonnefous and Commissaire Osvald boarded *Vauquelin* when the dockyard was at its quietest on the afternoon of Sunday, 2 November. Led by capitaine de frégate Robinet de Plas, they made their way to Aubert's cabin, burst in and found the spy copying the latest Mediterranean Fleet ciphers. Aubert would later admit under interrogation that he had already given Abwehr almost all of the current ciphers in use by the Marine Nationale. Indeed the French had themselves intercepted one of his letters, sent from Toulon in late October complete with a Mediterranean Fleet cipher, part of which is reproduced on p. 164.

This meant that, had war broken out as it so nearly did in 1938, the Kriegsmarine would have had advance warning of every move made by the Marine Nationale and could have speedily shared this with its Italian allies. Worse still, and of serious concern to the Royal Navy, had a French ship simply repeated verbatim the text of an enciphered signal sent from one of their ships, this could have given the Germans a break into British naval ciphers.[18]

One useful spin-off from the Aubert case was the opening up of a fruitful line of communication between MI5 and the Irish military intelligence service, G.2. A request for information on Mrs G. Brandy, the mailbox used by Marc Aubert, was sent to Dublin on 12 September 1938. Colonel Liam Archer's initial report, which

Variation des clefs à utiliser dans le Tac K biff"

VARÉTRA A N° 10

Variation normale

1° combinaisons

N° des jour	janvier novembre	février décembre	mars septembre	avril août	mai juillet	juin octobre
1	1234	4231	3214	4312	1432	3124
10	3142	3241	1342	2431	3412	1243
20	2314	2341	3241	1234	1432	3124

2° Lettre repère

n° du jour	Lettre
1	B
2	F
3	C
4	E
5	A
6	H
7	A
8	D
9	G
10	D
11	H
12	C
13	F
14	C
15	E

n° du jour	Lettre
16	F
17	B
18	H
19	A
20	G
21	E
22	D
23	B
24	D
25	G
26	A
27	D
28	E
29	F
30	B
31	-

Part of a Marine Nationale cipher key copied for his Abwehr spymasters by Marc Aubert. (National Archives) reached London on 14 October, identified her as Gertrud Brandy, the widow of German machine tools salesman Reinhard Brandy who had died in Dublin in February 1937. Gertrud had left for Germany in July 1937, but her daughter Edith had come to the notice of the Irish authorities because of the pro-Nazi company she kept at her home, 20 Harcourt Street in Dublin, and elsewhere. And MI5 had by then picked up one letter from Agent Charles on its way to the Harcourt Street address, confirming that Edith had taken on her mother's Abwehr role.

Political sensitivities meant that any cooperation between MI5 and Irish military intelligence had to be handled with extreme discretion. But Liam Archer travelled to London on 5 November 1938 and had a lengthy meeting with the MI5 Deputy Director General, Brigadier Oswald 'Jasper' Harker, who briefed him on the French side of the case. Harker wrote later that Colonel Archer, who recognised the Nazi threat for what it was but had precious few resources, was anxious to assist in any way he can but could offer little in the way of practical help. The secret liaison between Archer, a doughty former Irish freedom fighter, and his MI5 counterparts would mature into the valuable Dublin Link that remained in place through the critical period until July 1941 when, as MI5 officer Guy Liddell noted in his diary:

> Archer has been made Asst. Chief of Staff in Eire. This is rather a serious blow, as I doubt whether his number two is sufficiently strong to resist pressure from above.[19]

* * *

In November 1961, as files on Christopher Draper, P.O. Box 629, Jessie Jordan, Gertrud Brandy and Marc Aubert were being weeded and placed into storage, the MI5 archivist added the following case summary:

> Taken together, these files show how the false step of recruiting Major DRAPER led to; (1) the discovery of the Hamburg post box of the German Secret Service; (2) to the

identification of Mrs JORDAN as an intermediary; (3) to the arrest and conviction of four German agents in America; (4) to the discovery of Mrs BRANDY as another intermediary; (5) to the unmasking of a German agent in France.[20]

Marc Aubert's immensely damaging treachery had only come to light as a direct result of the letter from Gustav Rumrich in Prague being picked up in the mail intercept on Jessie Jordan in Dundee. And this only happened because Scottish housewife spy-catcher Mary Curran had persuaded Dundee Police that Jessie Jordan was a spy. Had Mary failed in her mission, and had the Dundee mail intercept not been put in place in time, Gustav's letter would have reached Jessie Jordan undetected and been forwarded to Abwehrstelle Hamburg. Gustav would then have started using Mrs Brandy's address in Dublin, again undetected, and both MI5 and the Irish would have remained unaware of the Dublin connection. Marc Aubert and Marie-Jeanne Morel could have continued their immensely damaging treachery into the opening months of the Second World War and possibly beyond. And none of this would have been possible but for double agent Christopher Draper securing the P.O. Box 629 address from Hamburg spymaster Hilmar Dierks.

A serious security breach had been closed. Now, as in previous espionage cases, justice had to be seen to be done.

Chapter 8

Confessions of a Nazi Spy

I want to propose a toast to Warner Bros, the only
studio with any guts!

Groucho Marx, December 1938

Jessie Jordan's trial at the High Court in Edinburgh was a brief
affair. Forty-two witnesses had been cited to appear on Monday,
16 May 1938, chief among them Edward Hinchley Cooke and
Mary Curran, but a guilty plea meant that none were required to
give evidence. Jessie appeared calm as she sat in the dock awaiting
sentencing, blonde hair immaculately styled and wearing the same
black coat and green hat she had put on when she was arrested
at Kinloch Street. Her defence counsel skilfully portrayed her as
an unloved illegitimate child who was the victim of circumstances
largely beyond her control. But there was no escaping that she
was an active, albeit inept, Nazi spy who could have had no illusions about the malign intent behind the tasks she had been set by
Abwehr. She was sentenced to four years in jail and, as she was
taken down, smiled briefly at Edward Hinchley Cooke and said,
'Auf Wiedersehen.' She was then driven away to begin her sentence
in Saughton Prison. Had she been caught just two years later she
would, like many of Abwehr's wartime agents, have faced a possible
death sentence.

In New York, the Federal Grand Jury hearings that had precipi-
tated Griebl's escape were already under way. One of the first to
testify was Senta Dewanger who told what she knew of Lonkowski's
activities in 1935. Günther Rumrich was another early witness and

spent more than two hours almost boastfully recounting his part in the affair. Maria Griebl and Kay Moog enlivened proceedings when they happened to arrive at the same time on Thursday, 19 May, and started a furious row while waiting to give evidence. Others to appear included Otto Voss and his wife, Christian Danielsen, Eleanor Böhm and a squalid parade of anti-Semitic Griebl associates and seedy New York Nazis.

Captain Adolf Ahrens of the *Bremen* and four of his crew were brought to Foley Square for questioning on 25 May, the next time the ship was in New York. Asked why he had not put Griebl ashore at Cherbourg as requested by American diplomats, Ahrens replied enigmatically, 'I had my orders.' Ahrens was allowed to leave and take his ship on her return voyage to Germany, but Wilhelm Böhnke, a pantryman who doubled as the *Bremen*'s Ortsgruppenleiter, or Nazi Party group leader, was one of four who were detained. A bulky, ungainly figure believed to have played a key role in the Griebl escape, Böhnke shuffled into the Grand Jury courtroom the next morning, glared resentfully at Judge Vincent Liebell and threw his arm up in a Nazi salute.[1]

The *Bremen* crew were still testifying the following morning when, as Turrou recalled, the proceedings were interrupted by a breathless Captain William Dreschel, New York Marine Superintendent for the Hamburg-Amerika Line, who burst in with news that the outbound *Hamburg* had discovered a stowaway named Gudenberg. The FBI made some hurried phone calls and discovered that Lonkowski informant Werner Gudenberg had returned home to Bristol, Pennsylvania, after testifying to the Grand Jury on 24 May, then left the following morning and vanished.

As a very public row kicked off between FBI Director J. Edgar Hoover and Federal Attorney Lamar Hardy over who was responsible for the embarrassing disappearance of two of the most important witnesses, Maria Griebl had wasted no time selling her husband's thriving practice and all of his medical equipment; even the large portrait of the late President Hindenburg that once adorned the wall of the waiting room had been sold. She had also sent a trunk filled with her husband's clothes to his mother's address in Würzburg and arranged for his Buick sedan to be shipped to Germany. Then, believing that she had nothing further to add to the legal process, she booked passage to Bremerhaven on 15 June.

Maria's fire sale dispelled any lingering official hopes that her husband would return for trial and, amid mounting suspicions that she knew a great deal more about his escape than she was letting on, she was ordered to appear before the Grand Jury on 9 May. Back in 1933, when she appeared before a Grand Jury investigating the Newark Schwabenhalle riot, an insufferably arrogant Maria had infamously demanded that she had a right to be questioned by a Gentile. This time she presented a very different figure, weeping and nervously twisting a handkerchief between her fingers as Lamar Hardy demanded she be held on $5,000 bail. 'I haven't $5,000,' she replied. 'I have no money; that's why I sold his effects, because I have no money. I intended to go to Germany because there is nothing for me here. I told Mr Hardy and the others where I was going.' And she had a point; she had made no secret of her intention to return to Germany, but Judge Liebell replied, 'I sympathize with you, but your husband has gone to Germany and, if you are given an opportunity, you won't return either.' Wiping away tears, Maria replied, 'I really won't go. If they had told me I couldn't go, I wouldn't have bought a ticket . . . My husband has $300 or $400 in the bank, but I can't get at it. I have no power of attorney.'

Judge Liebell then asked why her husband had not returned as promised, not least because that would bring an end to her problems. 'You see, madam, the government has been confronted with the disappearance of witnesses. Your husband was one of them and then there was another who went to Germany. The government must see that no more witnesses go on German boats. Send a message to your husband and ask him to come back here. Then all your trouble will be relieved.'[2]

Led away to the Womens' House of Detention, Maria was now a hostage against her husband's return, something that she knew was not about to happen. Partial relief would come from the eccentric publisher Seward Collins, a fervent admirer of Hitler and Mussolini, who put up the bail money two days later. Maria promptly disappeared to the Tompkins Corners cottage, quietly ignoring the fact that it was now technically the property of the Berliners, and hid herself away for another three months before finally being allowed to leave. By then it had emerged that she had indeed been lying and had known that her husband had been planning his escape for some weeks before he left.[3]

On 20 June 1938 the Grand Jury indicted eighteen people, only four of whom were actually in custody, to stand trial later in the year. The list included Udo von Bonin, Hermann Menzel, Erich Pfeiffer, Ernst Müller and 'Sanders' as the supposed German officials who had masterminded the plot; Otto Voss, Erich Glaser, Werner Gudenberg and Günther Rumrich as working agents; Ignatz Griebl, Wilhelm Lonkowski and Günther Rumrich who had acted as intermediaries; and Johanna Hofmann, Karl Schlüter, Theodor Schütz, Carl Eitel, the mysterious 'Schmidt' and Herbert Jänichen as couriers. Also named on the indictment was Mrs Jessie Jordan who was then beginning her four-year jail sentence in Scotland.

The Grand Jury trial in *United States of America v. Otto Herman Voss et al* began on 14 October 1938, Rumrich surprising his co-defendants, Voss, Glaser and Hofmann, with a guilty plea. Setting out the government's case, Lamar Hardy described a spy plot directed from Germany with contact men aboard German transatlantic liners. There was Wilhelm Lonkowski, the supposed piano tuner who had got aircraft secrets from Otto Voss and there was Dr Griebl, 'a great believer in the National Socialist Party', who had met with senior intelligence officers in Germany, among them Dr Erich Pfeiffer who had boasted of having an agent in every major North American aircraft plant. There were spies sending intelligence on the US Navy on the east coast of America and there were the spies who had forged the signature of President Roosevelt in order to get the designs of the latest US Navy aircraft carriers. Hardy was overstating the prosecution case on several counts, but he did refer to the information Rumrich had sent on the defences of the Panama Canal Zone, one of the world's most strategically important waterways. And, with an impeccable sense of timing, four German spies had managed to get themselves caught just the previous day while photographing gun batteries at the northern, Atlantic end of the canal.

In contrast to Jessie Jordan's brief court appearance in Edinburgh, the New York trial lasted an exhausting seven weeks. Star turns included Kay Moog who claimed that she had been nothing but an innocent dupe, then launched into an extraordinary account of her trip to Germany with Griebl the previous June. 'Germany was beautiful in summer,' she cooed in what witnesses recalled as a silken voice, then regaled the court with tales of meeting a tall and handsome Erich Pfeiffer at a champagne reception and of numerous friends and admirers who sent her 'loads of flowers'. She did, however, suffer from curious lapses of memory when cross-examined about the meetings at the Eden and the Astoria, saying, 'I was there to dance and have a good time. I wasn't interested in spies. Get that straight!' Kay Moog's endless and utterly pointless flights of fancy on Berlin and Bremen nightlife eventually proved too much for Judge John Knox who slammed his fist down on the bench and ordered, 'Stop that now!'

There was a frisson of excitement when Leon Turrou recounted an incident in his office after Johanna Hofmann had identified Griebl as her New York contact. 'Dr Griebl told Miss Hofmann he would have her shot for the information she gave.' Asked if he had done anything about the threat, Turrou replied, 'No, I just cautioned him not to threaten her again.' Defence lawyers for Hofmann, Voss and Glaser did their best to discredit Turrou, suggesting that he had been bribed to allow Griebl to escape. Turrou's former colleague Special Agent John McLaughlin, who had travelled to Berlin to take an affidavit from Griebl, recounted on allegation that Turrou had offered Griebl his freedom in return for $5,000. Griebl, McLaughlin said, had also alleged that Turrou had coached both himself and Kay Moog to give the right sort of testimony. There was no evidence to support either allegation and Turrou was cleared of any wrongdoing.

British newspapers, whose interest in the New York trial had waned rapidly, did latch on to Rumrich's revelation in court that he had been instructed that, were he to be arrested by the Americans, he was to say that he was working for a Major Christopher Draper, c/o Plane Advertising Ltd., Brettenham House, Strand, London WC2. Tipped off by a telephone call from a theatrical friend who said she had been approached by a Fleet Street reporter who was trying to trace him, Draper contacted MI5 and was told to keep his head down. But the press had turned up in force at the Playhouse Theatre where he was in rehearsal, eventually forcing their way on to the stage, taking photographs and shouting offers of £30 and £50 for an exclusive. Returning to his basement flat at 2 Southampton Street in London that evening, he found two reporters camped, quite literally, on his doorstep and demanding an interview.

The next morning's post brought a letter firing Draper from the Playhouse Theatre and a reporter from the *Daily Express* shouting an offer of £75 from the street. There was also a curious call from Draper's unidentified MI5 contact asking for permission to tell his superiors that he would sell his story to the press if there was not an immediate official announcement confirming his innocence. MI5 were obviously intent on making it appear that their hand had been forced should there be any repercussions, but Draper had no choice other than to agree. He then slipped out of his flat the back way, met his contact at Cannon Row Police Station and was told to go to the Balmoral Hotel in Broadstairs where a room had been rented for him in the name of George Mannering, his stage name.

Priming Rumrich to say that he had been working for Draper was clearly Hilmar Dierks' way of taking his revenge on Draper, the supposed Abwehr spy who had played him as a double agent. An announcement from the Air Ministry the following afternoon confirmed that 'the loyalty and integrity of Major Christopher Draper D.S.C., late of the Royal Air Force, is not in any way called into question'.[4]

In New York, the jury was finally able to retire to consider its verdicts at 6 p.m. on 29 November, returning guilty verdicts on Hofmann, Voss and Glaser. Before sentences were handed down on 2 December, Johanna Hofmann was first to make a personal plea for mercy. She stood at the bar for two minutes, hyperventilating and unable to speak before delivering her appeal so quietly that most of those in the courtroom were unable to hear what she said. It was a fine, doubtless well-rehearsed performance and a visibly moved Judge Knox said:

> For the defendant Hofmann I have a feeling of the deepest sympathy. A young girl, filled, undoubtedly, with love of her fatherland and thrilled perhaps with a belief that she was loyally serving a government which without question has restored the national pride of the German people, she was as clay within the hands of the potters of intrigue. Deserted now by the persons who enmeshed her in espionage, separated from her family and put to the necessity of being made an example for the benefit of stewards and other employees of the Hamburg and North German Lloyd Lines, she is a pathetic creature. If she alone were involved I would be glad to withhold sentence and return her to Germany. But that I cannot do.[5]

Hofmann was sentenced to four years in prison. Otto Voss, whose arrogance had done little to endear him to the court, received a six-year sentence which he would serve at Lewisburg Penitentiary in Pennsylvania before being interned for the duration. Erich Glaser was jailed for two years; moving to Vermont on his release, he was kept under surveillance by the FBI. Günther Rumrich, who had pleaded guilty and served as the chief witness for the prosecution, received a plea bargain sentence of just two years.

* * *

Justice only remained to be served in the case of Marc Aubert and Marie-Jeanne Morel, Erich Pfeiffer's star agents in France. There had been a delay while the Deuxième Bureau officer André Bonnefous took on the role of Aubert and fed Erich Pfeiffer bogus intelligence. This ploy could only have a short life as it entailed the Marine Nationale continuing to use the ciphers already compromised by Aubert, but it did last long enough to expose one of Pfeiffer's couriers, an attendant on the Wagons Lits sleeping car service between

Paris and Cologne named Harri Frahm. Wilfred Dunderdale, the MI6 Head of Station in Paris, reported that Frahm had been carrying messages from Pfeiffer to Paris and posting them on to Morel's apartment in Rennes. He had also sent payments hidden in the hollowed-out pages of books and collected return correspondence from a café near the Gare du Nord. Frahm was picked up on 29 December 1938 after the Deuxième Bureau left a fake letter at the Paris café letter box as bait. He was jailed for five years.[6]

On 31 December, two days after Frahm's arrest, Pfeiffer finally realised that his 'goldmine' agent Marc Aubert had been caught. The Bremen spymaster would later learn from revelations in the French press, repeated in British newspapers, that Aubert's capture had been down to the 'British Secret Service' who had tipped off their French counterparts. These revelations, which Edward Hinchley Cooke commented could only have come from someone in the Deuxième Bureau, wrecked the surveillance operation on the Dublin mailbox. 'Between ourselves,' he wrote to Valentine Vivian at MI6, 'this is a confounded nuisance from the point of view of the Dublin end . . . Thanks to this disclosure we must now assume that that particular channel has become completely brulé [burned].'[7]

The Aubert case was tried by the Tribunal Maritime in Toulon on 10 January 1939. Marc Aubert was brought into the courtroom first, his head down, face pale and drawn. Marie-Jeanne Morel followed moments later, one journalist ridiculing her as a sharp-faced brunette with a thin, reedy voice who possessed 'une beauté relative'. The proceedings were heard in camera and journalists were only allowed into the courtroom at 10 p.m. for the sentencing. Morel, who had confessed to her part in the affair soon after her arrest, broke down in tears when she received three years in jail. Aubert appeared oddly unmoved when, by a majority of five to two, the court sentenced him to death.[8]

That day's French newspapers were already linking the Aubert case to the mysterious disappearance of Jean Verdot, a merchant naval officer and Marine Nationale reservist who, according to unnamed naval sources, was to have been a witness for the prosecution. Verdot's ship, the cargo vessel *Oued Sebou II*, had been at Casablanca in Morocco on 10 November 1938 when a woman passenger, a beautiful, green-eyed blonde, asked him to pick up some cosmetics from a certain *parfumerie* in the city. Verdot agreed, went ashore and vanished. Then the blonde passenger vanished. A dismembered male torso was found in a Casablanca swimming pool early in January 1939 and, while there was not enough left for a positive identification, some French newspapers suggested that he had been silenced to prevent him giving evidence at the Aubert trial. It all made good copy, but the date of Verdot's disappearance just a week after Aubert's arrest, then still a closely guarded secret, made any connection most unlikely.[9]

Aubert's legal team lodged an appeal against his death sentence at the Cour de Cassation, the court of last resort in France, but there was little sympathy for a man whose treachery could easily have led to the deaths of thousands of his fellow sailors and the appeal was rejected. Execution of sentence was set for Monday, 6 March, and Marcelle Marie Aubert, the condemned man's mother, arrived in Toulon the Saturday before only to be told that her son was refusing to see her and that President Lebrun had rejected her final appeal for mercy. A distraught Mme Aubert was eventually persuaded to leave the city on the Sunday evening, partly to avoid the press and partly because it was feared that she might try to interrupt the following morning's proceedings. She was, however, allowed to return to collect her son's body once the firing squad had done its work.

* * *

As Marc Aubert met his bloody end in Toulon, shooting of a very different sort was under way on a locked and guarded Warner Bros sound stage in Hollywood. Back in June 1938, within hours of the Grand Jury indictments being issued in New York, Leon Turrou had resigned from his $4,600 per annum post as an FBI Special Agent. The investigation had undoubtedly been stressful, but he was a very fit 43-year-old and his decision appeared very odd given that the trial, in which he would be a star witness, was due to take place in a few weeks. That something had gone very wrong became apparent when, just a week later, a furious Director Hoover cancelled Turrou's resignation and fired him with prejudice and without three months' pay or retirement benefits.[10]

Hints during the Grand Jury preliminary hearings that Turrou was being set up as a fall guy for the Griebl and Gudenberg escapes might go some way towards explaining his decision. There were also indications that all was not well within the New York Field Office. Morale would undoubtedly have taken a downturn after Hoover announced that, as the Bureau had overrun its $6 million annual budget, half of the 110 staff in the New York office would be laid off for the month of May 1938, the other half being laid off for the month of June. Hoover's threat was clearly linked to a bid for an increased Bureau budget, but it is telling that Turrou's highly regarded former boss, New York Special Agent in Charge Reed Vetterli, also resigned in August 1938.

The real reason for Hoover's anger became apparent when, within hours of Turrou his resignation, the *New York Post* announced that it would be publishing a series of articles entitled *The Inside Story of the Spy Conspiracy in America – Revealed by Leon Turrou, former Ace G-man . . .* And the FBI Director had a point as Special Agents were under an obligation not to share, or profit from, information they had gained while on duty. Turrou fired back that the FBI Director was only 'jealous' and accused Hoover of raiding FBI files to write articles and books on Bureau cases. He too had a point as it is known that royalties from articles and books, written by Bureau staff but credited to Hoover, had a habit of disappearing into something called the FBI Recreational Association.[11]

Yet there had to be more behind Hoover's fury than the former G-man's stated intention to write articles for a New York newspaper, articles that the *Post* was in any case speedily barred from publishing ahead of the trial. Far more likely to have been behind the Director's ire was his discovery that Turrou had also, within hours of resigning, signed a contract with publishers Random House to produce a condensed version of the *Post* articles in book form and, worse still from Hoover's point of view, sold his story to movie moguls Warner Bros for $25,000. Given the rapid order of events, Turrou could never have prepared a series of articles, arranged a book deal and signed a film contract on his own while still a serving Special Agent fully engaged on a major investigation. He must have had professional help from an agent and this suggests strongly that, just as Ignatz Griebl had been preparing his escape from justice well ahead of actually leaving, Turrou had also been preparing his lucrative exit from the Bureau for some time.[12]

Heavily promoted in full-page advertisements as 'An Important Document That Should Be Read by Every American', the *New York Post* articles, ghost-written by *Post* journalist David Wittels, finally appeared on Monday, 5 December 1938, and *Nazi Spies in America* was published by Random House in January 1939. Later retitled *The Nazi Spy Conspiracy in America*, the book was an immediate best seller, a *New York Times* reviewer writing that it was 'intensely interesting, without being unduly sensational . . . the reader is constantly surprised by the combination of the fantastic and the apparently silly in the spy's assignments and risks . . . they are recounted here in gripping detail'. In truth, particularly as it clearly relies heavily on the New York Field Office case summary that had been written by Turrou ahead of the June 1938 Grand Jury hearings, a copy of which he must have taken with him when he resigned, the curious tone of naïve surprise at the antics of America's Nazi fellow travellers that he adopts in the text does seem at odds with the harsh reality of the time. Yet the book was written ostensibly to alert Americans to the dangers posed by Nazi aggression, so perhaps an element of faux astonishment is understandable.[13]

Turrou's story was also immensely attractive for movie moguls Harry and Jack Warner, long-standing vocal opponents of the Nazis. Harry Warner, a quietly devout Jew and family man, had been particularly keen to make an overtly anti-Nazi movie since withdrawing the studio's business from Germany in 1934, a year after Hitler was ushered into power. Restrictions on the industry and attacks from American fascist and anti-Semitic groups had made this impossible, but the story of the New York spy ring was different as it dealt with recent events already well covered in the media and could be handled in a quasi-documentary format. In another indication that

Turrou's FBI exit was planned well in advance, Warner Bros had a draft screenplay completed by October 1938 and this was sent to the Production Code Administration for approval immediately the Grand Jury trial was over. As the screenplay was largely based on sworn testimony given at the New York trial, the PCA gave the go-ahead for the movie, albeit with stern warnings about breaches of 1934 Production Code strictures on the unfavourable portrayal of another country's institutions.

Reaction to the news that the script had been approved was predictably mixed. Groucho Marx was unequivocal in his support, commenting, 'I want to propose a toast to Warner Bros, the only studio with any guts.' Georg Gyssling, the German Consul in Los Angeles, took a very different view and threatened that Germany would ban all future productions from any Hollywood studio if *Confessions of a Nazi Spy* conflicted with German interests. There were also difficulties with casting as many German-American actors, reputedly including Marlene Dietrich, turned down roles for fear of reprisals against their families in Germany. Early versions of the screenplay had called for an actor to play the part of Hitler and some nineteen candidates were approached, but all turned the role down. Even the Make-Up Men's Association made it clear that they would refuse to prepare an actor to play the part of the Führer. The names of the principal parts also had to be changed after a court ruling that people involved in a trial could not be portrayed without their consent.[14]

Edward G. Robinson, born Emanuel Goldenberg in Romania, was an early signing for the starring role of Edward Renard, the G-man character modelled on Leon Turrou. A lifelong liberal and vocal opponent of fascism, Robinson was, along with Groucho Marx and Harry and Jack Warner, a prominent member of the Hollywood Anti-Nazi League formed in 1936. Others to join the cast included Hungarian actor Paul Lukas who played Nazi fanatic Dr Kassel, a thinly disguised Dr Griebl, with German-born Lya Lys as his mistress Erika Wolf. Czech-born Francis Lederer took on the role of Kurt Schneider, the Rumrich character, British star George Sanders gave a suitably menacing performance as Franz Schlager, a part modelled on Karl Schlüter, and Dorothy Tree portrayed

Hilda Kleinauer, the movie version of Johanna Hofmann. Other cast members would be listed under assumed names. Russian-born Anatole Litvak directed and the writers were Milton Krims and John Wexley.

Confessions of a Nazi Spy began filming in January 1939 with Leon Turrou as technical advisor. The screenplay largely sticks to the version of events set out in Turrou's book; there is even an opening scene showing a Scottish postman delivering mail to a forbidding Mrs McGregor, albeit in a village set more akin to Brigadoon than grimly industrial Dundee. Kassel's fiery Nazi rhetoric accurately echoes that of Griebl at Madison Square Garden and a disturbance at another Nazi meeting addressed by Kassel mirrors the infamous Newark Schwabenhalle riot in 1933. The scenes that portray Rumrich getting the venereal disease statistics and the attempt to steal passports are faithfully rendered, as are the interrogations in Turrou's office. Even an accurate copy of Schlüter's match-book cipher makes an appearance during a search of Kassel/Griebl's office. Newsreel montages, including some footage simply stolen from Leni Riefenstahl's *Triumph of the Will*, are used effectively, particularly when the movie was rereleased with a revised ending after the Nazis had overrun much of western Europe in 1940. Less convincing, however, are the specially written scenes, not in Turrou's book, that show senior Nazi figures, among them a thinly disguised Goebbels, and a pair of sinister Gestapo thugs apparently able to wander the foggy streets of New York City, beating up and kidnapping seemingly at will.[15]

The completed movie was shown to a preview audience on 28 April 1939 with 110 police officers ringing the Beverly Theater in Beverly Hills to protect an apparently 'jittery' invited audience from attacks by American Nazis and their supporters. Adding to the theatricality of the occasion, Jack Warner turned up in a limousine with no fewer than five bodyguards. *Confessions of a Nazi Spy* was generally well received and grossed a healthy $45,000 in its first week on general release. Critical reaction was mixed with the *New York Times* praising the director and stars, but bemoaning the fact that, 'the film's promised revelations have long been in the public domain'. *Variety* observed perceptively that 'historians will one day take note of this daringly frank broadside from a picture company'. Predictably, however, the German-American Bund, a successor to Griebl's Bund der Freunde des Neuen Deutschland, or League of Friends of The New Germany, was quick to denounce cast and crew alike in rabidly anti-Semitic terms:

> Produced by Jew Jack Warner, story by Jew Milton Krims, acted by Jew Emmanuel Goldenburg (Edward Robinson), Communist supporter of Leon Trotsky, acted by Francis Lederer, Communist peace advocate; directed by Jew Anatole Litvak . . . historical director Jew Leon Turrou . . .[16]

Bund President Fritz Kuhn launched a $5 million lawsuit against Warner Bros claiming that he had been libelled in the movie, and lost. Isolationist American politicians worried about the movie's effect on public opinion and, in 1941, *Confessions of a Nazi Spy* would be one of eight productions named by the Senate Investigation into Motion Picture War Propaganda. Other films the committee believed likely to generate warlike sentiment among Americans included Charlie Chaplin's sharply satirical *The Great Dictator* and *That Hamilton Woman* starring Laurence Olivier as Lord Nelson with Vivien Leigh in the title role.

Elsewhere, countries with large ethnic German populations such as Argentina and South Africa vetoed the movie outright. Others, among them Norway, Denmark, Holland, Switzerland and Hungary, that were either determinedly neutral or understandably unwilling to provoke a powerful neighbour, refused to show it. And in Ireland, where it was quaintly deemed subversive to public morals, it was banned. At the end of July 1939 a worried Sir Geoffry Northcote, the Governor of Hong Kong, sent an urgent telegram to the Colonial Office in London asking for advice on whether to permit *Confessions of a Nazi Spy* to be shown in the British colony. He had apparently, and, it must be said, rather oddly, invited German consular staff to a review showing of the movie and they had asked that it be prohibited as it was 'anti-German propaganda of repulsive, mendacious type'. The advice from London was to allow it to be shown. The German Consul General in Calcutta (modern-day Kolkata) requested that *Confessions* be withdrawn from public exhibition in India, as 'it offends German sentiment'. The movie was shown and it would be the Consul General who had to withdraw from India when the Second World War broke out two weeks later.[17]

The outbreak of war brought new dangers, particularly for distributors and exhibitors in Poland. On 4 October 1939 *Variety* reported that 'WB fears for Safety of Its Rep in Warsaw due to Nazi Spy Pic'. In the event, Boris Jankolowicz, Warner Bros managing director in Poland, would walk over 300 miles to escape Nazi reprisals for showing *Confessions of a Nazi Spy* and told journalists on reaching Paris unsubstantiated tales of Polish cinema owners showing the film when the Nazis invaded having been hanged. The story of hangings is unconfirmed, but Poznań businessman Stefan Kalamajski was sentenced to 20 years forced labour by the Nazis because his Kinoteatr Słońce, then one of the largest cinemas in Poland, had shown the picture.[18]

Anathema to isolationists, indeed so blatantly interventionist as to have Edward G. Robinson's Renard character suggest that America was already at war with Germany, 'It's a new kind of war, but it's still war,' *Confessions of a Nazi Spy* was Hollywood's first openly anti-Nazi film. Largely forgotten today, it had nevertheless been a brave gamble by Warner Bros in 1939 and it would pave the way for future classics from the studio, not least their 1942 masterpiece *Casablanca*. And it all started with a letter steamed open over a boiling kettle in a Scottish post office.[19]

Chapter 9

The Alliance That Saved the West

An eye-opener to the State Department, War Department
and the FBI.

Guy Liddell, Deputy Director of MI5, March 1938

What had Abwehr achieved with the sequence of spy cases that
started with Christopher Draper and culminated with the arrests in
Britain, the United States, Czechoslovakia and France? The answer
has to be almost nothing of any tactical, strategic or political value
that could not have been found by other, less diplomatically damaging means. Of the only two agents who had supplied intelligence
of any real value, Marc Aubert had the most potential and, had he
been able to operate under wartime conditions with all its communication difficulties, his information, if used properly, would have
been of value to the Kriegsmarine and the Italian Regia Marina. But
he was condemned by a combination of his own crass behaviour
and the complacency of Erich Pfeiffer. Otherwise, of the cases covered here, only René Defauwes' intelligence on the construction of
Fort Eben Emael would have any real tactical significance.

In truth, Abwehr's blundering, illogical and poorly coordinated
espionage in Britain, the United States and France did considerably more harm to German interests than good. Enormous risks
were run to collect worthless trivia that was either freely available
from open sources, as in the case of Jessie Jordan's sketches of the
British Army base at Aldershot, Hermann Görtz' information on
RAF airfields and Otto Voss' data on American military aircraft,
or utterly valueless as in Günther Rumrich's statistics on venereal

disease. Inept spymasters like Hilmar Dierks, their tradecraft, such as it was, not having moved on since 1914 or earlier, employed ridiculous recruits like the ham-fisted drunkard Wilhelm Lonkowski and the garrulous, conceited Ignatz Griebl, while allowing fanatical Nazi couriers like Karl Schlüter to pursue their own mad schemes unchecked. It was a recipe for the wholesale disaster that it became.

As for the objects of Abwehr's espionage, German aircraft did target Royal Navy cruisers moored near Rosyth naval dockyard in the Firth of Forth on 16 October 1939, the first air raid on mainland Britain of the war, but no attack was ever made on the nearby Crombie naval armaments depot sketched by Jessie Jordan. RAF Manston, so carefully sketched by Hermann Görtz and Marianne Emig, was well known as a First World War airfield and the Luftwaffe was able to take high-quality air reconnaissance images of it, including low-level obliques showing its location relative to Ramsgate, at the start of the war in 1939. The airfield was, by virtue of its location, in the front line during the Battle of Britain and both it and the nearby towns of Ramsgate and Broadstairs suffered heavy bombing, yet there is no evidence that these raids were in any sense influenced by intelligence provided by Görtz. The aircraft carrier *Graf Zeppelin*, for which Abwehr's New York spy ring was tasked with spying on the latest American carriers, was launched in December 1938, but never completed. A victim of materials shortages, petty rivalries and the strategic incoherence that dogged the Nazi command structure, the part-completed carrier was captured by Soviet forces in 1945 and sunk as a practice bombing target off Gdansk in Poland in 1947.

Abwehr would have its counter-espionage successes during the Second World War, most notoriously Operation Nordpol (North Pole), also known as Der Englandspiel (England Game), in which British Special Operations Executive networks in Holland were, along with associated Dutch resistance networks, penetrated and played back against SOE between 1942 and 1944. Fifty captured Dutch SOE agents were executed at Mauthausen Concentration Camp and the distrust engendered by Der Englandspiel would contribute to the failure of Operation Market Garden, the September

1944 Allied airborne operation to capture strategic bridges in
Holland and drive into the Ruhr. Among the French resistance
networks uncovered by Abwehr was the réseau Gloria, more than
80 members of which were executed after it was betrayed by corrupt, double-dealing Catholic priest Father Robert Alesch. The
Franco-Polish Interallié network was broken in 1941 and one of its
founders, Mathilde Carré, was turned into an immensely damaging
double agent.[1]

Yet Abwehr's counter-espionage successes were far outweighed
by its espionage failures, a classic case being Operation Lena, the
infiltration of an advance guard of 21 agents into Britain, ostensibly
to pave the way for a German invasion. All but one of this ill-chosen,
ill-prepared band of so-called spies were captured and some were
turned into double agents to be played back against their German
employers. Increasingly distrusted by Hitler, the failing Abwehr was
broken up in February 1943 and the remnants absorbed into the
Sicherheitsdienst, the Nazi Party intelligence organ. Its former head,
Admiral Wilhelm Canaris, was arrested in the aftermath of the July
1944 plot to kill Hitler and hanged in Flossenbürg Concentration
Camp in April 1945.[2]

As for the British, when war broke out in 1939 MI5 could reflect
with some pride on having effectively neutralised the threat from
Abwehr, particularly as this was just one of many threats that the
small, pre-war B Division investigation staff of just fifteen officers
had to deal with. Yet this masked the harsh reality that the threat
had been minimal and that MI5's approach to counter-intelligence,
a victim of both chronic underfunding and increasingly ineffective
leadership, was becoming seriously outdated. Their success against
agents of the low calibre of Hermann Görtz and Jessie Jordan owed
much to the fact that Abwehr's espionage methods were likewise
stuck firmly in the past.

With war increasingly likely, changes would have to be made,
and, on 16 March 1938, the day after Hitler swept into Vienna
and delivered a speech hailing the *Anschluss* to 200,000 enthusiastic Austrians in Heldenplatz, MI5's B (Investigation) Division
Deputy Director Guy Liddell boarded the liner *Queen Mary* at

Southampton bound for New York. Armed with letters of introduction from Herschel Johnson, Counselor at the American
embassy in London, Liddell was on a mission to make permanent
the lines of communication with the FBI established during the
Jordan/Rumrich case.[3]

Initially at least, Liddell's discussions seemed to go well:

> I called on the State Department in Washington on March
> 24th with a letter of introduction to Mr Pierrepoint Moffat,
> head of the European Section. Mr Moffat was in confer-
> ence at the time so I went over to the War Department with
> a letter of introduction to Colonel E. R. Warner McCabe,
> Assistant Chief of Staff, G.2. Colonel McCabe passed me
> on to Colonel Strong and finally to Colonel Busbee who
> had been intimately connected with the German espionage
> case. He was in fact one of the officers who had been sent
> to the Military Station at Governor's [sic] Island on receipt
> of the American Military Attaché's wire from this country
> about the plot to overpower Colonel Eglin at the Macalpin
> [sic] Hotel, New York.
>
> Colonel Busbee gave me a brief outline of the case and
> it was arranged I should call the following morning at
> 10 o'clock when Colonel McCabe would take me down to
> see Mr Edgar J. Hoover [sic], head of the Federal Bureau of
> Investigation of the Department of Justice (F.B.I.).[4]

This was encouraging, particularly as the State Department
habitually viewed the British with intense suspicion, but Liddell had
unwittingly stepped into the still-simmering jurisdictional dispute
that had followed the arrest of Rumrich the previous month. There
had been what he would delicately term 'some slight contretemps'
between the War, State and Justice departments over his arrival
and both Hoover and his assistant Ed Tamm were now said to be,
'out of town for a few days'. This unsubtle slight aside, the British
spycatcher was impressed by James Clement Dunn, 'one of the real
live wires in the State Department', anglophile senior FBI officer

Percy Foxworth and Colonel Charles Busbee, who opened the War Department files on the case and allowed him to take notes. Liddell responded to this openness by detailing the part played by double agent Christopher Draper and how that had led to the discovery of Jessie Jordan.

Returning to New York, Liddell had two meetings with Leon Turrou and wrote later that he had been very impressed by the thoroughness of the FBI Special Agent's investigation:

> Having uncovered the two principal agents in the case and got them to the point where they were quite ready to incriminate anybody but themselves, he began making use of these people to obtain information about others . . . The results of these enquiries have been very much of an eye-opener for the State Department, War Department and the FBI . . . the FBI hope in due course to improve their position vis-a-vis the public by appearing in the role of guardians of state secrets.[5]

Liddell would have much preferred to have returned from Washington with a formal counter-intelligence liaison agreement in his pocket. In his report on the visit he noted that the Americans were well aware that 'had it not been for the information supplied from this side of the Atlantic, it is quite possible that the facts now disclosed would never have been known'. The army and FBI officers he had met had been eager for a liaison agreement that would cover German, Italian, Soviet and Japanese espionage and subversion, but they were hamstrung by a State Department whose default position was to avoid both diplomatic embarrassments and awkward repercussions in a non-interventionist Congress.

With the benefit of hindsight, it was unfortunate that Liddell was not given the opportunity to canvass the views of FBI Director Hoover who had commented ruefully in 1921 that the British, who had set up an MI6 Bureau in New York in 1915, had been 'much better informed on radical activities in this country, at least in New York, than the United States government'. The suspicion has to be that, at least in 1938, he had no intention of allowing that to happen again, hence his decision to be 'out of town' during Liddell's visit. Liddell had nevertheless made useful contacts in Washington and, as he boarded the liner *Queen Mary* for the passage home on 7 April, he was more than ever convinced that the Jessie Jordan case had opened up an opportunity for renewed transatlantic cooperation.[6]

Yet there were, as Colonel Valentine Vivian of MI6 pointed out after Liddell returned, two significant flies in the transatlantic intelligence cooperation ointment. One was Frederick Rutland, a former British Royal Naval Air Service officer and Japanese spy. Code-named 'Shinkawa' (New River) by the Japanese, Rutland had escaped prosecution in Britain because, as in the Sempill case, the evidence against him had come from diplomatic telegrams decrypted at the British Government Code and Cipher School (GC&CS) and that was a source too valuable to compromise. In April 1938, when his case was being discussed by Liddell and Vivian, Rutland was living the high life in Beverly Hills at vast expense to the Japanese and giving Tokyo little of value in return. As the MI6 official historian writes, Liddell would have been well aware that the British had been watching Rutland since his move to California five years before, mainly in the hope of picking up useful insights into Japanese intelligence gathering operations. They had, however, omitted to tell the Americans about this particular cuckoo in their nest.[7]

The other fly in the ointment revealed by Vivian, and one that seems to have come as a complete surprise to Liddell, was that MI6 was actively spying on both the American aviation and the US Navy. Indeed, if only because they had not been caught, they were clearly doing a far better job of it than Abwehr. In what MI6 historian Professor Keith Jeffery suggests was probably a considerable understatement, Vivian wrote that Liddell was 'definitely not happy' about this. And Liddell had every right to be furious, not least because he should at least have been briefed on this prior to his trip to Washington. On 7 June 1938, after what must have been some rather frank discussions, MI6 Director General Admiral Hugh 'Quex' Sinclair ordered that all espionage operations against American targets were to be closed down as soon as possible.[8]

These hurdles aside, it seemed that, thanks to the Jordan/Rumrich case and Liddell's visit to New York and Washington, the way was now open to a discreet intelligence and security alliance with the Americans. Yet the honeymoon would be a short one as, just two weeks after Sinclair's decision to stop clandestine MI6 activity in the United States, Leon Turrou resigned from the FBI and announced that he had sold the story of the investigation to the press. This was anathema to MI5, an organisation whose very existence was, like that of MI6, still an official secret. They had, after all, given the lead on Agent Crown to Colonel Lee on the strict understanding that their part in the investigation would never be made public and now Turrou, the very same FBI special agent on whom Liddell had lavished such effusive praise, was betraying that trust. And the situation would only get worse with the publication of Turrou's book and the movie *Confessions of a Nazi Spy*.

British faith in American security had been shaken by Turrou's revelations, and worse was to come. On 8 October 1939, just over a month after the outbreak of war, MI5 Watchers tailing a suspected German agent by the name of Ludwig Matthias followed their quarry into the lounge at the Cumberland Hotel opposite Marble Arch in London and watched as he met a resident identified by hotel staff as Tyler Kent, a 29-year-old American diplomat. The two men, who clearly knew each other, visited Kent's room and emerged a few minutes later, Matthias carrying a package under his arm.[9]

Tyler Kent then dropped off the radar until, on 14 February 1940, a Mr Gill of the British Foreign Office called on Herschel Johnson, Counselor at the American Embassy in London, with news that correspondence between Ambassador Joe Kennedy and President Roosevelt was falling into German hands. The mysterious Mr Gill was actually MI6 officer Felix Cowgill and the tip-off about the leakage of the Kennedy-Roosevelt correspondence had come from a Soviet defector, Walter Krivitsky, and an anti-Nazi German intelligence officer, Kurt Jahnke. Naïvely perhaps, Herschel Johnson was adamant that the source of the leak could only be in the London embassy or Washington. But, as MI5 would later point out, the British were routinely intercepting American diplomatic cables and the recent case of Foreign Office Communications Department clerk John King jailed for ten years for selling intelligence to the Soviet NKVD suggested that the source of the leak could just as easily be British.[10]

Ten days after Cowgill's meeting with Johnson, on 24 February 1940, MI5 agent Marjorie Mackie reported that Anna Wolkoff, a dress designer of White Russian extraction and member of the Right Club, a clique of generally stupid right-wing extremists, had befriended a John Kent of the American Embassy. Mackie corrected the American's forename to Tyler in a subsequent report and, by mid-April 1940, it was apparent that Kent, a code clerk at the embassy, was the source of the leaked documents which, MI5 now knew, included the correspondence between President Roosevelt and Winston Churchill, then First Lord of the Admiralty. Kent had also allowed Right Club members Captain Archibald 'Jock' Ramsay, a pro-Nazi Scottish MP and deranged anti-Semite, and Anna Wolkoff to access the documents and Wolkoff was, in turn, passing copies to the Italian assistant military attaché, Colonel Don Francesco Maringliano, Duke del Monte.[11]

The Kent case came to a head on Saturday, 18 May 1940. That morning, as the Wehrmacht blitzkrieg was scything through northern France, Guy Liddell asked Herschel Johnson to see an MI5 colleague, Captain Max Knight, about a delicate matter. Knight set out the case against Kent and wrote later that Johnson was both profoundly shocked by the revelations and furious that MI5 had not shared their suspicions sooner. Knight placated Johnson somewhat by pointing out that MI5 had to be sure of their ground before making damaging allegations against an American diplomat, though the real reason for leaving Kent in place had been a high-risk strategy to keep a watch on the defeatist, isolationist Ambassador Joe Kennedy. Johnson and Knight agreed to meet again the following day to coordinate action against Wolkoff and Kent. Meanwhile, Johnson would speak to Ambassador Kennedy about revoking Kent's diplomatic immunity and ensure that nothing was done to arouse the code clerk's suspicions.[12]

Sunday, 19 May 1940, brought a torrent of bad news from Europe. Antwerp, Amsterdam and Brussels were all in enemy hands and

French resistance was collapsing. The British Expeditionary Force was, along with the entire Belgian Army and two French armies, in imminent danger of being trapped and British Commander-in-Chief Lord Gort had begun planning a withdrawal towards the English Channel port of Dunkirk. That night, at 9 p.m., Winston Churchill delivered his first broadcast as Prime Minister, an address that did little to disguise the disastrous situation unfolding in France and Belgium, but finished with a stirring call to arms:

> Today is Trinity Sunday. Centuries ago words were written to be a call and a spur to the faithful servants of Truth and Justice: 'Arm yourselves, and be ye men of valour, and be in readiness for the conflict; for it is better for us to perish in battle than to look upon the outrage of our nation and our altar. As the will of God is in Heaven, even so let it be.'

The trouble was that arms were in desperately short supply so, the broadcast over, Churchill dictated a strongly worded telegram to President Roosevelt demanding urgent deliveries of ammunition, Curtiss P-40 fighter aircraft and surplus American destroyers. Handing it to his Assistant Private Secretary John Colville, the Prime Minister said, 'Here's a telegram for those bloody Yankees. Send it off tonight.' Colville was taken aback by the less than diplomatic language, particularly as the Prime Minister was himself half 'bloody Yankee' on his mother's side. Yet Churchill's bluntness is understandable when set against the background of the extreme stress that he and those around him were operating under and pressure from irresolute members of his own administration to seek a settlement with the Nazis. But he quickly concluded that the desperate tone of his appeal to Washington would do the British cause no favours and, at 2.30 a.m., asked for the telegram to be returned.[13]

The original of Churchill's message was reclaimed unsent by Downing Street, but not before it had been handed to American Embassy night-duty code clerk Tyler Kent for encryption. And Kent had a furtively scribbled copy in his pocket when he went off duty the following morning. Looking forward to a morning in bed with his mistress, Irene Danischewsky, the wife of a Russian-born businessman serving in the British Army, and unaware that he was being followed by Special Branch detectives, Kent made his way to his second-floor apartment at 47 Gloucester Place near Hyde Park. Later, he was due to have dinner at La Coquille, an exclusive seafood restaurant in St Martin's Lane, with Right Club member, racing driver and socialite Enid Riddell and the Italian Duke del Monte.[14]

Three hours later, at 11.20 a.m., there was a commotion on the landing outside Kent's room and someone tried to open the locked door. Twice the American shouted, 'Don't come in!' but the burly Special Branch Detective Inspector Joseph Pearson shoulder-charged the door and Max Knight, Detective Constable Stanley Buswell and Second Secretary Franklin Gowen from the Embassy crowded in behind him. They found a furious Kent, clad only in his pyjama bottoms, standing beside his unmade bed. As Buswell moved towards the door to the bathroom, Kent called out, 'You can't go in there . . . there's a lady.' Sure enough, on the other side of the door the detective found a frightened Irene Danischewsky, naked apart from the top half of Kent's pyjamas.[15]

Kent was driven away to a cell in Cannon Row Police Station and, after begging the detectives not to expose her infidelity to her husband, Danischewsky was allowed to go home. Max Knight and the detectives searching the American's room found a leather-bound and locked ledger that, on being broken open, turned out to be a list of Right Club members. There was also a cache of more than 1,500 neatly filed documents stolen from the American Embassy, among them copies of the Churchill-Roosevelt telegrams. Kent would later claim that he planned to use the documents to prove that Churchill and Roosevelt were communicating behind the back of the then Prime Minister, Neville Chamberlain, and conspiring to drag the United States into the war in the spring of 1940. He was unaware that the correspondence had been undertaken with Chamberlain's full approval.[16]

British reaction was swift and decisive. On 23 May, three days after Kent and Wolkoff had been arrested, Parliament passed the

Treachery Act, making it easier for those convicted of espionage and treason to be executed. Defence Regulation 18B was also extended to allow the internment without trial of those who held views sympathetic to the enemy and Enid Riddell would be among a tawdry parade of 1,000 pro-Nazi small fry detained by the end of 1940. Many of those named in Ramsay's red ledger were, however, prominent establishment figures or members of both Houses of Parliament, Christopher Draper's sponsor Lord Sempill among them, whose arrest would have caused a national scandal at a time when Britain could least afford one. These people were quietly removed from sensitive positions and discreetly but firmly warned to keep their views to themselves.[17]

Kent's treachery caused acute embarrassment in American diplomatic circles. A furious Ambassador William Bullitt, under whom the code clerk had recently served in Moscow, told a British diplomat in Paris, 'I hope you will shoot him, and shoot him soon. I mean it.' Bullitt also claimed that Kent had been found to be in the pay of the Russians during his posting in Moscow. Kent would always vehemently deny that he was a Russian spy, but Bullitt's allegation does suggest that the code clerk's subsequent posting to London was imprudent. The view from Washington was no less bleak, Assistant Secretary of State Breckinridge Long writing, 'Nothing like this has happened in American history. It means not only that are our codes cracked . . . but that our every diplomatic manoeuvre was exposed to Germany and Russia . . . It is a terrible blow – almost a major catastrophe.'[18]

There was also considerable unease in the White House at the prospect of the Churchill-Roosevelt correspondence being led as evidence for the defence should Kent be extradited to stand trial in the United States as it would be seized on by isolationists determined to wreck the re-election campaign of the President. MI5 were, however, at pains to pass on a reassuring message through Ambassador Kennedy to the effect that Kent would be held incommunicado and tried in camera under British law. In November 1940, once Roosevelt was safely back in the White House, Tyler Kent was jailed for seven years and Anna Wolkoff, who had stupidly handed a letter she was sending to Nazi propaganda broadcaster William Joyce, otherwise known as Lord Haw-Haw, to one of Max Knight's moles, was sentenced to ten years.

***

Among the documents found in Tyler Kent's room were copies of two messages from MI5, sent in October and November 1939, warning the FBI about Soviet spies operating in the United States. It turned out that these messages, sent at a time when the FBI was barred from reciprocal contact with the British by an American neutrality directive, had been passed along diplomatic channels from the American Embassy to the State Department and had not reached the FBI. The issue of MI5 establishing a direct line of communication with the FBI without offending the American Embassy and the State Department would be solved with the help of MI6.[19]

In June 1940, a month after Tyler Kent's arrest, MI6 Director General Sir Stewart Menzies had appointed Canadian businessman William Stephenson as Head of Station in New York. Through a mutual friend, boxer Gene Tunney, 'Little Bill' Stephenson had quickly established an effective working relationship with FBI Director Hoover and went on to lead British Security Coordination (BSC), an MI6 offshoot based in New York's Rockefeller Plaza. Legend has it that it was Hoover who suggested the British Security Coordination name, perhaps in the pious hope that the new organisation would limit its activities to office-based coordination. But Stephenson and MI6 had other ideas and BSC would expand rapidly to employ over 1,000 people and carry out intelligence, security and propaganda operations across the United States, Canada, the Caribbean and Central and South America.

Hoover was well aware that the Bureau lacked experience of counter-espionage operations, a failing thrown into sharp focus by the clumsy handling of the Jordan/Rumrich case. With Stephenson's help, he arranged for two Special Agents to travel to Britain in November 1940 'to make a survey not only of intelligence matters but all matters dealing with functions of police in times of national emergency'. MI5's reaction on hearing of the impending visit by Hugh Clegg, Assistant Director in charge of the Bureau's Domestic Intelligence Division, and his assistant Florence Hince reflects the damage that had been done by Leon Turrou's revelations. Guy Liddell commented:

> I presume we shall have to entertain these people to some extent. I am all for telling them as much as we possibly can, but having Leon Turrou in the back of my mind I should feel inclined to be a bit cautious. There is I presume no harm in giving them a copy of the memo we prepared for Colonel Lee some time ago. This would give them something to work on. Would you like me to get in touch with the embassy about their arrival? It is possible of course that the embassy know nothing about them.[20]

When Liddell met the Americans at Waterloo Station in London on 10 December 1940 he found that BSC in New York had made an embarrassing error and Florence Hince was actually Lawrence Hince. 'We had all expected to see a glamour [sic] platinum blonde and were much disappointed,' he later recorded in his diary. 'We told him so and he seemed to think it was a good joke.' Still apparently unable to recall Hince's name correctly, Liddell met the FBI men for lunch the following day:

> I had lunch with Hugh Clegg and Clarence Hince of the FBI and had a long talk with Clegg. They have an enormous programme which covers everything from SIS [MI6] to the fire brigade. They were desperately anxious to wipe out the impression left by the Leon Turrou incident. Clegg told me that he now covers the whole of the western hemisphere both for espionage and counter-espionage. He looks as tough as a gangster but is, I think, a very good fellow.[21]

Clegg and Hince were in Britain for six weeks at the height of the Luftwaffe blitz, often spending the night in the basement shelter at

Claridge's, their London hotel. They were given briefings on British espionage and counter-espionage including the operation of under-cover agents, mail and telephone interception, hidden cameras, the tracking of suspects and the protection of infrastructure. The sensitive subject of signals intelligence remained off limits until, on 10 January 1941, Liddell met Valentine Vivian of MI6 to discuss how much the Americans should be told about traffic between an Abwehr radio in the United States and Abwehrstelle Hamburg that the Voluntary Interceptors of MI5's Radio Security Service were monitoring. It was agreed that Liddell should first try to find out how much the FBI knew before revealing how much the British knew, so he broached the subject over lunch with Clegg and Hince at Claridge's on 17 January and wrote later:

> Clegg has come clean about the Group 10 messages. He tells us that he has some 30 XX [double-cross] agents placed in various factories and that he is feeding the Germans with misleading information.[22]

The radio messages were, Clegg told Liddell, being sent from a short-wave wireless on Long Island that Abwehr believed was being operated by a spy ring led by South African fraudster Frederick Joubert Duquesne. A German-American double agent, William Sebold, had infiltrated the Duquesne ring and the Long Island wireless was actually being operated by FBI special agents. Thirty-three members of the Duquesne ring would be rounded up in June 1941, but the fact that MI5 had been reluctant to reveal that they were intercepting the Duquesne traffic which they believed, until told otherwise by Clegg, was being generated by genuine Abwehr agents is a measure of the caution that still persisted on the British side. Likewise, the fact that the Americans had said nothing about their double-cross operation points to an equally understandable measure of wariness on their part. Yet real progress had been made and Liddell commented after their final meeting on 22 January 1941 that Clegg 'seemed thoroughly satisfied with his visit, which I am sure will be very profitable to us both'.[23]

Liddell and Clegg agreed that MI5 counter-espionage material would in future be shared with the FBI through MI6's British Security Coordination office in New York, thus bypassing the State Department logjam. MI5 officer Major John Maude was attached to the New York operation to handle the traffic and more than 100,000 messages would be passed to the FBI during 1941. Better still for the FBI, MI6 wanted its New York operation to remain a closely guarded secret so the Bureau would be able to take all of the credit for any successful counter-espionage operations this link generated. A grateful Hoover wrote to MI5 Deputy Director Oswald 'Jasper' Harker, on 7 March 1941:

> I want to express to you and, through you, to the members of your staff, my sincere appreciation of the helpfulness and cooperation which you extended to Mr Clegg and Mr Hince of this Bureau on the occasion of their recent visit to England. I appreciate the many evidences of your thoughtfulness and interest, as well as the many helpful suggestions which you very kindly made to them.
>
> Please do not hesitate to let me know whenever I may be of service.
>
> With assurances of best wishes and highest regards, I am
>
> Yours sincerely,
>
> J. Edgar Hoover.[24]

Nine months before Pearl Harbor, and despite their differences of culture and method, it seemed that MI5 and the FBI were inching towards a working agreement. Hoover submitted two memoranda to the President based on what Clegg and Hince had learned, and almost certainly drafted by Clegg, along with his proposal that the Bureau be expanded into a global intelligence and counter-intelligence role, in effect a hybrid organisation that combined the remits of MI5 and MI6. But much of the goodwill generated by Stephenson and the Clegg Mission would evaporate in June 1941 once Hoover had convinced himself that Menzies and Stephenson had influenced the President to appoint his hated rival, war hero Colonel William Donovan, head of the Office of the Coordination of Information, America's first attempt at a global intelligence service. This was, of course, precisely the role Hoover had had in mind for himself.

American intelligence officer David Bruce would credit Stephenson's deputy Charles Ellis with helping to establish the Office of the Coordination of Information. But whether MI6 really exerted any meaningful influence over the appointment of 'Wild Bill' Donovan, who had met Menzies and other British intelligence officers during two visits to Britain in 1940, is debatable. Indeed Stephenson was probably flattering both himself and Menzies when he wrote:

> Bill [Donovan] accuses me of having 'intrigued and driven' him into the appointment. You can imagine how relieved I am after three months of battle and jockeying for position in Washington that 'our man' is in a position of such importance to out efforts.[25]

BSC's habit of overstepping the mark by smearing isolationists, manipulating the American press and, on one occasion, ineptly tailing Under Secretary of State Adolf Berle, who wanted to severely limit Stephenson's activities, did not help matters. And the already strained relationship plunged to a new low after the Bureau almost wrecked a delicate British double-cross operation at the end of 1941. Dušan 'Duško' Popov, a wealthy Serbian playboy, committed anti-Nazi and British double agent code-named Tricycle had landed in New York in August 1941 ostensibly, at least as far as his Abwehr controller was concerned, to set up a network of Nazi spies in the United States. His baggage included four telegrams containing eleven microdots disguised as punctuation marks, a torn business card that would identify him to an Abwehr contact, a Virginia Woolf novel to be used as a cipher key, $70,000 in cash and an Abwehr questionnaire on Pearl Harbor.[26]

The telegrams with the microdots and the Pearl Harbor questionnaire were passed to the FBI and, as with so much that involved
Hoover, there are conflicting accounts of what happened next. But
it seems that, three days later, Popov was summoned to a meeting
with Percy Foxworth, Reed Vetterli's replacement as Special Agent
in Charge of the Bureau's New York field office. The meeting was
not a success and 'Sam' Foxworth dismissed the Pearl Harbor
questionnaire, which had clearly originated in Japan and sought
information on the precise location of airfield buildings and dockyard installations, as a fake.

A subsequent meeting with Hoover would prove an acrimonious
affair, the Director belittling Popov, who had meanwhile resumed
both his playboy lifestyle and an affair with French actress Simone
Simon, as immoral and a 'bogus' spy only interested in money and
sex. Critically, he too refused to take seriously the Pearl Harbor
questionnaire, the significant wording of which, as a civilian, he was
probably unable to comprehend. Later, after 2,400 Americans had
died at Pearl Harbor on 7 December 1941, Hoover would deny ever
having met Popov, whom he had placed under 24-hour FBI surveillance, or knowing anything about the questionnaire. According to
MI5 officer Tommy Robertson, one of Popov's controllers, 'No one
ever dreamed that Hoover would be such a bloody fool.'[27]

The failure of the Tricycle operation in the United States was
down to something that Guy Liddell had first recognised during
his visit back in 1938, namely that the FBI was essentially a police
force whose primary interest lay in catching criminals, or spies for
that matter, and ideally doing so in circumstances that would attract
maximum favourable publicity for John Edgar Hoover. They were
simply not interested in the complex task of running double agents,
nor did they possess the skills to do so. Now, with the threat of even
a partial breakdown in liaison with the FBI all too real in the aftermath of the Tricycle affair, Guy Liddell returned to the United States
at the end of May 1942. He met Hoover two weeks later, on 16 June:

> I saw [Deputy Director Ed] Tamm who took me into Hoover.
> Hoover is obviously the prima donna type. He was cordial

and held forth at great length about his organisation and his difficulties. I gave him some picture of our experiences in England whenever he showed signs of drawing breath, which was not often. It was obviously no good discussing with him such matters as XX agents.[28]

Assistant Director Milton 'Mickey' Ladd was more forthcoming, telling Liddell that the FBI was under the impression that MI5 was constantly holding back information and that, as a result, was doing likewise. Yet there was fault on both sides and, on visiting the New York Field Office, Liddell found Percy Foxworth both seriously overworked and 'singularly narrow in his outlook . . . There is no doubt that the Tricycle case has been seriously mishandled.'[29]

Despite the inauspicious start, Liddell and his MI6 colleagues from BSC did reach an agreement with the FBI on measures to improve collaborative working and the exchange of information. Before leaving for a long, uncomfortable flight home lying on a mattress in the bomb bay of a Liberator bomber, he had also put in place specific arrangements to jointly run any British XX agents operating in the United States and made a concerted effort to improve the Bureau's understanding of double-agent operations. The icy reception that MI5 and MI6 personnel had become accustomed to from the FBI thawed, but developments elsewhere, particularly in the field of cryptography, were already transforming the wider Anglo-American intelligence relationship.

* * *

On 8 July 1940 British Ambassador Lord Lothian wrote to President Roosevelt proposing 'an immediate and general exchange of secret technical information with the United States, particularly in the field of ultra short wave radio'. The President agreed and the British Technical and Scientific Mission, led by scientist Sir Henry Tizard, arrived in Washington at the end of August 1940. Tizard's small team brought 21 ground-breaking technologies developed in Britain, not least the cavity magnetron, a powerful vacuum tube that made possible the manufacture of centimetric radar sets small enough to be carried in ships and aircraft. They also briefed the Americans on the development of self-sealing fuel tanks, the jet engine and a range of other subjects including the research into nuclear fission being undertaken at Birmingham University in England by émigré German-Jewish physicists Otto Frisch and Rudolf Peierls.[30]

The Tizard Mission foreshadowed both Roosevelt's December 1940 declaration that America must become 'the great arsenal of democracy', and the March 1941 Lend-Lease logistical lifeline to Britain. Tizard's brief had not, however, included any exchanges on signals intelligence (SIGINT) and it would be an American, Brigadier General George Strong, who first proposed, during a meeting in London on 31 August 1940, that British and American codebreakers should work together to break German, Italian and Japanese ciphers. Strong cabled Washington five days later, on Thursday, 5 September, to ask

> Are you prepared to exchange full information on German, Italian and Japanese code and cryptographic information therewith? Are you prepared to agree to a continuous exchange of important intercept in connection with the above? Please expedite reply.[31]

The birth of the signals intelligence alliance between the MI6 codebreakers at the Government Code and Cipher School, Bletchley Park, and their American opposite numbers that followed would prove no less protracted and fraught as that between MI5 and the FBI. There were serious concerns in the wider British intelligence community, shared by the British codebreakers at Bletchley Park, about American security, partly down to Leon Turrou's indiscretions and partly down to the well-known insecurity of America's own ciphers. Prime Minister Churchill intervened in October 1940 to halt the sharing of even heavily disguised Enigma decrypt derived intelligence with the Americans.[32]

On the other side of the Atlantic the Army was enthusiastic about a cryptography exchange with the British, but the US Navy, notably Commander Laurance Safford, the hidebound head of the codebreaking section OP-20-G to which Agnes Driscoll belonged, was strongly opposed. Yet the Tizard Mission, with its hard-headed but generous sharing of military technologies in return for manufacturing capacity, had generated goodwill in Washington and the President's envoys, among them William Donovan, were reporting Britain's determination to continue the war. So, just as the British clamped down on signals intelligence sharing, the President overruled the Navy's objections and, at the end of October 1940, gave his approval for a secret American cryptography mission to Britain.[33]

Captain Abraham 'Abe' Sinkov and Lieutenant Leo Rosen from the US Army Signals Intelligence Service and Lieutenant Robert Weeks and Ensign Prescott 'Pres' Currier from OP-20-G sailed into this impasse aboard the Royal Navy battleship HMS *King George V*. Arriving at Scapa Flow in the Orkney Islands on 6 January 1941, the Americans transferred to the cruiser HMS *Neptune* for the journey south and, after being bombed and strafed by enemy aircraft off the east coast of Scotland, arrived at Bletchley Park, 50 miles north of London, after dark on 8 January. Ushered in through blackout curtains to the ground floor office of GC&CS operational head Commander Alastair Denniston, they were greeted by some of Britain's top codebreakers and handed a glass of sherry by Denniston's somewhat awestruck personal assistant, Barbara Abernethy. 'I hadn't the faintest idea what they were doing there, I wasn't told,' Abernethy recalled. 'But it was very exciting and hushed voices.'[34]

The next morning Leo Rosen handed the Bletchley codebreakers a gift that matched anything the Tizard Mission had taken to Washington the previous summer. One of only four American 'Magic' decryption machines then in existence, it had been developed to break into Japanese diplomatic traffic super-enciphered in the 'Purple' code. Given Japan's growing belligerence and consequent rising tensions in the Pacific in 1941, handing the British a very rare 'Magic' machine along with a partially reconstructed JN25 Imperial Japanese Navy code book was what the brilliant codebreaker Lieutenant Colonel John Tiltman rightly called 'a magnificent gesture'. Abe Sinkov and his colleagues quickly won the respect of the Bletchley Park codebreakers, but there could be little reciprocity while the British ban on the sharing of cryptography secrets remained in force.

The British reluctance to share one of the most closely guarded secrets of the war with a nation that was then still neutral is understandable and was soundly based on the 'need to know' principle. Indeed, such was the level of security surrounding the Bletchley Park operation, only a very few people had a comprehensive picture of what went on there. Opening it up to four visitors from a country then still at peace with Germany would have been an extraordinary lapse, despite the gift of the Purple machine. Yet Lieutenant Colonel Tiltman was understandably embarrassed by the one-way traffic in information and asked Commander Denniston for permission to reveal more on, for example, the successful break into Luftwaffe 'Red' Enigma. Denniston refused, though he did allow Tiltman to raise the matter with MI6 Director General Stewart Menzies, who had overall responsibility for Bletchley Park. Apparently sympathetic, Menzies approached the Prime Minister who gave his approval on 27 February subject to the Americans signing an oath of secrecy. Sinkov's team were then introduced to the only two completed Bombe decryption machines designed by Cambridge University mathematicians Alan Turing and Gordon Welchman.

Some historians have suggested that the 1941 Sinkov Mission was short-changed at Bletchley Park, the Americans giving the British much more than they got in return. Laurance Safford wrote later that the American delegation had been 'double-crossed' and that the British had refused to hand over a captured Enigma machine, an accusation that blithely ignores the fact that the British did not actually capture a complete Enigma until May 1941, two months after the Americans left Bletchley Park. In reality, Sinkov's team were given the next best thing to a real Enigma, a 'Paper Enigma' that set out what was known of the functions of the real German machine, and both Leo Rosen and Prescott Currier were given full briefing on the workings of the Bombes before twice watching one of the Turing-Welchman machines cycle through intercepted enemy cipher text.[35]

What the critics either tended to forget or chose to ignore is that the sheer scale, complexity and experimental nature of the Bletchley

Park operation meant that a small team of four young American officers would never be able to assimilate it all in a matter of weeks. Interviewed for a National Security Agency oral history project in 1979, Dr Sinkov, a Brooklyn mathematics teacher before he became a codebreaker, offered a more balanced view:

> Well, if you leave out for a moment the ENIGMA then I think we were probably giving them cryptanalytically more than we were getting, because of the PURPLE which was a pretty good accomplishment. But when the ENIGMA information is added in I think that throws the balance in their direction, because the solution of the ENIGMA was quite an accomplishment and of extreme importance in the conduct of the war.[36]

As the Sinkov Mission left Bletchley Park at the end of March 1941, British codebreakers were monitoring Wehrmacht and Luftwaffe units massing on the Soviet border in eastern Europe. Under Secretary of State Sumner Welles had, by then, handed Konstantin Umansky, the unpleasant Soviet Ambassador in Washington, a detailed account of Hitler's Führer Directive 21 to invade the Soviet Union derived from a source in Berlin. On 3 April, the British Ambassador in Moscow, the erratic Sir Stafford Cripps, passed on a message from Churchill to Stalin alerting the Soviet leadership to the impending German invasion; the 'reliable agent' referred to being actually Ultra intelligence derived from Enigma decrypts:

> I have at my disposal sufficient information from a reliable agent that when the Germans considered Yugoslavia caught up in their net, that is, after March 20, they began transferring three of their five tank divisions from Romania to southern Poland. As soon as they learned of the Serbian revolution, that transfer was revoked. Your Excellency will easily understand the meaning of these facts.

Stalin, although fearful of German intentions, recklessly dismissed the clear British and American warnings as a ploy to drag the Soviet Union into the war on the Allied side and took no action. He did secure the Soviet Union's eastern border by signing a neutrality pact with Japan later in April 1941, but more warnings of German intentions, not least intelligence from the British traitor John Cairncross, were likewise ignored and Operation Barbarossa, the unsubtly code-named invasion, began on 22 June 1941.[37]

On 9 August 1941, with the Wehrmacht driving towards Moscow and Stalin loudly demanding Allied help, President Roosevelt and Prime Minister Churchill met for a four-day conference at Placentia Bay in Newfoundland. Constrained by political and public opinion at home, Roosevelt was unable to declare war or sign any binding treaties. But newsreel film of the two leaders and their senior staffs singing hymns on the quarterdeck of HMS *Prince of Wales* sent an immensely powerful message around the world, a message reinforced by putting their signatures to the Atlantic Charter, a joint statement of policy that looked forward to 'the final destruction of the Nazi tyranny', and set out eight common principles that would do much to shape the post-war world.

Eight decades on from the Atlantic Charter, the wider Anglo-American relationship is not particularly special. Always asymmetric and, as during the botched 2021 withdrawal from Afghanistan, all too easy to lose sight of amid a chaotic geopolitical landscape, it is just one among a number of useful alliances involving two nations that will ultimately pursue what they see as their own best interests. Yet this somewhat opaque wider relationship is underpinned by the most formidable intelligence and security alliance the world has yet seen, an alliance that can trace its origins back to that Saturday afternoon in January 1938 when MI5 handed Jessie Jordan's intercepted Agent Crown letter to American Military Attaché Colonel Raymond Lee.

From that small beginning, Guy Liddell's subsequent visit to the United States and, three years later, the decision to share critical elements of the Enigma secret with the Sinkov Mission, an Anglo-American intelligence and security alliance was born. Formalised in 1943 with the BRUSA Agreement, it would significantly shorten the route to Allied victory in the Second World War. Rationalised post-war as the 1946 UKUSA Agreement and expanded to include Australia, Canada and New Zealand as members of what would become known as the 'Five Eyes', it would weather the treachery of Kim Philby, Aldrich Ames and others on both sides of the Atlantic and survive avoidable low points such as the ill-conceived Anglo-French Suez Crisis in 1956. It would hold the line in the Cold War, contribute to British victory in the 1982 Falklands War and inform Allied strategy in the 1990–91 Gulf War. There have been serious failures, notably the critical five-week delay in detecting and accurately interpreting the Soviet missile build-up in Cuba that took the world to the brink of nuclear war in 1962. And, after the September 2001 terrorist attack in New York, fragmentary and inconclusive intelligence on weapons of mass destruction was wilfully misinterpreted to make the case for the 2003 Iraq War. Once again, however, the alliance survived and, for better or worse, would go on to play a key role in the so-called War on Terror.

Early in the second decade of the 21st century, as the brittle globalist world order fragments and increasingly bitter and protracted conflicts over territory and resources threaten world stability, the Western intelligence and security alliance remains remarkably resilient and adaptable. The 2021 AUKUS agreement between Australia, the United Kingdom and the United States was conceived to counter the growing threat from an economically and demographically troubled but still expansionist China. Initially dismissed by some as merely symbolic, AUKUS will see three of the Five Eyes, possibly soon to be joined by Japan and perhaps India, the latter two nations being already members of the Quadrilateral Security Dialogue (QUAD), enhance intelligence cooperation and military capability in the Pacific theatre. Given the nature of the threat, AUKUS has the potential to become every bit as important to geopolitical stability in the Pacific theatre and beyond as the NATO alliance was in containing Soviet expansionism in Europe during the first Cold War.

Elsewhere, the CIA, MI6, the American National Security Agency (NSA) and the British Government Communications Headquarters

(GCHQ) accurately predicted the February 2022 Russian invasion of Ukraine. In sharp contrast, Général Éric Vidaud, head of the French Direction du Renseignement Militaire (DRM), was sacked for his organisation's failure to forecast the Russian invasion. And, despite warnings from Washington and London, Bruno Kahl, head of the German Bundesnachrichtendienst (BND), had to be hurriedly evacuated after unwisely finding himself in Kyiv just as the invasion began. Not that the French and Germans were alone in their shortcomings prior to the Ukraine war: serious operational intelligence failures, born of a tendency to give an authoritarian leader only data that he would want to hear, are believed to have led President Vladimir Putin to purge around 150 senior staff of the Russian Federal Security Service (FSB). General Sergey Beseda, head of the FSB's Fifth Service Operational Intelligence Division, was sacked and jailed.

Anglo-American intelligence successes in Ukraine, albeit gained against a notably low-tech and vulnerable target, have done much to restore reputations damaged by failures in Iraq and Afghanistan. And, at the time of writing, both the British and the Americans are continuing to provide Ukraine with the timely and actionable signals intelligence (SIGINT), satellite imagery (IMINT), human intelligence (HUMINT) and advanced cyberdefence capabilities that have allowed its numerically inferior military to slow the Russian advance to a grinding, attritional crawl. Once again, as Russian aggression and Western declinism threaten to plunge Europe into a new and dangerous Cold War, the Anglo-American intelligence and security alliance is proving critical to events of immense and lasting global significance. And it all started with a letter steamed open over a boiling kettle in a Scottish post office in January 1938.

Afterword

The Woman with Auburn Hair

The Jordan/Rumrich case, Leon Turrou's book and the movie *Confessions of a Nazi Spy* sparked an epidemic of spy fever across Britain and the United States. In Dundee, where it had all begun, suspicions centred on Elizabeth 'Elly' Robertson, the estranged wife of Merchant Navy wireless operator Robert Robertson. The couple had married in 1930 and had a son, Charles, a year later, but Robertson had disappeared in 1936 leaving a poverty-stricken Elly in a squalid Dundee boarding house. Yet, just when her fortunes appeared to have hit rock bottom, in 1937 Elly was able to move into a new bungalow at 11 Rescobie Avenue in the suburb of Craigiebank and send her son to the fee-paying Dundee High School. Asked where all the money was coming from, she would claim that her husband, said to be working for Marconi Wireless in Calcutta (modern-day Kolkata), was sending it from India. A year later, the upwardly mobile Elly was on the move again, this time to another new bungalow in leafy Broughty Ferry.

With the Jordan case front page news, Dundee Police began taking a close interest in Elly Robertson and discovered that she had been born Elisabeth Joosten to Dutch parents living in Viersen, Germany, in December 1901. She was reported to be very close to an Arbroath solicitor named James McLeay who was described by police and legal colleagues as 'a dubious character'. McLeay had, it seems, received a substantial part of a £50,000 estate being handled by his firm by 'unscrupulous means'. Elly had also bought a car and Arbroath garage owner William Cromarty confirmed that his customers Mr McLeay and Mrs Robertson were 'very friendly' with each other. They were also, according to Cromarty, very keen on fishing, though their angling expeditions were 'generally confined to the vicinity of places of interest to foreign powers, such as aerodromes, power stations, etc.'.

Elly, who had a decidedly chequered career as a motorist, collided with a road sign and gatepost in the Angus village of Monifieth amid a violent thunderstorm late on 26 August 1939, a week before the outbreak of war. Police arrived at the scene to find that she had been driving home from a party and was too drunk to stand unaided. Banned from driving for a year, she then became a frequent passenger on the bus service that ran between Broughty Ferry and Dundee. Conductor Frank Reilly later told police that she appeared to be very pro-German and, on one occasion in May 1940, had told him, 'I suppose it will soon be your time to go to the war . . . Why should you have to fight? You have nothing to fight for. Let the people with the money do the fighting.' Elly was also, Reilly recalled, in the habit of sitting on the longitudinal seat at the back of the bus that gave a clear view of the River Tay. She was, Reilly continued, forever asking about shipping in Dundee Harbour and, 'One day she pointed out a building in Broughty Ferry Road and asked what it was. When I told her it was the Orphanage, she said, "Yes, it was an Orphanage, but it is not that now, are there not soldiers in it?" I said, "Not that I know of," and she replied, "No, it's not soldiers, it's sailors, how many are there?" I told her I had no idea.'

Then, just as it seemed that the suspicions about Elly Robertson were justified, Detective Constable Ian Macdonald reported that 'This woman lives very expensively and during the last winter she has acquired three very expensive fur coats . . . According to my information, it is a usual occurrence to see men of all ages leaving her house at all hours of the day and night.' In view of this, MI5 concluded that Elly's interest in sailors was purely professional and that 'it is quite clear that there is another explanation of Mrs Robertson's apparent affluence since the departure of her husband to India'.[1]

Elly Robertson would not be Dundee's last brush with Nazi espionage, either imagined as in her case, or, as in the case of Dutch double agent Folkert van Koutrik, all too real. Van Koutrik, who had managed to infiltrate both MI5 and MI6 while working for Abwehr before the war, would surface in 1943 living close to Elly Robertson's former home in Broughty Ferry and working in the wartime Allied submarine base in the city. That, however, is another story.

* * *

Sixty-four-year-old American widow Etta Shiber resigned herself to a second night cooped up in an overcrowded railway carriage at Hendaye Station in south-west France. It was the evening of 18 May 1942 and, ill and half-starved after eighteen months as a prisoner of the Gestapo, Etta could now see freedom tantalisingly close, just yards away across the railway bridge over the River Bidassoa that divided France from neutral Spain. Yet nothing seemed to be happening.

Seventeen years earlier, while Etta and her husband William had been visiting Paris, she had visited a dress shop in rue Rodier owned by Kate 'Kitty' Bonnefous, the British-born estranged wife of a French wine merchant. Despite the difference in their ages, Kitty being almost a decade younger, the two women had struck up a close friendship and, when Etta was widowed in 1936, Kitty suggested that she come over to France and move in with her. War broke out three years later and, as the German Army approached Paris on 13 June 1940, the two women and their three dogs joined the flood of refugees desperately trying to make their way south along the N20.

After three days stuck in a vast traffic jam they happened across an RAF pilot who had been shot down during the Dunkirk evacuation and was trying to avoid capture and get home. Hiding him in the boot of their car, the two women returned to Paris and looked after him in their rue Balny d' Avricourt apartment until, with the help of friends, Kitty was able to arrange his escape to Britain. Before long, Etta and Kitty were players in a network smuggling dozens of evading Allied soldiers and airmen into the unoccupied southern half of France from where they could make their way home through neutral Spain. But the network was betrayed to the Gestapo by a collaborator and, on 26 November 1940, Etta was one of the first to be arrested and thrown into Cherche-Midi military prison. Others, among them Kitty Bonnefous, were rounded up in the ensuing days.

Kitty and another member of the network were sentenced to death while Etta and two others received lengthy terms of hard labour. Etta spent the next fourteen months at Cherche-Midi and Fresnes prisons, then a freezing, overcrowded cell at Troyes Penitentiary where conditions were appalling, even for wartime, and she witnessed the suicide of one of her cellmates. Finally, in April 1942, came news that she was to be paroled. It seemed that, as an American citizen, she was to be exchanged for an important German woman being held prisoner in the United States.

So it was that, having been assured by the Gestapo that Kitty was still alive, Etta found herself in that crowded railway carriage at Hendaye. Another night would drag by before, at midday on 19 May, a train approached from the Spanish side of the border. A band began to play and an oddly familiar young woman with wavy auburn hair stepped down to be greeted by a party of Nazi officers. As she hurried along the platform to board the train before it crossed back into Spain, Etta was convinced that she had seen the auburn-haired woman's picture somewhere, perhaps in a newspaper. It was only two days later, once she was safely aboard the Swedish liner *Drottningholm* and on her way to New York, that she learned that she had been exchanged for Abwehr courier Johanna Hofmann.[2]

Appendix

The Players
The Spymasters

CHRISTOPHER DRAPER

Born at Bebington on Merseyside in April 1892, Christopher Draper was inspired to become an airman by Louis Bleriot's cross-Channel flight in 1909 and gained his Royal Aero Club certificate in October 1913. He joined the Royal Naval Aviation Service in January 1914 when his contemporaries included a Captain H.C.T. Dowding who, as Air Chief Marshal Hugh Dowding, would lead RAF Fighter Command during the 1940 Battle of Britain. Despite being described by one superior officer as having 'very little idea of discipline, but a brilliant pilot', Draper went on to command Naval 8 Squadron with distinction in France in 1918 and was credited with nine victories. Like so many wartime airmen, he found it difficult to adjust to life in peacetime and drifted from job to low-paid job as a bit-part actor and stunt pilot.

Following his brush with espionage, Draper rejoined the Royal Naval Air Service on the outbreak of the Second World War in 1939 only to find himself, as a former Squadron Commander, reduced to the rank of Sub-Lieutenant and armaments officer. He would rise to Lieutenant Commander and command a squadron before being demobbed again, aged 55 in 1945. Out of work and angered by the treatment of veterans, in May 1953 he repeated his 1935 Thames bridges stunt, this time flying under no fewer than fifteen bridges. Conditionally discharged at Bow Street Magistrates Court on payment of ten guineas costs, the flight had nevertheless had the desired effect as he was a minor celebrity once more and soon back in both work and funds. By the time he died in 1979, this remarkable man could boast of a flying career that had begun with lessons in a primitive Bristol Boxkite in 1913 and progressed to taking the controls of a Gloster Meteor fast jet fighter more than four decades later.

NORMAN BAILLIE-STEWART

Baillie-Stewart was born Norman Baillie Wright in London in 1909. His father was Captain, later Colonel, Hope Baillie Wright of the 67th Punjab Regiment of the Indian Army and he spent three of his infant years in India. Educated at a small private school in Britain while his parents remained in India during the First World War, he went on to the Royal Naval College at Dartmouth only to have to leave in October 1925 after a bout of illness. Recovering his health, he won entry to Royal Military Academy Sandhurst with a prize cadetship, changed his name to the more aristocratic Baillie-Stewart and joined the Seaforth Highlanders. Sailing for India with his regiment, he seemed destined for a successful military career. Yet a sizeable chip on his shoulder allied to a deeply unpleasant, insolent personality would lead him into constant disputes with senior officers and, on his return to Britain in 1931, an attachment to the Royal Army Service Corps. Variously described by his fellow officers as arrogant, careless, temperamental, tactless and unable to get on with the men he commanded, he first acquired an admiration for all things German after an affair with a German girl named Irma Steidelmann.

Two years into his five-year sentence for espionage, Baillie-Stewart was described by Major Ben Grew, the Governor of Maidstone Gaol, as 'a troublesome prisoner'. Released in 1937, he moved to Vienna and took German citizenship in 1940, four months after the outbreak of war. By then he had begun broadcasting on the Reichsrundfunk English language service, his affected upper-class drawl credited by some with earning him the original title 'Lord Haw Haw' coined by *Daily Express* critic Jonah Barrington. His broadcasting career was brief and he spent the rest of the war as a civil servant and English teacher. Arrested in Austria in 1945, he narrowly escaped execution for treachery thanks to his German citizenship and was sentenced to another five years in jail. Released in 1949, he settled in Raheny, Dublin, married and had two children. He dropped dead in the street, aged 57, in June 1966.

HERMANN GÖRTZ

Much of what we know about Hermann Görtz' early life comes from his *lebenslauf* or curriculum vitae which, as we have seen, was subtly flexible according to who he thought would read it and must be treated with caution. Born in Lübeck on 15 November 1890, in April 1910 he joined the army as a one-year volunteer. But he was determined to follow his father, Heinrich, into the legal profession and, on leaving the military, his studies took him to Heidelberg, Paris, Edinburgh and Kiel before they were interrupted by the outbreak of the First World War. Rejoining the army, he was wounded in the chest and arm during an advance in Upper Silesia and spent three months in hospital. Transferring to the Imperial German Air Force, by 1918 he had found that both his languages and his legal training had equipped him well for interrogating captured Allied airmen.

Returning to his wife, Admiral's daughter Ellen Aschenborn whom he had married in July 1916, he served briefly in a right-wing militia before settling in Hannover, where the couple had three children, and resuming his legal career. Armed with a doctorate in international law, in 1925 and 1926 he worked in New York and Chicago before returning to Germany and setting up his own practice in first Lübeck, then, in 1929, in Hamburg. In 1930 he was engaged in the Siemens-Halske case at the High Court in London, the case that would bring him into contact with the habitués of the Chelsea Arts Club and set him on the road to both financial ruin and espionage.

Imprisoned along with Baillie-Stewart in Maidstone Gaol, Hermann Görtz was released in February 1939. Repatriated to Germany, he joined the Luftwaffe and, having met a number of Irish Republican Army prisoners while in Maidstone, suggested to Abwehr once war had broken out in September 1939 that the IRA could be useful to the German cause and that he was the man to bring this about. Parachuted into Ballivor, County Meath, on 5 May 1940, he had to hike for four days before making contact with leading republican figures. His mission, code-named Unternehmen Mainau, got off to a bad start when he had to leap over a garden wall to escape a Garda Síochána raid on the Dublin home of leading republican Stephen Held. Disillusioned after having been in Ireland for nineteen months and achieving precisely nothing, Görtz was arrested at Clontarf on 27 November 1941. Released from internment in February 1947, he found work as Secretary of the Irish charity Save the German Children Fund, but was rearrested after a change of Irish government policy towards former internees. He committed suicide in Dublin on Friday, 23 May 1947, swallowing cyanide after being mistakenly threatened with deportation to Germany.[1]

MARIANNE EMIG

Marianne resurfaced in Hamburg at the end of May 1947 after seeing a newspaper report of Görtz' death in Dublin. Interrogated by Captain Mark Lynton of the British occupation forces, she said that she had been born at Mainz on 4 July 1916 and, after moving to Hamburg with her family early in 1934, had found work as a secretary in Dr Görtz' legal practice in Rathausplatz. She went on to describe their 1935 trip to England and, at first, was adamant that she had not seen him do anything that could be construed as spying. Clearly still loyal to her newly dead lover, Marianne was at pains to make Görtz appear nothing more menacing than 'a temperamental and somewhat scatter-brained literary dilettante'. The pair's hurried departure from Broadstairs had, she claimed, been down to her parents, who had been against the trip, insisting that she come home. She had been waiting for the call to rejoin her lover in England when she received a letter saying that he had been imprisoned for espionage. She had met Görtz twice following his release in the spring of 1939 and had received a letter from him that July, then heard nothing of him until she spotted the newspaper article on his death.

In 1945 Marianne had found work as a secretary and interpreter for the British Port Controller at Hamburg and, at the time of her 1947 interrogation, was working for Radio Hamburg. Described by Layton as 'an ingenuous though not a particularly effective liar relying very much on her good looks and general "jeune fille" appearance', she was eventually forced to admit that she had been well aware of the real purpose of the 1935 trip to England and that she had willingly taken on the role of attractive femme fatale, but claimed that it had been merely a youthful lapse. A Marianne Emig giving her occupation as a redakteur (editor) is shown in the 1980 Hamburg directory as living in a Parkallee apartment she had occupied since the early 1950s.[2]

JESSIE JORDAN

Briskly business-like as ever and keen to capitalise on her own notoriety, Jessie Jordan arranged to have the contents of her Dundee hairdressing salon auctioned off just three weeks after her arrest. A sizeable crowd laid siege to the Kinloch Street salon and auctioneer Charles Boe struggled to make himself heard, but everything including the Fortschritt permanent waving machine, furniture, basins, hairbrushes, cards advertising Jordan's Vienna perms, books, magazines, even the linoleum on the floor found buyers and the sale raised £90 which she instructed her solicitor to invest.

Jessie's daughter, Marga, had meanwhile remarried over the anvil at Gretna Green, this time to a Glasgow salesman named Tom Reid whom she had met just two months earlier. The couple, who sat together at the back of the court during Jessie's trial, had set up home in Glasgow. But there was no escaping her mother's notoriety and both Marga and her four-year-old daughter Jessie were being harassed by the press and abused by neighbours. To escape the constant pressure, Marga and her daughter sailed for Hamburg in November 1938 intending to wind up the family's affairs in Germany, then return to Scotland once the fuss had died down. Then came news that she had died in Hamburg's Finkenau Frauenklinik women's hospital, the cause of death being recorded as a perforated uterus that may have been the result of a botched abortion. Young Jessie Wobrock was placed in a German orphanage.[3]

Jessie Jordan was shattered by the news of her daughter's death which was broken to her while she was recovering in her cell at Saughton Prison in Edinburgh from an operation to remove her appendix. Transferred to Aberdeen Prison, she was due for release on licence in January 1941, but was immediately interned for the duration of the war. Locked up once more, this time in London's Holloway Prison, she was able to put her professional skills to good use, hairdressing for other internees including Diana Mitford, the wife of British fascist leader Sir Oswald Mosley. Repatriated to Germany in 1945 after her application to renounce her dual nationality and take British citizenship was refused, she was eventually reunited with her granddaughter who would become a nurse. Having become a Christian Scientist while in Holloway, Jessie Jordan died at her home in Limmerstrasse, Hannover, on 25 November 1954. The corner shop in Dundee's Kinloch Street where she once briefly plied her trade as a hairdresser fell victim to a post-war redevelopment scheme.[4]

WILHELM LONKOWSKI

Lonkowski was born at Worlienen in Prussia (modern-day Worliny in Poland) on 20 January 1896. He served in the Imperial German Air Force during the First World War and his service record, unearthed at the Bundesarchiv by Professor Rhodri Jefferys-Jones, shows that he survived being shot down and badly injured during a dogfight with a French aircraft. Towards the end of the war he married Auguste 'Gunny' Krüger, a barber's daughter from Obornik, also then in Prussia. Having seen their homeland of Prussia carved up by the 1919 peace settlement that ceded large swathes of territory to the newly created state of Poland, the Lonkowskis emigrated to the United States in 1929 and settled on Long Island where Wilhelm found work at Ireland Aircraft in Garden City and struck up a friendship with another German émigré, Otto Voss.

Returning to Germany in February 1934, the Lonkowskis were back in New York the following January, this time with Wilhelm as a fully-fledged Abwehr spy. His would be a short career as a spy and, just nine months later, the hapless pair were speeding over the border to Canada in Ignatz Griebl's car, desperate to escape American justice. Safely back in Germany, Lonkowski was given a civilian post in Hermann Göring's new Air Ministry. The fondness for alcohol and high living continued unabated and this would lead to an unwelcome brush with the Gestapo after one of their rowdy parties was found to have breached wartime rationing regulations. Whether they survived the war and, if so, what happened to them thereafter remains a mystery.

Günther Rumrich

Günther Rumrich was released in 1940 and dropped from view until, on 29 June 1943, he was sacked from his job as a welder at the Swan Island Shipyard in Portland, Oregon, when it was discovered that he had registered for the Coast Guard pass that allowed him into the waterfront under the false name Joseph Rumridge. That evening he told the bemused owner of the Ramapo Hotel, where he was then living and, at various times, entertaining no fewer than eight women, that he had to travel to Montana where his wife was in a critical condition in childbirth. And that was the last the hotel heard of him until FBI agents arrived two weeks later to search his room. Rumrich had meanwhile returned to his old trade as a dishwasher at Skipper's Seafood Restaurant in Seattle, leaving behind a trail of dud cheques signed using the alias Joseph de Bors of Omaha, Nebraska. Guri Bloomquist had divorced her errant husband while he was still in jail in 1940 and remarried as Guri Livesey, but they had clearly kept in touch as it was she who sent cash to cover the bounced cheques.

The FBI were now hot on Rumrich's heels once more, but he stayed one step ahead of the G-men by signing on aboard the Alaska-bound US Navy auxiliary USS *Baranof* as Joseph de Bors, a messman. Wanted posters complete with FBI mugshots were being circulated, but he still managed to step ashore at Seattle when his ship returned there on 26 August and disappear once more, this time to San Francisco where he found work on the night shift at a Coca-Cola bottling plant. He was finally picked up on 15 October and did subsequently try to reform, even attempting to re-enlist. One of life's perennial losers, he died on 8 December 1983 in New York.

Dr Ignatz Theodor Griebl and Maria Griebl

Ignatz Griebl was born at Straubing in Bavaria on 30 April 1898 and spent his early years in the city of Würzburg where his father was a schools inspector. The family's values were energetically Christian and robustly patriotic, Ignatz' father penning mawkishly jingoistic song lyrics after war broke out in 1914. Ignatz joined 2nd Bavarian Field Artillery Regiment on 1 April 1915 and, serving on the Italian front, was awarded the Iron Cross second class in September 1916. Post-war, and after a failed attempt to become a doctor in Munich, in 1924 he joined the stream of Germans disillusioned and embittered by defeat who crossed the Atlantic in search of a new life in the United States. Griebl had an added motive for emigration in the form of his girlfriend, Austrian-born nurse Maria Glanz, whom he had met while recovering from wounds during the war.[5]

Fourteen years later, on 10 May 1938, Griebl was a failed spy who had to abandon his wife in a Manhattan street at the dead of night and sneak aboard the German liner *Bremen*. Two weeks later the Nazi Party newspaper *Völkischer Beobachter* announced that Dr Ignatz Theodor Griebl, a stowaway from New York, had been arrested when the *Bremen* docked at Bremerhaven and would be expelled after severe punishment. But this was just a smokescreen to placate the American authorities and Griebl went straight on to Vienna where he took over the busy Reichsratsstrasse practice of a Jewish gynaecologist and surgeon, Dr Herbert Kulka. And, aside from his meeting with the Assistant Federal Attorney Lester Dunigan and the FBI agents sent to Berlin to take his affadavit in 1938, that was the last anyone in the United States would hear of him for six years.[6]

Maria Griebl followed her husband to Vienna on being released from bail in New York in November 1938 and found that he had sold the Giessen property extorted from the Berliners and used the money to buy a newly built apartment block at Dionysius-Andrassy-Strasse 7 in Vienna from an emigrating Jewish family, the Fischers. The reunion with her husband was not a happy one and the Griebls separated in August 1939. They divorced in May 1942 and Ignatz married Helen Forster, a Viennese woman with whom he would have one child, the very next day. He was arrested in Salzburg, Austria, in August 1945.

Otto Fischer, a member of the family of Viennese Jews who had been forced to sell their apartment block to Griebl at a knock-down price, was then working as a civil servant at the War Department in New York. Interviewed by the FBI, he recalled how, after repaying the mortgage, his family had seen the remaining 40,000 Reichsmarks from the sale confiscated by the Nazi state. In June 1946 the Property Control Section of the US Military Government of Austria confiscated the property, which had suffered only slight war damage, from Griebl and handed it back to the Fischer family.[7]

That, however, was just the start of Griebl's post-war troubles. On 20 July 1947 an advertisement in the *Neues Österreich* newspaper invited women who had been abused or inhumanely treated by Dr Griebl to communicate with the Regional Criminal Court in Vienna. Evidence was taken from a number of women, many of whom were still too traumatised to testify in court, and, on 9 February 1938, Griebl was arraigned on a charge of torture and violation of human dignity. One woman, identified only as Frau K and heard in camera, recalled how Griebl had called her a mongrel and insulted her before examining her in such a brutal manner that she fled from the consulting room in tears. A nurse who had worked for Griebl also denounced him as a sadist. Regretting that it was unable to proceed on the cases of the women who had been abused and had come forward but just wanted to put the trauma behind them, the court struck Griebl off as a medical practitioner, declared his remaining property, such as it was, forfeit and sentenced him to eight months in prison.[8]

Kay Moog

Kay Moog, Maria Griebl's simpering rival for her husband's unsavoury affections, made a brief return to the headlines in February 1941 when she claimed damages of $75,000 from Warner Bros for the way in which she had supposedly been portrayed in *Confessions of a Nazi Spy*. Kay alleged that actress Lya Lys had played the Erica Wolf character as a very obvious impersonation of herself and that this had caused her so much distress that she had even considered suicide. An unimpressed Judge Abruzzo ordered the two women to stand side by side in the courtroom, noted that Lya Lys, who was five foot five inches tall and blonde, looked nothing like the six-foot-one-inch brunette Kay Moog and dismissed the case. Kay Moog died at Palm Beach, Florida, in December 1984.

Tyler Kent

Born on 24 March 1911 at Newchang in Manchuria where his father was the American Consul, Tyler Kent spent his early years as a Consular Service child in Germany, Switzerland, Ireland and Bermuda. Athletic and a gifted linguist and mathematician, he did well at school and went on to Princeton, but was something of a loner and dropped out during his second, or sophomore, year. After a few months studying Russian at the Sorbonne and Spanish at the University of Madrid, in 1933 he joined the staff of William Bullitt, the first US Ambassador accredited to the Soviet Union, as a clerk. Once in Moscow the weaknesses in Kent's character led to him falling prey to the alcohol and attractive girls dangled in front of bored diplomats by the Russian intelligence services. Taking up with blonde NKVD agent Tatiana Ilovaiskaya, he began passing over documents stolen from the embassy and the grateful Russians supplemented his modest salary so that he was able to buy a car, a rare luxury in 1930s Moscow.

Kent left Russia on 23 September 1939 bound for his posting in London, stopping en route in Stockholm where he met Ludwig Matthias, a double agent believed to have been working for both

Abwehr and the NKVD and was given the bulky envelope Matthias was seen carrying out of Kent's room at the Cumberland Hotel a few days later. Kent had brought the envelope into Britain using his diplomatic privilege and, under interrogation, would claim it held only cigars.

Kent served his sentence at Camp Hill Prison on the Isle of Wight, visited twice a month by the ever loyal Irene Danischewsky whom he promptly forgot about on being repatriated to the United States in December 1945. In 1946 he married Clara Hyatt, a wealthy heiress thirteen years his senior and spent the next 30 years successfully working his way through her fortune. Unrepentant to the last, he died a pauper while living in a Texas trailer park in November 1988. Anna Wolkoff, his partner in crime, was released in 1947 and died in Spain in August 1973 when she was thrown from a car being driven by her friend and fellow Right Club member Enid Riddell whose eyesight was failing. By the time Irene Danischewsky died in 1977, her niece Helen Mirren was carving out a successful career as an actress.

THE SPYMASTERS

HILMAR DIERKS

Jessie Jordan's Abwehr recruiter Hilmar Dierks was born at Leer in East Friesland on 5 January 1889. A professional soldier, he was involved in the German advance into France and Belgium in the early autumn of 1914, but was recruited into Abteilung IIIB before the year was out. Dutch historians Kluiters and Verhoeyen have traced two attempts that Dierks made to get to Britain as a spy, once posing as a Belgian prisoner of war and on another occasion through Sweden, but both missions failed. His subsequent activities centred on recruiting and training agents destined for espionage missions in Britain, many of them Dutch seamen. Dierks' First World War operation, which was based in Rotterdam, was well known to the British and seven of his agents, among them Dutchmen Willem Roos and Haicke Janssen, were caught and executed by firing squad in the Tower of London.

Dierks' 1925 offer to spy for the British, made while posing as an arms dealer, was almost certainly an attempt at infiltration and suggests that he had maintained some intelligence contacts, most likely at that time with the Deutscher Überseedienst. The approach was wisely rebuffed by the British and, after a decade spent in the motor trade, he returned to full-time intelligence work with Abwehrstelle Hamburg in the mid-1930s.

Spymaster Dierks adroitly offloaded the fallout from the arrest of Jessie Jordan and the collapse of the New York spy ring in 1938 on to Erich Pfeiffer. He was later heavily involved in preparations for Operation Lena, an operation to land an advance guard of Abwehr agents in Britain ahead of the planned German invasion in 1940. On 2 September 1940 he joined three of his Lena agents, Werner Wälti, Karl Theodor Drücke and Vera Schalburg in a Hamburg wine bar to celebrate the completion of their training but was killed when their car crashed later that night. Wälti, Drücke and Schalburg were flown from Norway to Scotland by seaplane and paddled ashore in a rubber dinghy near Buckie in the early hours of 30 September 1940. Described by MI5 as having been 'thrown to the wolves' by Dierks, they were all speedily arrested. Both Wälti and Drücke were hanged, but Vera Schalburg, who had operated unsuccessfully as an Abwehr agent in London before the outbreak of war, was interned, spending some time along with Jessie Jordan in Holloway Prison. She is thought to have been repatriated to Germany in 1945.

ERICH PFEIFFER

Bremen spymaster Erich Pfeiffer ended up shouldering, at least in public, much of the responsibility for the antics of Griebl, Rumrich and the others in America. Transferred to open a Nebenstelle at the port of Brest in newly occupied France in July 1940, then to Paris and Berlin, by 1943 he was becoming disillusioned due in part to increasing conflicts with the Nazi Party's intelligence arm, the Sicherheitsdeinst. An opportunity to escape the hothouse atmosphere in Berlin arose in May 1944 after Erich Vermehren, the anti-Nazi Abwehr stelleleiter in Istanbul, defected to the British and Pfeiffer was asked to take over. But he soon found himself under house arrest when Turkey severed relations with the Axis in August 1944 and was only able to leave Turkey towards the end of April 1945. Travelling aboard the neutral Swedish liner *Drottningholm* to Liverpool, he was detained for interrogation, then released. Erich Pfeiffer died in Oldenburg, Germany, in July 1959.[9]

THE SPYCATCHERS

EDWARD HINCHLEY COOKE

British spycatcher Edward Hinchley Cooke was for many years the public face of MI5, an organ of the state whose very existence was then still not officially acknowledged. The son of a British school-teacher and a German mother, he was born in Dresden in 1894 and still had a marked German accent when he joined what was then MO5 during the First World War as a stool pigeon, posing as a prisoner of war and extracting intelligence from German prisoners. Between the wars he was variously an interpreter for Prime Minister David Lloyd George and, for four years, a businessman with armaments giant Vickers. He also spent time with the City of Birmingham Police and is believed to have qualified as a barrister before returning to the secret world with MI5. Retiring with his wife, Dora, to a seafront house on Wellington Parade in Kingsdown near Deal in 1945 and becoming Deputy Lord Lieutenant of the County of Kent, Brigadier Edward Hinchley Cooke suffered a heart attack and died on 3 March 1955 aged just 61. An intensely private man, he remains a somewhat mysterious figure even today after the release of files on many of the cases that he was involved in.

LEON TURROU

Leon Turrou travelled to Europe in the summer of 1939 to promote his book and *Confessions of a Nazi Spy*, sailing for home from Le Havre on 16 July just as the continent was lurching towards war.

Much in demand as a public speaker, he travelled the United States warning of the dangers to America should Europe fall to the Nazis.

Teresa Turrou died at their Westbury home on 1 May 1942 and, a year later, aged 48, Leon enlisted as a private in the Corps of Military Police. Despite the churlish intervention of his old foe J. Edgar Hoover, he was speedily commissioned as a Lieutenant with the help of another high-profile former G-man who had fallen foul of the FBI Director, gangster John Dillinger's nemesis Mel Purvis.

In August 1943 came news that his younger son Victor, a Second Lieutenant bombardier with the 66th Bomber Group, had been shot down over southern Italy and killed. In May 1944 Leon and his other son Edward were able to locate Victor's body and recover it for burial in the American cemetery at Nettuno. Post-war, Leon remarried and joined the Paris-based Central Registry of War Criminals and Security Suspects (CROWCASS) to hunt down wanted Nazis, some of whom were recruited by the CIA to spy on the Soviet bloc. He decided to make his home in the French capital in 1949 and died there, aged 91, in 1986.[10]

FLORENCE JOHNSON

Florence Johnson, the widowed Broadstairs landlady whose home Hermann Görtz and Marianne Emig rented in 1935, lived quietly in Broadstairs until her death in April 1951. Her home 'Havelock' still stands today, much altered, in Stanley Road.

MARY CURRAN

Mary Curran, the intrepid housewife spycatcher whose dogged determination had uncovered Jessie Jordan's Abwehr mailbox in Dundee and led to the exposure of Nazi spies in the United States, Prague, Ireland and France, found herself embroiled in a dispute with MI5 and Dundee Police after she and her husband applied for a reward for their efforts in the Jordan case. The response from MI5 and Dundee Police was that the Currans had only been doing their patriotic duty and were, in any case, selling their story to the press. The Police and MI5 did have a point, but Mary and her husband John were a working-class couple with little money and four young children to bring up. They were also unaware that MI5 had been aware of Jessie Jordan since June 1937, five months before Mary alerted them to the Dundee connection, so would have understandably imagined their role in the affair to be more central than it actually was. An agreement was finally reached in May 1939 and a sum of £20 was handed over. Mary Curran died in 1988, John having predeceased her in 1971.[11]

Notes

Preface

1   KV2/267. Paillole: 2003 pp. 83–89. Paillole article in *Historama, hors serié No. 35* pp. 78–83.
2   Daladier was not shot. He returned to active politics after the war and died in his bed in 1970. Daladier quoted in May: 2000 p. 168. See also Horne: 1990 ch. 4 and Wheeler-Bennett: 1963.
3   KV2/267. *L'ouest-éclair* 5 March 1939. Paillole: 2003 pp. 83–89. *Historama, hors serié No. 35* pp. 78–83.
4   Jeffery: 2010 pp. 290–300.

Chapter 1

1   KV 2/871. KV 2/872. *The Times* 16 August 1930 and 10 March 1931. Born in British India in 1912, Harold Adrian Russell Philby was nicknamed 'Kim' after Kimball 'Kim' O'Hara, the young Irish orphan who spied against the Russians in India in Rudyard Kipling's eponymous novel published in 1901.
2   Draper: 1962 p. 120 *et passim.*
3   KV 2/871. Draper: 1962 p. 126.
4   The meeting was organised by Lady Margaret Dalton, the 83-year-old widow of distinguished barrister Sir Cornelius Dalton. Lady Dalton's nephew Hugh would be a Labour member of Winston Churchill's War Cabinet and a post-war Chancellor of the Exchequer.
5   For Draper's pro-Nazi letters see, for example, *The Times*, 3 December 1932. KV 2/954.
6   Draper: 1962 pp. 137–142.
7   Draper *ibid.* Andrew: 2009 pp. 209–210. Harker took part in the interview because MI5's German specialist Edward Hinchley Cooke was unavailable. KV 2/3534.

8   Born in Dresden, Germany, to a British father and German mother in January 1894, the multi-lingual Hinchley Cooke had been recruited by what was then MO(5) in 1915 to operate as a stool pigeon, successfully posing as a German in British POW camps and eliciting information from inmates. Details of his subsequent career are sketchy, but he was on an intelligence mission to Leipzig in January 1919, he was Prime Minister Lloyd George's interpreter at the Spa Conference in July 1920 and, that same year, he recovered sensitive pre-war archives of the British Consulate in Dresden. FO 371/4842. KV 2/952.

9   The six engineers were indeed linked to MI6 through their boss, Moscow representative of the Metropolitan-Vickers Electrical Export Company and long-standing MI6 asset Charles Richards. Five were found guilty at a Moscow show trial but were released a few weeks later. Richards escaped the round-up in Moscow, but mysteriously drowned while swimming during a trade mission to Brazil in January 1941.

10   KV 2/174.

11   *Ibid.*

12   *Daily Express* 12 May 1933.

13   In the intercepted correspondence, Marie-Louise had been mis-spelt as Marie Luise.

14   On 21 April 1933, soon after Baillie-Stewart had been jailed, Silvester received a letter from an Elise Schulz in Berlin asking him not to try to contact Marie-Louise as she was now classed as a spy.

15   *Illustrierte Kronen Zeitung* 31 December 1933.

16   Frogé had been identified by Stanislas Krauss, an Abwehr agent of Polish extraction who was caught offering French officers low-interest loans that would leave them vulnerable to black-mail. Krauss' intercepted correspondence with a Dutch contact bore a striking similarity to Baillie-Stewart's Marie-Louise letters and Frogé's Germaine correspondence. Delmer: 1961 p. 202 *et passim.*

17   An agent of fortune who would work for anyone with the right money, Geissmann would penetrate the Czech, Polish and American intelligence services while working for Abwehr. The

MI6 officer assigned to his case in 1945 was one H.A.R. 'Kim' Philby. KV2/1457.

18 Gordon Switz was recruited in New York in 1931 by Lydia Stahl's Soviet controller, GRU illegal Moishe 'Manfred' Stern. In London, where the Switzes had lived in some style at Soviet expense in the summer of 1933, socialising with writer Dylan Thomas and artist Augustus John at The Pheasantry, a louche nightclub on Kings Road, investigations focused on their controller, a mysterious Russian known only as 'Frank'. KV 2/1586. KV 2/1587. KV 2/1588.

19 Helsinki masseuse Ingrid Bostrom, one of the GRU agents interrogated by the EKP, gave evidence that solved the April 1932 murder of Volter Asplund, technical director of Finland's state arms factory Lapua/VPT. According to Bostrom, a GRU agent had wooed Jenni Anttilla, the Asplunds' housekeeper, and persuaded her to administer a sedative to her employer in a tankard of beer. This rendered Asplund sufficiently groggy for him not to notice that secret files had been stolen, but a second dose of what was probably scopolamine laced with arsenic, given so the files could be returned, killed him. Bostrom's statement led to Jenni Anttilla confessing and being sentenced to fifteen years in jail.

20 KV 2/177. KV 2/183. KV 2.1586. For the suspected link to Baillie-Stewart see *The Daily Telegraph* 23 December 1933. For the German Marie-Louise identification see *The People* on 6 December 1936, a story recycled in several American newspapers including *The Pittsburgh Post-Gazette* on 8 January 1942.

21 Harker's report of the Draper interview suggests that it was de Trairup who reported the case to Kell. The precise nature of the Russian's links to the head of MI5 are something of a mystery. For the official history version see Andrew: 2009 p. 210.

22 De Trairup would, in 1938, win a libel action against a British provincial newspaper, the *Wolverhampton Express & Star*, that had accused him of smuggling valuable works of art out of civil war-ravaged Spain. The plan bore striking similarities to the earlier gold smuggling scheme, including the use of a chartered yacht, but de Trairup was able to secure an out of court

settlement on a technicality. KV2/952. Andrew: 2009 p. 210.
KV 2/952, KV 2/954. J 13/15867. J 107/145. *London Gazette*
9 January 1934.

23 KV 2/952.

24 Still wrongly seen by many as a classic case of 'to the victor,
the spoils' and the root cause of Germany's slide towards
extremism, the Allied reparations bill was actually a small frac-
tion of the cost of the damage done by German aggression in
France and Belgium and it would, in any case, only be levied
when Germany was judged able to pay. When the scheme was
finally abandoned in 1932, Germany had paid just 21 billion
goldmarks, less than 16 per cent of the 132 billion gold marks
(£6.6 billion or $33 billion) originally demanded.

25 Chapayevsk remains one of the most toxic places on earth with
concentrations of arsenic in the soil some 8,000 times the inter-
nationally permitted maximum. Miscarriages run at three times
the Russian average, as do cancers of the throat, liver and kid-
neys, and a large but unknown number of children suffer from
'pathological ageing and intellectual degeneration'. On 28 May
1928 a tank containing 11,000 litres of phosgene exploded at
the Stoltzenberg chemical works in Hamburg. Fortunately it
was a Sunday, so only eleven people died and 369 were injured.
The Germans claimed that the gas was left over from the
war, but MI6 noted that the tank was dated 1924. Centre for
Defense Studies *Russia Weekly* issue 38, March 1999. Nekrich:
1997 pp. 52–55. Press reports April 2008. Ziemke: 2004 pp.
175–176. Wala: 2001 pp. 267–268. Mahnken: 2002 p. 144 *et
passim*.

26 For the early days of Abwehr see *Major General Friedrich
Gempp, German Intelligence Leader* by Kenneth Campbell in
American Intelligence Journal Vol. 25, No. 1 (Summer 2007),
pp. 75–81. See also Höhne: 1979 p. 153 *et passim* and, for the
Unberseedienst, KV 2/1116.

27 *Ibid.* WO 372/19/80613. *Lancashire Evening Post* 21 August
1896.

28 One of Stott's early tasks for the fanatically anti-communist
Makgill had been to infiltrate the National Union of Railway-
men and sabotage a national rail and dock strike by telling

union bosses that staff at Liverpool's Lime Street station were refusing to come out in sympathy with striking miners. Stott's intervention was exposed as a lie, but not before, on 15 April 1921, a date still infamous on the British Left as Black Friday, the Triple Alliance of rail, coal and docks unions had disintegrated. Kenneth Stott left just £349 when he died in 1959. Esther Jeanne Le Roy, born in London to Belgian parents in 1897, went on to manage a millinery shop and died in Wales in 1971. KV 2/1116. Bennett: 2009 pp. 74–77. *North Wales Weekly News* 20 May 1971. Census returns.

29   General Friedrich Gempp was promoted out of Abwehr in 1927. Retiring in 1943, he died aged 70 while in Soviet captivity in 1946. Campbell: 2007.

30   KV 2/391. Brammer: 1989 p. 23.

31   KV 2/365.

Chapter 2

1   'Source L' provided the French embassy in Berlin with eight dossiers of intelligence on German rearmament plans between June 1933 and April 1934. Von Natzmer and von Iéna were credited in contemporary German press accounts with stealing engineering drawings of both aircraft and their engines. Sosnowski was promptly jailed on returning to Warsaw as the Gestapo had deceived the increasingly paranoid Poles into thinking he was a double agent. His subsequent fate is aptly shrouded in mystery; some sources suggesting that he died in a Soviet gulag, others that he was killed in the 1944 Warsaw Uprising. *French Intelligence and Hitler's Rise to Power* by Peter Jackson in *The Historical Journal*, Vol. 41, No. 3 (September 1998) quoting SHAT, 7N 2594, Documents L.I 2, 30 Oct. 1933, pp. 795–824. Stehlin: 1964 pp. 24–26.

2   The medieval barbarity of the Berlin beheadings provoked a horrified reaction worldwide. But Gröpler's axe would fall again a few weeks later, this time on the neck of Reichsmarine signals rating Egon Bresz. A Leica film roll with images of what was probably a daily key settings book for the naval Funkschlüssel C Enigma cipher machine had been found in Bresz's apartment

after his girlfriend had begun 'throwing more money about than was expected of a petty officer's sweetheart'. If Bresz was working for Polish intelligence, it will have been no coincidence that he was beheaded on 3 July 1935, the same day that Polish Foreign Minister Józef Beck arrived in Berlin for an official visit. KV 2/267.

3   The Reichswehr had shipped Hauptmann Amlinger's body home from Russia in a crate marked 'Machinery Spares' and attempted to cover up the incident with a press release claiming that he had broken his neck in a riding accident. His widow's suicide exposed the lie. *Manchester Guardian*, 3 December 1926. Wala: 2001 p. 267 *et passim*. Ziedler: 2006 pp. 182–183.

4   *The True Condition of French Aviation* by Warrington Dawson, Special Assistant at the American Embassy in Paris, 24 March 1933. Accessed at https://www.fold3.com/image/46692775. See also *German Rearmament and the West, 1932–1933* by Edward W. Bennett. (Princeton University Press 2015).

5   CAB/24/249 Command Paper 113(34) Imperial Defence Policy Memorandum by Secretaries of State for War and Air, and the First Lord of the Admiralty 20 April 1934.

6   See Smith: 2011 ch. 20 for an account of the Air Ministry's wilful complacency which was matched by the wishful thinking of the Admiralty in respect of Germany's clandestine U-boat construction programme. See also Richelson: 1997 p. 83 and Kershaw: 2004 chs. 1–2.

7   The French intelligence was also leaked to left-wing journalist Dorothy Woodman, a former leading suffragette and mistress of *New Statesman* editor Kingsley Martin, who included it in a prescient if long-forgotten book, *Hitler Rearms: An Exposure of Germany's War Plans*, published in 1934. See also Overy: 1975, Jackson: 1998, Wark: 1982. Wark: 2010 p. 38. Deist et al: 1990 p. 481 *et passim*. Royal Commission on the Manufacture of and Trading in Arms 1935/36, Minutes of Evidence, Cmd. 5292. quoted in Edgerton: 2006 p. 42. Cabinet Report by the Ministerial Committee on Disarmament, July 1934, in CAB/24/250. KV 2/971. For the espionage ban in Britain, see Brammer: 1989 p. 93.

8   Sempill, who was also spying for the Imperial Japanese Navy,

was a member of the Japan Society, unaware that one of his fellow members, a Colonel Vernon Kell who had a vague job in the War Office, was actually the head of MI5. He escaped prosecution as the evidence against him came from intercepted Japanese telegrams. *The Next War in the Air: Civilian Fears of Strategic Bombardment in Britain, 1908–1941*. PhD thesis by Dr Brett Holman (University of Melbourne, 2009). See also Dr Holman's excellent website http://airminded.org/.

9 Quote from an unidentified former Abwehr officer in Leverkuehn: 1954 p. 93. Both the text and the context point to the quote being from Erich Pfeiffer. See also Leverkuehn: 1954 p. 81. Andrew: 2009 p. 133 *et passim*.

10 Landing cards in DPP 2/314.

11 Understandably eager to make his trip around southern England appear innocent, Görtz would later claim that he and Marianne were heading for The Lizard, the most southerly point on the UK mainland, at the time of the accident. If that really was the case, they were taking an extraordinarily roundabout route. See itinerary in CRIM 1/813.

12 Departure and landing cards along with a hotel bill for 23–28 August 1935 at Hospiz am Gendarmenmarkt, Berlin. Görtz was careful not to tell his creditors that he was back in Germany. See letter to Dr Heinrich Rohl dated 31 August 1935. According to a receipt found in his belongings, Görtz had three rolls of film developed from which were taken 52 enlargements and two sectional enlargements. CRIM 1/813. KV 2/1319.

13 Letter from Barclays Bank International Branch, 168 Fenchurch Street, London, dated 23 November 1935 in KV 2/1319.

14 Görtz statement to police dated 18 November 1935. CRIM 1/813. KV 2/1319.

15 RAF Manston Operations Record Book AIR 28/512.

16 Eitel had been recruited by a customs official prepared to turn a blind eye to his currency smuggling racket if he would bring back American newspapers from New York. Invited to lunch with a Dr Ederhof in Bremen a few weeks later, Eitel was asked to gather information on French and American coastal defences and naval vessels whenever the Bremen called at Cherbourg and New York. Eitel then spent a day at Ederhof's Bremen office

getting detailed instruction, by the end of which he knew that Ederhof's real name was Erich Pfeiffer and that he used the alias 'Spielman'. KV 2/267. KV 2/384.

17 Arrival of Wilhelm and Auguste Lonkowski at Ellis Island on 7 February 1929 from the passenger list for SS *Berlin* accessed via Ancestry.com. Turrou: 1939 records Lonkowski as being in the United States and working at the Ireland Aircraft Co, Roosevelt Field, Long Island, in 1928, but offers no source for this. Fellow Abwehr spy Otto Voss, who immigrated to the United States on 22 October 1928 and started work at Ireland Aircraft, 'shortly after arriving,' confirms that he knew Lonkowski while both men were working at Ireland Aircraft in 1929. Under FBI interrogation, Lonkowski's American brother-in-law Ernest Beck confirmed that Lonkowski first visited the United States in 1929. NARA FBI HQ file 65–748–783, pp. 95–98.

18 NARA FBI HQ file 65–748–783 p. 28 *et passim*.

19 Gudenberg and Voss, who were the same age, sailed together on the *Deutschland* from Hamburg, arriving at Ellis Island on 22 October 1928. *Deutschland* passenger manifest via Ancestry.com.

20 Gudenberg could not recall the precise dates of Lonkowski's first visit to Buffalo when questioned by the FBI in 1938, but voyage records and crew lists for the *Europa* suggest it must have taken place in the first two weeks of August 1935.

21 NARA. FBI SAC report dated 7 July 1938 Bureau HQ file 65–748–783 p. 99 *et passim*. Turrou: 1939 p. 145 *et passim*.

22 NARA. FBI SAC report dated 7 July 1938 in Bureau HQ file 65–748–783 pp. 99–102. Turrou: 1939 p. 152 *et passim*.

23 Lonkowski was not the Putnam Valley's first spy. On September 1780 American militiamen captured Major John André, a British go-between with turncoat American General Benedict Arnold, at nearby Tarrytown village. André was later hanged. The captain of the German ship the Lonkowskis tried to board was at first reluctant to take them. The situation was resolved after Lonkowski phoned Griebl who sent a telegram to Pfeiffer who, in turn, contacted the ship and asked for the captain's assistance. KV 2/384.

Chapter 3

1 KV 3/1319.

2 *Ibid.*

3 Information from Kent Police Museum, 6 December 2012.

4 KV 3/1319.

5 The sequence of events in the Görtz case given in Nigel West's *MI5*, first published in 1981 though reissued as recently as 2019, is wrong. West makes no mention of the central role played by Marianne Emig, nor does he make any reference to Kenneth Lewis. Curiously, the MI5 official historian Professor Christopher Andrew does not include the Görtz case, one of the Security Service's most high-profile cases between the wars, in his seminal work *The Defence of the Realm – The Authorized History of MI5.* (Allen Lane 2009). Andrew: 2009. West: 1981.

6 The female staff at MI5 christened Thomas Argyll Robertson 'Passion Pants' in honour of the tartan trews he wore as an officer in the Seaforth Highlanders. For some reason, Robertson's biographer makes no mention of his involvement in this, his first major case. Frank Foley, MI6 Head of Station in Berlin, was asked to trace Suhr but was only able to report that he must have had some official standing as Nazi currency regulations made sending such a large sum abroad all but impossible. Later, the French Deuxième Bureau would identify 'Otto Suhr' as one of several aliases used by a Luftwaffe intelligence officer. Elliott: 2011. KV 2/1319.

7 Josephine Lewis née Becker had been born in Paris to a German father and British mother. She and her husband, Harley Street surgeon John Lewis, had been divorced for nine years. Kenneth Lewis had last seen his father five years prior to the events described here. See census 1891 and 1911 for Josephine Lewis origins and KV2/1319 for Kenneth's relationship with his father.

8 The Home Office warrant authorising interception is in KV 2/1319.

9 Lewis statement in KV 2/1319.

10 DPP 2/314.

11 KV 2/1320.

12 Görtz' travel records to the United States and Las Palmas are available online at Ancestry.com.

13 See, for example, article entitled *RAF Expansion – Six New Bomber Squadrons* in *The Times* on 10 April 1935, *Royal Air Force – Six New Flying Training Schools* in *The Times* on 5 July 1935 and *Royal Air Force – Contracts For New Base* in *The Times* on 15 July 1935, four days before Görtz landed at Southampton.

14 Two letters from Rahardt of 4 Portnall Road, Paddington, London, dated 30 and 31 October 1935 were found among Görtz' papers following his arrest. KV 2/1319.

15 Görtz CV in KV 2/1320. See also *Niemeyers Zeitschrift fur Internationales Recht. T. XXXI. Fasc. 1–4 (1929)* and *Hanseatische Rechts – und Gerichts-Zeitschrift* July 1931 p. 427 *et passim*. The British branch of the Siemens concern would later find it expedient to deny any association with Görtz – see letter from Siemens Brothers & Co. dated 29 November 1935 in KV 2/1319 and a short summary of his involvement in KV 2/3313.

16 Nicholls' career with the Pavlova company can be traced from travel documents and contemporary press coverage. See, for example, BT27/1033 via Ancestry.com for the passenger manifest of the liner *America* bound from Southampton for New York on 27 September 1923. In this, Sylvia gives her address as the Opera House, Covent Garden, but lies about her age, claiming to be seventeen when she was born the daughter of a well-to-do engineer on 15 September 1908 and was actually only just fifteen. On her return from Australia aboard the P&O liner *Narkunda* in 1926, she gives Anna Pavlova's studio at Ivy House, Golder's Green, as her address. The discrepancy in her age had by then shrunk as she claimed to be nineteen when the ship docked on her eighteenth birthday. Sylvia would return to the theatre following her dalliance with Haybrook, touring in variety reviews such as The Co-Optimists with Stanley Holloway, the Fol-de-Rols and The Bouquets. She also made occasional appearances on the BBC. She died in 1983.

17 *New York Evening Post* 15 June 1931. *The Pictorial Review*, Albany, New York, 25 February 1951.

18 Starr Faithfull's death remains a mystery, though a least one author has suggested that she was murdered by gangsters looking for information they could use to blackmail her abuser, Boston Mayor and former Assistant Treasury Secretary Andrew J. Peters. Rudolf Haybrook (1898–1965) had been door-stepped by reporters after his initials and the allegation that he was 'a bit too rough' was found in a diary Starr had left in a London hotel. See contemporary press coverage and *The Passing of Starr Faithfull* by Jonathan Goodman published by Kent State University Press: 1996. CRIM 1/813.

19 McLeish v McLeish & Haybrook J 77/2926/498.

20 For international coverage, see, for example, '. . . cette affaire d'espionage sensationelle' in *Le Matin* 20 November 1935. *Daily Express* 22 November 1935.

21 Smith report dated 11 January 1936 in KV 2/1320.

22 Kell to Atkinson 6 December 1935 in KV 2/1319.

23 Josephine Lewis to a reporter from the *Daily Sketch* as published 20 November 1935.

24 KV 2/1319.

25 Thost, a persistent thorn in the British side since his arrival in October 1930, had been served with an expulsion order on 29 October 1935, eleven days before Görtz was arrested at Harwich. One piece of evidence from 'Havelock' that had clearly not been deemed expedient to produce in court was a letter of introduction to Paul Rykens, the pro-Nazi Dutch founder of chemical industry conglomerate Unilever.

26 Sir Reginald Powell Croom-Johnson (1879–1957) resigned his Somerset parliamentary seat two years later in 1938 on being appointed a Judge of the High Court of Justice, King's Bench Division.

27 DPP to Kell 10 March 1946 in KV 2/1319. *Daily Mirror* 10 March 1936.

28 Five-part serial entitled *Brigitte* by Dr Hermann Görtz published in the *News Chronicle* in March 1936. KV 2/2642.

29 'Something of a dipsomaniac' Pfeiffer to MI5 interrogators at Camp 020, Interim Report, October 1945. KV 2/267.

30 The 2020 value of the Pratt & Whitney contract is expressed as contemporary opportunity cost. In 1967 American industrial

giant ITT successfully sued the American government for $25,000,000 as compensation for war damage to its business interests in Nazi Germany. Included in this was $5,000,000 for damage inflicted by US Air Force bombers on the Focke-Wulf factories in which ITT had a share and which had been building the very same aircraft that had shot down many of these US Air Force bombers. *The (F)utility Factor: German Information Gathering in the United States, 1933–1941.* Thomas H. Etzold in *Military Affairs*, Vol. 39, No. 2. April 1975.

31 General Erhart Milch, Hermann Göring's deputy, attended the June 1936 air show at Hatfield north of London and was shown several new RAF aircraft including the prototype Hawker Hurricane and Supermarine Spitfire fighters. Dining with influential British airmen including the pro-Nazi Japanese spy Lord Sempill at London's Carlton Hotel, Milch startled senior RAF officers by asking how their supposedly secret experiments with radiolocation, now better known as radar, were progressing.

32 MI5 noted ruefully that Pye-Smith only admitted to £10 of the £20 delivered to him by courier in November 1936. KV 3/007. KV 2/365.

33 There were seven questions, all concerned with the French official reaction to recent events in Austria where a Nazi coup had been suppressed, though not before the anti-Nazi Austrian Chancellor, Engelbert Dollfuss, had been assassinated. Berlin was concerned that, egged on by Austrian royalist émigrés in Paris, the French might be pressuring Kurt Schuschnigg, Dollfuss' successor, to restore the Hapsburg monarchy. The last thing Hitler wanted was to spark a revival of monarchism in Austria or, for that matter, Germany, so who better than Bernhuber, with his much-vaunted contacts in the Elysée Palace, to find out what the French were up to in Vienna? *Miroir du Monde* issue number 265 dated 30 March 1930 for account by Armand Avronsart (born Anton Gorecki in Poland) 1904–1983.

34 *Ibid.*

35 Bernhuber had, it seems, first spied in Belgium and Poland during the First World War, playing piano in a Vienna nightclub for some months after the war before being sent first to Spain

where he operated undercover as a tobacco salesman. In Paris from early 1934, he posed as a playboy and pharmaceutical salesman while spying on the French government. *Miroir du Monde* issue number 265 dated 30 March 1930. Dina Saronni interviews and trial transcripts from *Le Matin*, *Figaro* etc.

36 France-Marguerite Labbatut's body drifted inshore later that morning and was recovered for burial. Suicide from *New York Times* and *Petit Parisien* 30 August 1936. As for the couple's Abwehr handler, Hussinger mysteriously disappears from the case soon after his arrest and Altmeyer was exchanged for a French spy in German hands on Christmas Day 1937. See also *Etoile de l' A.E.F.* issue dated 16 August 1936 for a reasonably full description of what rapidly became a notorious and widely reported case.

37 KV 2/267. KV 2/1924. KV 2/1925. KV 2/2277. KV 2/2278. KV2/83. See also *Spionnen aan de achterdeur: de Duitse Abwehr in België 1936–1945* by Etienne Verhoeyen, Maklu-Uitgevers nv, Antwerp, 2011 (Governance of Security Research Report Series (Gofs), vol. IV). For the fall of Eben Emael, see Horne: 1990 ch. 9. See also *The Fall of Fort Eben Emael: The effects of emerging technologies on the successful completion of military objectives*. Research paper by Major Thomas B. Gukeisen US Army, University of South Dakota, 1993.

38 Sebag-Montefiore: 2000 p. 46 *et passim*.

39 Gestapo agents were also suspected of involvement in the suspicious deaths of anti-Nazi émigrés Dora Fabian and former Reichstag delegate Mathilde Würm in London in 1935. Barnes J. & Barnes P.: 2010 ch. 6. See also *National Socialist Germany: The Politics of Information* essay by Michael Geyer in *Knowing One's Enemies: Intelligence Assessments Before the Two World Wars*. Ernest K. May (ed.), Princeton University Press 1984.

40 A chilling Abw.III memorandum issued on 8 March 1935, stated that, 'The private life of those privy to official secrets requires constant surveillance. Sporadic checks are essential, both on duty and off.' Abw.III *Merkblatt über spionage, Spionageabwehr und Landes verrat* 8 March 1935 quoted in Höhne: 1979 p. 188.

41 Leverkuehn: 1954 p. 90. KV 2/267.

42 Pfeiffer's agents included several of Ludwig Dischler's former assets. One was Ulrich Blum, a wartime German U-boat officer then the Technical Director of Ingenieurskantoor voor Scheepsbouw, a Dutch front company building U-boats in violation of the Treaty of Versailles. Another was German-born Ludwig 'Louis' Fischer who worked in the Rotterdam office of the inland shipping company Damco Scheepvaart Maatschappij, the same Louis Fischer given to Christopher Draper as a contact address two years before. KV 3/209. KV 2/267. Höhne: 1979 p. 182.

43 Quite why Canaris favoured Pfeiffer, who had only been working in Abwehr for ten months, over more experienced intelligence officers is not clear. Perhaps he was taking the opportunity to clear out dead wood, perhaps it was because Pfeiffer had an economics degree and had recently worked as an industrial statistician, or perhaps it was because Pfeiffer was, like the new Abwehr chief, a former U-boat officer. KV 2/267, KV 3/205. Newman-Hall report to Nicholson in KV 2/1924. For Pfeiffer's admiration for Max Ronge, see KV3/206. *Kriegs und Industrie Spionage*: (Amalthea-Verlag, Zurich, Leipzig & Vienna, 1930), *Meister der Spionage* (Johannes Günther Verlag Leipzig und Wien, 1935).

44 See KV3/205 for statement by Leutnant-zur-see Addicks (no relation the Pfeiffer's agent Henry Addicks) given to British 21st Army Group 23 May 1945 and KV 3/206 for Newman-Hall's *vertrauensmann* or agent number and code name.

45 KV 2/1924.

46 *Ibid.*

47 NARA. FBI HQ file 65–748–783.

48 *The Kriegsmarine and the Aircraft Carrier: The Design and Operational Purpose of the Graf Zeppelin 1933–1940* by Marcus Faulkner in *War in History*, Vol. 19, No. 4, November 2012, pp. 492–516.

49 *Bremen* arrived in New York on Friday, 6 December 1935, so Eitel's meeting with Griebl and Voss must have taken place over that weekend. One of Pfeiffer's claimed informants, a director of the Bremen Atlaswerke engineering firm working in Glasgow with the G & J Weir pump manufacturing concern,

brought back nothing of interest as doing so would have excited suspicion. Eitel post-war interrogation at Camp 020. KV 2/384.

Chapter 4

1   Before handing over the agreed price of £70 for Jolly's Saloon, Jessie pointed at the name plate over the door that read T. Jolly and asked who the mysterious Mr Jolly was. It was explained to her that James Curran was a devout Catholic whose motto was 'Thou Jesus Our Lord Liveth Yet'. The term 'saloon' rather than 'salon' was still in common usage, particularly for those establishments that also offered hairdressing for men. Dundee was not the, 'sleepy little farming town in central Scotland', as described by unofficial FBI historian Dr Raymond J. Batvinis. This is but one of several fundamental errors in Batvinis' account of these events. *Daily Record and Mail* 24 May 1938. Curran family recollections to journalist Theo Long in 1938. Batvinis: 2007 ch. 1.

2   *Daily Record and Mail* 24 May 1938.

3   Despite the risk of Jessie realising she was under some sort of surveillance, the police never did return the sketch to the shop. Carstairs memorandum dated 29 November 1937 in KV 2/193. Carstairs witness statement in KV 2/3534.

4   Neilans letter dated 1 December 1938 in KV 2/194. *Daily Record and Mail* 24 May 1938. Annie Ross (1905–1962) was appointed Dundee's first woman police officer in January 1935.

5   Carstairs precognition in KV 2/3534. B Division at Thames House between 1934 and 1939 from Andrew: 2009 p. 134.

6   Detective Inspector Tom Nicholson witness statement in KV 2/3534. Curran family recollections. *Daily Record and Mail* 24 May 1938. Contemporary weather reports for 19 November 1937.

7   KV 2/194. Jessie Wallace birth certificate from Scotland's People.com.

8   *Sunday Mail* 22 and 29 May 1938.

9   Karl Friedrich Jordan's brother Heinrich Wilhelm Jordan (b. 24 April 1886 in Hannover) died on 7 April 1908 when condemned

buildings in East Castle Street, London, that were being used as staff quarters for Berners Hotel collapsed. See Ancestry.com *Germany, Select Births and Baptisms 1558–1898*.

10 Margarethe Freida Wilhelmine Jordan birth from Ancestry.com *Hamburg, Germany, Deaths, 1874–1950*. Friedrich Jordan death certificate from Ancestry.com *Hamburg, Germany, Deaths, 1874–1950*. Estimates of deaths in the 1918–1920 influenza pandemic vary from 30 million to 50 million and higher. In two years, the pandemic killed many more than the 21 million who died of war causes in four years of conflict. See *The Geography and Mortality of the 1918 Influenza Pandemic* by K. David Patterson and Gerald F. Pyle in *The Bulletin of the History of Medicine*, Spring 2001, pp. 2–21. (Johns Hopkins University Press.)

11 Jordan-Baumgarten marriage and divorce certificate from Ancestry.com *Hamburg, Germany, Marriages, 1874–1920*. Frau Jessie Jordan-Baumgarten, Friseurin, Hartungstrasse 15, from the Hamburg address book for 1925. Werner Tillkes born 29 August 1914 was one of five children of Richard Tillkes and his wife Alice *nee* Riebenstein. Tillkes genealogical data from Ancestry.com.

12 *Sunday Mail* 5 and 12 June 1938.

13 *Daily Express* 28 January 1939.

14 For Hauptmann Conrad Ontjes in Referat IIIH and Hilmar Dierks in Referat IM, see KV 3/204. Contemporary Hamburg address books have C. Ontjes living at Isestrasse 30. KV 2/365.

15 The creepy Owens was promptly dropped by MI6, though his espionage career was far from over and, as a wartime double-cross agent, he would play a key role in the deception plans ahead of the 1944 D-Day landings. KV 2/444.

16 KV 2/365.

17 KV 2/193.

18 KV 2/193. KV 2/3534.

19 *Sunday Mail* 12 June 1938.

20 Mary Wallace was a partner in Felin Newydd House convalescent home near Talgarth in Brecon. There is no record of the material gathered at Southampton being intercepted, so it must have been sent separately to an address not yet on the MI5

intercept list. *Dundee Courier* 27 July 1937. *Sunday Mail* 12 June 1938.

21 One letter intercepted en route to Jessie Jordan that did cause some concern was from a Flight Lieutenant J.B. Wallace stationed at RAF North Weald, a front-line fighter base. John Wallace turned out to be Jessie's nephew and the correspondence was entirely innocent. He retired in 1966 as Air Vice-Marshal John Brown Wallace OBE MB Ch.B (1907–1980), Deputy Director of Medical Services for the RAF. For Wallace correspondence and other details, see Dundee City Police memorandum by Carstairs dated 29 November 1937 in KV 2/193. KV 2/194.

22 *Daily Record* 24 May 1938.

23 KV 2/193. KV 2/3534.

24 KV2/193.

Chapter 5

1 Assistant Director Edward Tamm memorandum to Director Hoover, 5 April 1938. Bureau HQ file 65–748–320. Turrou: 1939 p. 17 *et passim*.

2 *Ibid.*

3 Bureau HQ file 65–748–783.

4 *Ibid.*

5 Guy Liddell (MI5) report in VNST II 2/21, Vansittart Papers, Churchill College, Cambridge University.

6 *Ibid.* Rumrich 'Life History' in Bureau HQ file 65–748–783.

7 Turrou identified his father, whom he claimed died before he was born, as a Frenchman named George Turrou. The father might have been French, he might even have been George or Georges, but he was not George Turrou as Leon only adopted this surname when he was 22 years old. Even the correct date of his first arrival in the United States remains a mystery; when his wife applied for an American passport, she stated, doubtless at Leon's prompting, that he had lived in the United States since 1909. He would then have been just fourteen years old. In Leon's own 1921 and 1924 passport applications the date of his arrival in the US moves randomly forward to March and August 1913. The 1940 census return for the Turrou household

in New York includes Leon's 66-year-old mother-in-law Anna Zakshenska. Jeffreys-Jones: 2020 p. 44.

8   See, for example, *The Times* of Hudson, Ohio, dated 12 March 1943 for a report on a public address by Turrou. See *SS Pocahontas* passenger list 22 November 1920 and Teresa Turrou passport application filed in Warsaw on 13 July 1922, both sourced via Ancestry.com. Edward and Victor Turrou birth details from their Second World War Service Registration Cards also sourced via Ancestry.com.

9   USMC Muster Roll, 28 May 1921 and SS *Paris* Le Havre to New York passenger manifest 27 – 24 March 1923 via Ancestry. com.

10   Turrou: 1939 pp. 54–55.

11   Turrou would later suggest that he accused Rumrich of being Crown because the letter found in his apartment was signed 'N. Spielmann'. But there is no evidence that this alias, used by Erich Pfeiffer during Addicks case in Britain two years before, was among the information that MI5 had passed to the FBI at this early stage in the investigation. The Eglin message was, in any case, much clearer evidence of Rumrich's identity as Crown. Turrou: 1939 p. 56.

12   *The Forgotten Treason: The Plot to Overthrow FDR* by Emily Lacy Marshall, Wesleyan University, Middletown, Connecticut, April 2008. Yeadon & Hawkins: 2008 p. 129 *et passim*.

13   See various press reports on Camp Wille und Macht (Will and Power) at Griggstown, NJ, in August 1934. FBI agents discovered that some of the weapons purchased by the Silver Shirts had come from the US Navy base at San Diego. See *The Failure of Nazism in America: The German American Bund, 1936–1941* by Leland V. Bell in *Political Science Quarterly*, Vol. 85, No. 4 (Dec 1970), pp. 585–599 and *William Dudley Pelley, An American Nazi in King Arthur's Court* by Kevin J. Harty in *Arthuriana*, Vol. 26, No. 2, pp. 64–85.

14   Healey, who published the anti-Semitic hate sheets *Healey's Irish Weekly* and *Nordics Awake!* was jailed in June 1935 for inciting violence against Jews. Un-American Activities Committee co-chairman Rep. Sam Dickstein subsequently became a Soviet spy. The Russians had, however, a low opinion of their man

in Congress, describing him as 'a complete racketeer and a blackmailer'. Yeadon & Hawkins: 2008 p. 129 *et passim*. *Soviet Spies: Did they make a difference?* Review article by Tim Weiner in *World Policy Journal* Vol. 16, No. 1, pp. 101–103. For German immigration to the US see *Deutsche in den Vereiniten Staaten: Räumliche Verteilung und Bestimmungsgründe ihrere Binnenwanderungen* by Sabine Henning in *Erkunde* Vol. 53, pp. 177–190. *'It Can't Happen Here': Fascism and Right-Wing Extremism in Pennsylvania, 1933–1942*. Author: Philip Jenkins. Source: *Pennsylvania History*, Vol. 62, No. 1 (Winter 1995), pp. 31–58. President conference with Hoover, Treasury Secretary Morgenthau *et al* on 8 May 1934. Gentry: 2001 p. 201 *et passim*.

15   With more than 30 such cases crowding his in-tray by October 1933, Ambassador William E. Dodd was understandably irate when German Foreign Minister Konstantin von Neurath kept him waiting for six hours while he lunched with a visiting Chilean diplomat. It was a coldly calculated snub, delivered in part because the Ambassador, a feisty liberal democrat, had given a speech in Berlin the previous evening condemning totalitarianism and economic nationalism.

Isabel Steele later wrote and starred in *I Was a Captive of Nazi Germany*, a truly dire movie based on her experiences. Her seventeen-year-old sister Marian announced that she was returning to Germany to wed the very same army officer, Kurt Lamprecht, who had denounced Isabel to the Gestapo. Brigitte Helm was considered guilty of 'race defilement' as she had once been married to a Jew. Interrogated and briefly imprisoned, she subsequently married a rich industrialist and went to live in Switzerland. She never acted again.

British, Dutch, Czech, Austrian, Russian and Swiss citizens also suffered at the hands of the Gestapo. English teacher W.W. Mann spent three days in Alexanderplatz jail in 1933, *Daily Telegraph* journalist Noel Panter was jailed for several weeks and elderly British train spotter Rawdon Charlewood spent six weeks in Moabit Prison after he was seen noting down details of rolling stock in Frankfurt Station. Ill and traumatised, he was released on 7 December 1935. See contemporary press accounts and *Hollywood and Hitler* by Thomas Docherty, a Columbia University Press e-book published in 2013.

16 Thompson was paid from a San Francisco bank account managed by one Eisuke Ono, whose daughter Yoko would become the artist wife of John Lennon. *Japanese Intelligence – A Suitable Case for Treatment* by John W.M. Chapman in *Intelligence and International Relations 1900–1945*. Gentry: 2001 p. 205. KV 4/443.

17 President meeting with Hoover and Hull, 25 August 1936. Gentry: 2001 p. 201 *et passim*. See also Summers: 2012 and *Informing FDR: FBI Political Surveillance and the Isolationist-Interventionist Foreign Policy Debate, 1939–1945* by Douglas M. Charles in *Diplomatic History*, Vol. 24, No. 2 (Spring 2000), pp. 211–232.

18 Rumrich 'Life History' in Bureau HQ file 65–748–783. Tamm memorandum *op cit*.

19 The Gestapo had, apparently, some difficulty with their search as Senta had changer her name from Dirlewanger to Dewanger on emigrating to the US. There is no evidence that her relatives were harmed. See OSS Washington Secret Intelligence Special Funds Records, WASH-SPDF-INT-1 document 9404 p. 3. Accessed via Fold3.com.

20 *Ibid.*

21 Turrou: 1939 p. 64.

22 Tamm memorandum *op. cit.* Turrou: 1939 p. 68 *et passim*.

23 Arrival date and biographical details from www.ellisisland.org.

24 The former Schwabenhalle at 593 Springfield Avenue survives in 2022 as a bar. As a Jew, mobster Abner 'Longy' Zwillman was no lover of the Nazis. But his thugs were equally prepared to crack heads at socialist and communist meetings and sending his men to break up the Schwabenhalle meeting was primarily about protecting his organised crime interests. Zwillman is perhaps better remembered for bribing Columbia Studios boss Harry Cohn to get his mistress, Jean Harlow, Hollywood's 'Platinum Blonde', a two-picture deal with Columbia Pictures. Walter Kauf spent six months in the County Penitentiary for his part in the night's events. See press accounts for the Springfield riot on 16 October 1933.

25 For the launch of *Die Brücke*, see the *New York Times*, 10 July 1933. The paper folded at the end of 1933 after just eight issues. It was relaunched in 1934 as *Das Neue Deutschland*, once again published by Dr I.T. Griebl. For Griebl's resignation from Harlem Hospital, see the *New York Times*, 21 November 1933.

26 *New York Times* 29 March 1935. Antoinette Heim was revealed as a deeply unpleasant con artist whose crimes included defrauding her own servants. She was sentenced to three years' jail in June 1942. *New York Times* 3 June 1942.

27 Griebl did not entirely lack a sense of humour, as Jewish journalist Arnold Levin recalled: 'At all his meetings which I covered diligently for the Jewish press, he would turn towards the press corner, shake his finger at me, and bowing with mock grace, smile and hiss, "The lying Jewish press . . ."' *The Canadian Jewish Chronicle* 31 August 1935. For the House Un-American Activities Committee hearing at the Bar Association Building in Manhattan on 18 May 1934, see various press accounts including the *New York Sun*, 18 May 1934, and the *New York Times*, 19 May 1934. For the Madison Square Garden meeting, see the *New York Times*, 7 October 1934.

28 Turrou: 1939 pp. 106–107.

29 Liddell to Vivian, 10 March 1938 in KV 2/3533.

30 Neilans notebook transcript from Tayside Police Museum. See also Neilans precognition in KV 2/3534.

Chapter 6

1 Many years after these events an old blue police notebook was found at the back of a desk drawer in the Dundee CID office. A remarkable find that survives today in the collection of Tayside Police Museum, it turned out to be a verbatim record of Jessie Jordan's first interrogation by Chief Constable Joe Neilans and Edward Hinchley Cooke recorded in neat Pitman's shorthand by Neilans.

2 This suggests that the version of the sketch found by Mary Curran must have been the original from which she had made a fair copy to send to Hamburg.

3 Nicholson precognition in KV 2/3534.

4   Neilans notebook transcript from Tayside Police Museum. Hinchley Cooke, Neilans, Ross, Nicholson and Carstairs trial precognitions in KV 2/3534.

5   KV 2/365. Else Duncombe's post-mortem was carried out by Sir Bernard Spilsbury (1877–1947) and her death certificate was signed by coroner William Bentley Purchase (1890–1961). These two officials were often used by intelligence services in sensitive cases, not least that of Glyndwr Michael, the tramp whose body was used in the Operation Mincemeat deception in 1942. While Spilsbury's case index cards and notebooks, held today by the Wellcome Collection Library in London, include a number of cases of suicide by aspirin overdose, there is, understandably, no record for Else Duncombe. Wellcome Collection ref. PP/SPI/B. Else's funeral was organised and paid for by Hugh Grant Langmore (1870–1953), a 69-year-old retired bank manager who had spent time in Germany in the early years of the 20th century and had married a German. Beyond that, while it is possible that Else may once have worked for the Langmores, it has not been possible to confirm a connection between Langmore and Duncombe. See Hendon Cemetery Register, 8 March 1938, accessed via Ancestry.com.

6   For Griebl's account of the Germany trip, see FBI New York Field Office case summary dated 7 July 1938 in Bureau HQ file ref.: 65–748–783.

7   Astoria summer variety programme for 1937 from *Bremer Zeitung* dated 4 June 1937.

8   KV 2/267. KV 2/1973. Bureau HQ file ref.: 65–748–783 and Turrou: 1939 pp. 7–16.

9   In his book, Turrou writes that it was he who, during the search of Griebl's office the night before, spotted the match book 'in a corner of Griebl's personal desk'. This is not borne out by FBI documents, not least the Tamm memorandum, which make it clear that the match book was in a desk drawer and was only found after Griebl was asked about enciphered letters the following day, 26 February, at the earliest. Tamm memorandum *op. cit.* p. 31. Turrou: 1939 pp. 109–110.

10   Bureau HQ file 65–748–783.

11   *Ibid*. Tamm memorandum *op. cit.*

12   *Ibid*. Zaech case from *Indifference to Internent: An examination*

of RCMP responses to Nazism and Fascism in Canada. Thesis by Michelle McBride, Department of History, Memorial University of Newfoundland 1997. From 1934 to 1941.

13 Guy Liddell (MI5) report in VNST II 2/21, Vansittart Papers, Churchill College, Cambridge University.

14 KV 2/1973.

15 KV 2/267.

16 For Driscoll see, *inter alia, The Neglected Giant: Agnes Meyer Driscoll* by Kevin Wade Johnson pub. in 2015 by The National Security Agency, Center for Cryptologic History. See also House of Representatives Committee on Claims Report No. 1099 dated 24 June 1937 *Maude P. Gresham and Agnes M. Driscoll.*

17 Tamm memorandum to Director Hoover, 5 April 1938. Bureau HQ file 65–748–320.

18 KV 2/267.

19 *Ibid.*

20 An MI5 memorandum dated 3 March 1938 shows that the British were quick to make the connection between the passport blanks scheme and the Ikal case, possibly after having been prompted do so by MI6. They passed their theory on to the FBI, also making the point that anyone entering the Soviet Union on an American passport, not least an Abwehr agent, would attract unwelcome attention. Arnold Ikal died in a Gulag. Ruth was released in 1939 and elected to stay in the Soviet Union as she faced arrest should she return to the United States. Morgan: 2020 pp. 159–160. Kern: 2008 pp. 200–201. Guy Liddell memorandum in KV 2/3533.

21 Bureau HQ file 65–748–783. William Butler Brown (1914–1959) served through the Second World War, rising to the rank of commander.

22 Crown letter, intercepted on 27 January 1938, in KV 2/193. For a template Rumrich had used President Roosevelt's memorandum to Cordell Hull, reproduced in the *New York Times*, on the sinking by Japanese aircraft of the Yangtse River gunboat USS *Panay* on 12 December 1937, four years almost to the day before Pearl Harbor.

23 Rumrich believed that 'Schmidt' was a crewman aboard the

Hamburg-Amerika liner *Hamburg*, and 'Schmidt's' recorded meetings with Rumrich, including that on 4 January 1938, do coincide with the ship's arrivals in New York. See relevant issues of the *New York Times* for shipping movements and KV 2/267 for Pfeiffer statement.

24 Bureau HQ file 65–748–320. Griebl actually had $162 in his wallet of which Ahrens took $156 to cover his fare in Tourist class.

25 *Ibid.*

26 Liddell report of meeting with Hardy in KV 2/3533.

27 Bureau HQ file 65–748–320.

28 Isidor (1887–1942) and Helene (1892–1942) are commemorated today in Giessen with brass plaques in the pavement outside Alicenstrasse 16. Their son Lothar (1914–1993) had emigrated to Palestine in 1935. Karla (1924–2015) escaped to Palestine with her brother's help in 1939. Berliners story from the *Bundesarchiv Memorial Book* and www.giessen.de. For Maria Griebl's letter see Turrou: 1939 pp. 219–220. For the transfer of the Tompkins Corners property see the *Peekskill Evening Star*, 21 May 1938.

Chapter 7

1 KV 2/3534.

2 *Names of Streets in Teplice in History and at Present*. Thesis by Ludmila Mráčková. Univerzita Hradec Králové, 2016.

3 KV 2/267.

4 KV 2/3534. KV2/3421.

5 Gibson's contact was almost certainly Colonel, later Brigadier General, František Moravec (1895–1966), in 1937 and 1938 the deputy head, and later head, of operations in Czech Military Intelligence. Jeffrey 2010.

6 Paillole: 2003 p. 83. Paillole article in *Historama No. 1* 1978. Born in 1899 the son of a successful Constantinople-based British businessman and a Russian countess, Wilfred Dunderdale went to school in the Ukraine and acquired the nickname 'Biffy' due to his prowess as an amateur boxer. More widely known as Bill Dunderdale, he was an extraordinary

character and friend of Ian Fleming who had a Bondesque love for fast cars and fast women, he wore hand-made suits and was often to be seen being chauffeured around Paris in a large, allegedly bullet-proof Rolls-Royce. He successfully combined a high-profile life with a very successful espionage career.

7 A copy of the letter handed over by Hinchley Cooke has unfortunately not survived in the MI5 archives. The description of both the meeting and the content of the letter is drawn from Paillole: 2003 p. 83 *et passim*.

8 KV 2/356. Paillole: 2003 p. 83 *et passim*. Paillole article in *Historama, hors serié No. 35* 1978 pp. 78–83.

9 For Lydia's arrest and contents of suitcases, see various contemporary press accounts.

10 Lydia would later claim to have fended off the advances of a fellow passenger on the *Santa Maria* who promised to make her a movie star in return for becoming his mistress, but none of the other passengers could be described as anything remotely resembling her 'fabulously rich businessman'. For Lydia's movements, see passenger manifests for SS *Montclare* sailing Cherbourg on 15 August 1929, SS *Champlain* sailing Le Havre on 10 August 1932 and SS *Santa Maria* sailing San Cristobal on 21 December 1932.

11 Lydia was not, however, a success as a journalist. Her career lasted only a few days before, as one colleague put it, 'we realised that this sort of work did not suit Lydia Oswald'. *Journal de Genève*, 14 March 1935.

12 There was, in fact, nothing revolutionary about the *Emile Bertin*'s weaponry. Her 550mm torpedo tubes, which the Germans seem to have been particularly interested in, were based on a 1920 design and the French Model 23D torpedo was a likewise tried and trusted design with broadly similar performance to the German G7A 533mm torpedo, though they were electrically propelled unlike the German torpedoes which were steam driven and left a tell-tale trail of bubbles. The only lead generated in St Malo concerned a nightclub singer who had travelled to Brest carrying glass jars similar to the one containing opium in Lydia's suitcase and there was a suspicion that she might be their drug dealer. It turned out that the girl's

mother was in the habit of sending her jam and the glass jars were merely empties being returned. One possible source of the opium was lieutenant de vaisseau Pierre Cherriere, a shipmate of de Forceville's, who was arrested in July 1935 while trying to smuggle a large quantity of opium out of Brest naval base. *Le Temps*, 26 July 1935.

13 Due to woeful French security, Lydia Oswald's story was covered in detail by the French and Swiss press. See also Reiss: 1941 p. 208 *et passim*, Mader: 1974 p. 306 and KV2/3386. Paillole: 2003 p. 12 *et passim* makes brief reference to the Oswald case, but Paillole conflates details of the Oswald case with that of Lydia Stahl and mistakenly captions a photograph of Lydia Oswald as Lydia Stahl.

14 Paillole: 2003 p. 83 *et passim*. Paillole article in *Historama, hors serié No. 35* 1978 pp. 78–83. Contemporary French press accounts covered Aubert's background and relationship with Morel in great detail.

15 KV 2/267.

16 *Ibid.*

17 Sources on the 1938 Munich Agreement are numerous. For the intelligence sources, see Andrew: 2009 pp. 200–207. For the diplomacy, see Stewart: 1999 pp. 295–309.

18 KV 2/356.

19 Harker memorandum dated 5 November 1938 in KV 2/356. For Archer promotion, see Liddell diary entry for 16 July 1941 in KV 4/188

20 KV 2/356. See also a case summary in the diary of MI5 officer Guy Liddell in KV 4/466.

Chapter 8

1 Bureau HQ file 65–748–320. Turrou: 1939 pp. 260–263. *New York Times* 29 May 1938 and 3 June 1938.

2 *New York Times* 10 June 1938.

3 *Ibid.* 10 and 12 June 1938. German Consul General Hans Borcher had also admitted that he had forwarded a letter in mid-April that granted Griebl permission to practise in Germany.

4 Draper: 1962 pp. 151–154.

5   *New York Times* 3 December 1938.

6   MI6 memorandum to Hinchley Cooke dated 10 January 1938 KV 2/356.

7   *Ibid.* KV 2/267. Paillole: 2003 p. 83 *et passim*.

8   *L'ouest-éclair* 11 January 1939 and *Petit Journal* 11 January 1939 have good coverage of the trial and sentencing.

9   For coverage of the Verdot disappearance see *L'ouest-éclair* 7 January 1939 among numerous other publications.

10 *New York Times* 1 July 1938.

11 *Ibid.* 2 July 1938. For Hoover and the FBI Recreational Association see Gentry: 2001 pp. 448–449.

12 Birdwell: 1999 p. 70.

13 *New York Post* 3 December 1938 *et passim*. *New York Times* 5 February 1939

14 The Groucho Marx comment, made at a Hollywood Anti-Nazi League meeting in Edward G. Robinson's home, was quoted in the *Hollywood Reporter* on 6 December 1938. For the Make-Up Men's Association decision see the *New York Times* 6 January 1939.

15 Birdwell: 1999 ch. 3.

16 *New York Times* 29 January 1939. *Variety* 3 May 1939. Extracted from *Deutscher Weckruf und Beobachter,* 6 August 39, as quoted in *Anti-Nazi sentiment in film: Confessions of a Nazi Spy and the German-American Bund.* Eric J. Sandeen. Published by the Mid-America American Studies Association in *American Studies*, Vol. 20, No. 2 (Fall 1979), pp. 69–81.

17 CO 859/6/9.

18 *Variety* 24 April 1940. Kalamajski, also a prominent industrialist, survived and died in 1949.

19 For an assessment of the film, see *Confessions of a Nazi Spy* by Jacqui Miller in *Film and Ethics – What Would You Have Done?* Cambridge Scholars Press 2013.

Chapter 9

1   Alesch was shot by firing squad in 1949. Carré, code-named La Chatte by Abwehr, persuaded her case officer Hugo Bleicher to send her to Britain early in 1942. She immediately confessed

and, after being run as a treble agent for a few months, was imprisoned. Handed over to the French after the war, she was tried for treason and condemned to death. The sentence commuted to life imprisonment, she was released in 1954 and died aged 94 in 2007.

2   The Lena agent who was not captured, Dutchman Jan Willem ter Braak, evaded capture until March 1941 when, having been abandoned by his Abwehr masters, he shot himself in a Cambridge air raid shelter. German historian Monika Siedentopf has written that the Operation Lena agents were deliberately chosen to fail by anti-Nazi elements within Abwehr. Siedentopf: 2014.

3   According to a 1938 internal directory, MI5 employed a total of just 45 staff, 26 of whom were officers and the rest support personnel, compared with around 4,400 in 2022. KV 4/127. See also Andrew: 2009 p. 182.

4   KV 4/394.

5   Liddell was taking notes in Turrou's office on 5 April when Griebl phoned in with news that three members of the Ordnungsdienst, small groups of American Nazis drilling in Nazi uniforms, were planning to leave aboard the liner *New York* the following day. Turrou secured a warrant for their arrest and, as he boarded the *Queen Mary* for his own passage back to Southampton two days later, Liddell read in the *New York Times* that Wilhelm Böning, Johann Unkel and Karl Hermann had been picked up. A warrant was also issued for the arrest of Ewald Rossberg, said to be a member of the Gestapo. They were not included on the Federal Grand Jury indictment. Vansittart Papers *op. cit.* Nobody, least of all Guy Liddell, could have foreseen the lengths to which an untouchable and increasingly paranoid J. Edgar Hoover would, along with a cabal of deeply unpleasant witch-hunters, not least the drunken Wisconsin Senator Joe McCarthy, stretch that self-acquired remit a decade later. KV 4/394.

6   'Much better informed . . .' Smith: 2011 p. 150.

7   The MI5 surveillance operation on Rutland, widely known as Rutland of Jutland for his exploits as a seaplane pilot during the eponymous sea battle in 1916, had its moments. There was the

time when he and his mistress were strolling through St James's Park one summer's evening in 1923, apparently too intent on each other to notice the MI5 Watchers following at a discreet distance. But if Rutland had missed the Watchers in the park, he certainly spotted them the next morning as he drove away from the RAF Club in Mayfair. Thinking they were private detectives employed by his jealous wife, Rutland swerved his car across the front of MI5's taxi and, as the MI5 B.4 Watcher Section history records:

> . . . jumped out, charged like a maniac towards us, opened the door of our cab, sprang inside and planted himself across the doorway. He was certainly angry – in fact, very angry. Roaring, 'Now I'll know who and what you are, and who instructed you to follow me,' he drew himself up and adopted a very threatening attitude. As Rutland had been a Service boxing champion we had visions of a rough house, so it was policy to go canny. When his invective had died down somewhat, he was quietly asked what all the trouble was about; this ridiculous talk of following him was all Greek to us, this was not the Continent, such things were not done in England, etc, etc. All we were concerned with was catching our train which went in a quarter of an hour from Victoria. The driver of our cab was one of the good old type and played up well, and when asked, 'Where did these men ask you to drive?' he replied, 'Victoria,' without blinking an eyelid. Then, to our great surprise and, needless to add, to our great relief, Rutland began to waver, and finally he apologised and departed.

Confronted later by MI5, Rutland was told that he had indeed been followed and, recalling the incident in Piccadilly, said, 'So I was right; but I thought my wife had put those on to me as she was trying to get a divorce.' Repatriated to Britain by the Americans early in the war and interned, he committed suicide in 1949. KV 4/443. Jeffery: 2010 ch. 8, *Working with the Americans*. See also *Japanese Intelligence – A Suitable Case for Treatment* by John W.M. Chapman in *Intelligence and International Relations 1900–1945.*

8   KV 2/394. Jeffery *ibid.*

9   KV 2/543. Bearse & Read: 1991 p. 64 *et passim.* Willets: 2015 pt. 3, ch. 1. Hemming: 2017 ch. 37.

10   For Cowgill's report of his 14 February 1940 meeting with Herschel Johnson, see KV 2/755. This file also contains Guy Liddell's response dated 16 February. For the case of Foreign Office clerk and Soviet spy John Herbert King, his mistress Helen Wilkie and others, see KV 2/815 and KV 2/816. For Kurt Jahnke see *K. A. Jahnke and the German Sabotage Campaign in the United States and Mexico, 1914–1918* by Richard B. Spence pub. in *The Historian*, Vol. 59, No. 1 (Fall 1996), pp. 89–112 and KV 2/755. For Krivitsky see TNA file series beginning KV 2/802.

11   KV 2/543. Bearse & Read *op. cit.*, Willetts *op. cit.*

12   KV 2/543. Masters: 1984 p. 88.

13   Colville: 1986 pp. 157–159.

14   For the pencil copy of the telegram in Kent's pocket, see Max Knight memorandum dated 20 June 1940 in KV 2/543.

15   Pearson report dated 22 May 1940 in KV 2/543.

16   Masters *op. cit.* p. 89. Sources on the correspondence between Roosevelt and 'Former Naval Person', Churchill's nom de plume, include Jenkins: 2001 ch. 29.

17   Sempill associated himself with a range of pro-fascist and pro-Nazi causes including the Anglo-German Fellowship, The Link, the Nordic League and the Right Club in the 1930s. Given what was to come, it was unfortunate that he lavished praise on two Japanese airmen, Iinuma (pilot) and Tsukagoshi, who had flown from Tokyo to London in 94 hours 17 minutes in 1937, their aircraft emblazoned with the words Kamikaze-Go (Divine Wind). Rejoining the Royal Naval Volunteer Reserve soon after the outbreak of war, he gave an undertaking that he would cease all contact with the Japanese. Yet MI5 surveillance revealed that, driven no doubt by an enormous back overdraft, he had maintained contact with Japanese diplomats and continued to pocket consultancy fees or, as he termed them, 'little presents from Japan'. Towards the end of 1940 a source told

MI5 officer Derek Tangye that the King's brother, the Duke of Kent, had described Sempill as 'a first-class swine'. MI5 maintained their surveillance and there is evidence that Sempill was considered for 18B detention though the proposal seems to have been dropped. Made aware of Sempill's conduct on 9 October 1940, two months before the Pearl Harbor raid that he had done so much to enable, Prime Minister Churchill minuted, 'Clear him out while time remains.' Sempill was duly 'invited to resign his commission' by the Second Sea Lord the following day. *The Guardian* 16 April 1937. He died in 1962. KV 2/871.

18 Bullitt, then US Ambassador to France, quoted in memorandum from Ronald Campbell to Sir Alexander Cadogan dated 8 June 1940. KV 2/543. Long quote from Andrew: 2009 p. 226.

19 Marked in pencil, 'Found in light brown suitcase' and 'Original found in property of Kent when he was searched . . .', two of the MI5 messages have survived in Kent's case file. One message, sent to consul Neal D. Borum at the American Embassy on 19 October 1939, two weeks after Kent arrived in London from his previous posting in Moscow, concerned Soviet NKVD agents Sonja Evelyn Strand and Terence Edward Stephens whom MI5 believed were then in New York. The daughter of Swedish immigrants and a Moscow-trained radio operator, Strand had been born in Boston, Massachusetts, in June 1910. Stephens, likewise a Moscow-trained radio operator, was from Bristol in England. Liddell's information that Terence Stephens was in America was wrong; he had died of blood poisoning in Barcelona in July 1938 while serving with the International Brigade in the Spanish Civil War and is recorded on the International Brigade Memorial in Castle Park, Bristol. Sonja Evelyn Strand married Charles Dibner in New York in 1941 and died in Florida in 1989.

The other surviving message, addressed to Herschel Johnson, referred to Soviet agents Mikhail Borovoy alias Willi Brandes and Jozef Volodsky alias Armand Labis Feldman. Borovoy alias Brandes alias Mr Stephens had been mixed up on the Woolwich Arsenal spy plot in Britain but had escaped the MI5 net. Hoover's biographer Curt Gentry claims that, during their first meeting on 16 April 1940, Stephenson had tipped off the

FBI Director about Tyler Kent. But the Kent case was still in its infancy when Stephenson left for the United States and was in any case, being run by MI5's Max Knight, who played his cards very close to his chest, while Stephenson was working for MI6. There is no known evidence that anyone in the United States was aware of Kent's treachery before Knight's meeting with Herschel Johnson on 18 May 1940. Gentry: 1991 p. 264. For Stephenson quote see Jeffery: 2010 ch. 13.

20　Bennett: 2009 pp. 193–194 and 253 *et passim*. Stephenson shared Hoover's tendency for brazen self promotion, later elevating his role to that of Churchill's personal representative in the United States even though, as Foreign Office historian Gill Bennett writes, there is no evidence that he ever met or even spoke to the Prime Minister. The name British Security Coordination was given to Stephenson's organisation by the FBI. For a precis of the formation of BSC, see MI5 memorandum dated 15 July 1941 in KV 4/394. Bennett: 2009 p. 253–254. Liddell diary entry for 30 November 1940 in KV 4/187. KV 4/446. KV 4/447.

21　Liddell diary entry for 11 December 1940 *op. cit.* In his explanatory note for the edited 11 December entry in the published version of Guy Liddell's diaries, *The Guy Liddell Diaries, Volume I: 1939–1942: 1939–1942: MI5's Director of Counter-Espionage in World War II* (Routledge: 2005), Nigel West wrongly credits Liddell with having personally taken the evidence that led to FBI to Rumrich to Washington. The evidence was, as we have seen, passed by MI5 to the American embassy in London. Nor did Turrou, as West suggests, claim all the credit for himself.

22　Clegg's claim of 30 double agents, assuming it was correctly recorded, is wildly overstating the case as Sebold was the only double in the Duquesne ring. The Voluntary Interceptors (V.I.s) of the Radio Security Service (RSS) were mainly pre-war amateur enthusiasts originally tasked in 1939 with tracking illicit transmissions from stations in Britain. In May 1940 the emphasis changed to the interception of enemy wireless traffic from outside Britain. Originally set up and run by MI5, the RSS was taken over by MI6 in 1941. Contrary to what David

Charles suggests in his 2005 on the subject, the two FBI representatives were not allowed anywhere near the Government Code & Cyper School at Bletchley Park. Liddell diary for 10 and 17 January 1941 in KV 4/187. David M. Charles (2005) *'Before the Colonel Arrived': Hoover, Donovan, Roosevelt, and the Origins of American Central Intelligence, 1940–41*, pub. in *Intelligence and National Security*, 20:2, 225–237.

23 Liddell *op. cit.* 22 January 1941. See also Weiner: 2012 ch. 12. Borne: 2015 ch. 7.

24 Much of the trans-Atlantic message traffic in 1941 was generated by the possible infiltration of enemy agents into the thousands of American personnel, among them 30,000 members of a Civilian Technical Corps tasked, more than five months before America joined the European war, with constructing bases for the US Navy and Army Air Corps. See MI5 memorandum dated 19 July 1941 in KV 4/394. For Hoover's 7 March 1941 letter see KV 4/446. Gentry: 2001 pp. 265–266.

25 *The Role of British Intelligence in the Mythologies Underpinning the OSS and early CIA* in *American-British-Canadian Intelligence Relations 1939–2000*. David Stafford and Rhodri Jeffreys-Jones eds. (Routledge 2000). For the Ellis role in the establishment of COI, see Dorril: 2000 pp. 50–51 quoting *The Last American Aristocrat: The Biography of David K.E. Bruce* by Nelson D. Lankford. Gentry *op. cit.* p. 266. Stafford and Jeffreys-Jones *op. cit.* p.7. Stephenson to Menzies quoted in Bennett: 2009 p. 257.

26 For the Hawaii questionnaire, see KV 2/849.

27 In fairness to Hoover, whether the service chiefs would have seen the questionnaire for what it was and taken appropriate action on the Hawaii defences is debatable. Hoover would, in an April 1946 *Readers Digest* article, dishonestly take the credit for having discovered the Germans' use of microdot technology, a breakthrough handed to the FBI by Popov and MI5. Knightley: 1986 p. 150. Gentry *op. cit.* pp. 270–271. Miller: 2005 ch. 6.

28 KV 4/190.

29 KV 4/190. KV 4/394.

30 For a detailed account of the Tizard Mission, see *Top Secret*

Exchange: The Tizard Mission and the Scientific War. David Zimmerman. Alan Sutton Publishing, 1996

31 Strong telegram to Chief of Staff General George C. Marshall dated 5 September 1940 in NSA Historical Papers https://www.nsa.gov/Helpful-Links/NSA-FOIA/Declassification-Transparency-Initiatives/Historical-Releases/UKUSA/smdpage14704/2/ *Early Papers concerning US–UK Agreement 1940–1944.*

32 The first Turing Bombe electro-mechanical code-breaking machine was operational on 18 March 1940 and the second, with important modifications designed by Welchman was put into operation on 18 August 1940. Sebag-Montefiore: 2000 pp. 55–56.

33 In what must have been an attempt to hoodwink his less cryptographically aware superiors, Safford even suggested that cooperation against Axis ciphers would somehow lead to the British being able to read American ciphers (which they had been doing for years anyway). Safford was notoriously averse to sharing US Navy cryptology information with anyone, even the US Army. Safford was sidelined after Pearl Harbor. Smith: 2001 pp. 99–100. See also Smith: 2011 ch. 7.

34 National Security Agency (NSA) oral history file NSA-OH-02–79 to NSA-OH-04–79 Dr Abraham Sinkov, May 1979 accessed via https://www.nsa.gov/Helpful-Links/NSA-FOIA/Declassification-Transparency-Initiatives/Historical-Releases/UKUSA/ That extraordinarily important late-night sherry party is commemorated today by a plaque on the wall of Denniston's office at Bletchley Park. Barbara Eachus née Abernethy quoted in Smith: 2001 pp. 100–101.

35 *The First Americans: The 1941 US Codebreaking Mission to Bletchley Park.* Paper by David Sherman published by The National Security Agency Center for Cryptologic History, 2016.

36 Sinkov oral history interview, NSA *op cit.*

37 Hughes-Wilson: 2017 pp. 237–238. Sebag Montefiore: 2004 p. 357 *et passim.* See also Gabriel Gorodetsky. *Grand Delusion: Stalin and the German Invasion of Russia.* Yale University Press, 1999.

Afterword

1 HO 45/25733.

2 Etta Shiber returned to New York and died in 1948. Kitty Bonnefous was released from a prison camp in Poland by Russian forces in 1945. Born Kate Robins, the daughter of stationer and printer Charles Robins and his wife Emily in London in 1886, after the war she was awarded both an MBE and a Croix de Guerre. She died at her London home in November 1965. The womens' story was told in somewhat bowdlerised form in Etta Shiber's ghost-written book *Paris Underground* published in 1943 and in a movie of the same name released in 1945.

The Players

1 *German Espionage in South County Dublin*. Paper by James Scannell read to the Old Dublin Society, 28 March 2001.

2 KV 2/1322.

3 Marga's marriage to Tom Reid, a divorcee, was almost certainly bigamous. Tracked down by a journalist after the war, Marga's first husband, Hermann Wobrock, denied ever having divorced her following their 1935 separation. Marga Reid death certificate from Hamburg, Germany, Deaths, 1874–1950 accessed via Ancestry.com.

4 Jessie Jordan's death in 1954 is recorded on her 1912 marriage certificate. Accessed via Ancestry.com.

5 Among the patriotic verses composed by Ignatz Griebl (sen.) was *Heimatliebe*, a song for chorus and piano accompaniment published in 1916 and held today by the Bayerische Staatsbibliothek in Munich. Translated from German, it reads:

> Oh I love you, my homeland,
> My delightful, sunny Franconia? -
> O heavenly home! I greet you!
> My home soil! I kiss you!
> You are ever in my thoughts.
> Fly high, brave red and white flag,

May my Franconia flourish forever!
Do I love you, my Bavarian country,
You pearl in German waters? -
From snowy white cornfields up to the high Rhon,
Your valleys, your mountains,
Are so beautiful to behold!
I wrap your blue and white flag around my heart,
My dearest, my dearest, my Bavaria!
How much do I love you, my Germany,
this bloody contested earth? -
I give you all my possessions and property;
My meaning and my being and my last drop of blood
Belong to you, my splendid country.
Show us the way to victory, black and red flag,
God protect you, God protect you, my Fatherland!

6   For Griebl's arrival at Bremen, see *Völkischer Beobachter* for 22 May 1938. A Czech-born Jew, Dr Herbert Kulka escaped with his wife, Helene, first to Britain and then, in March 1940, to the United States. Dr Kulka died in San Francisco in 1964 and Helene Kulka died in 1995. Genealogical data accessed via Ancestry.com.

7   Maria would find herself involved in a similar dispute with a Jewish family over another apartment block in Neuwaldgasse, Vienna. See US Army Property Control Branch files PC/V/XIX/94 Ignatz Theodor Griebl and PC/V/I/3 Maria Griebl accessed via Fold3.com.

8   *Welt Express* 9 February 1948. *Welt am Abend* 10 February 1948 accessed from Österreichische Nationalbibliothek via onb.ac.at.

9   KV 2/267.

10   Jeffreys-Jones: 2020 pp. 191–193.

11   KV 2/194.

Acknowledgements

Many individuals and organisations have contributed to this project in the years since my interest in the short, unsuccessful career of Jessie Jordan, Nazi spy, was first kindled in the late 1980s. I am grateful to them all, but must make special mention of members of the Curran family, in particular the late Catherine Gray and her daughter Sharon Gray; members of the Haddow family, in particular Donald Haddow; the late Ralph Erskine; Professor Rhodri Jeffreys-Jones; the late Peter Fletcher; and Wilma Milne. My thanks also to the excellent team at Birlinn Publishing, notably Hugh Andrew and Andrew Simmons, to my copy-editor Ian Greensill, and to my literary agent, Tom Cull.

Select Bibliography

Published works

Andrew, Christopher. *The Defence of the Realm – The Authorised History of MI5*. Allen Lane, 2009

Baillie-Stewart, Norman. *The Officer in the Tower*. Leslie Frewin, 1967

Barnes, James and Barnes, Patience. *Nazis in Pre-War London, 1930-1939: The Fate and Role of German Party Members and British Sympathizers: The Fate & Role of German Party Members & British Sympathisers*. Sussex Academic Press, 2010

Bassett, Richard. *Hitler's Spy Chief – The Wilhelm Canaris Mystery*. Weidenfeld & Nicolson, 2005

Batvinis, Raymond J. *The Origins of FBI Counterintelligence*. University Press of Kansas, 2007

Bearse, Ray and Read, Anthony. *Conspirator – The Untold Story of Churchill, Roosevelt and Tyler Kent, Spy*. Macmillan, 1991

Bennett, Gill. *Churchill's Man of Mystery – Desmond Morton and the World of Intelligence*. Routledge, 2009

Birdwell, Michael E. *Celluloid Soldiers – Warner Bros' Campaign against Nazism*. New York University Press, 1999

Borne, Ronald F. *Troutmouth – The Two Careers of Hugh Clegg*. University Press of Mississippi, 2015

Brammer, Uwe. *Spionageabwehr und Geheimer Meldedienst – Die Abwehrstelle im Wehrkreis X Hamburg, 1935–1945*. Rombach GMBH, 1989

Colville, John. *The Fringes of Power – Downing Street Diaries Volume One: 1939–October 1941*. Sceptre, 1986

Delmer, Sefton. *Trail Sinister: An Autobiography, Volume One*. Secker & Warburg, 1961

Diest, Wilhelm, et al. *Germany and the Second World War: Volume 1: The Build-up of German Aggression.* Clarendon Press, 1990

Doherty, Thomas. *Hollywood and Hitler 1933–1939.* Columbia University Press, 2013

Dorril, Stephen. *MI6 – Inside the Covert World of Her Majesty's Secret Intelligence Service.* The Free Press, 2000

Draper, Major Christopher, *The Mad Major.* Air Review, 1962

Edgerton, David. *The Shock of the Old: Technology and Global History Since 1900.* Oxford University Press, 2006

Elliott, Geoffrey. *Gentleman Spymaster – How Lt. Col. Tommy 'Tar' Robertson Double-Crossed the Nazis.* Methuen, 2011

Gentry, Curt. *J. Edgar Hoover – The Man and the Secrets.* Norton, 2001

Gilbert, Martin. *Finest Hour – Winston S. Churchill 1939–1941.* Minerva, 1989

Hayward, James. *Hitler's Spy, The True Story of Arthur Owens, Double Agent Snow.* Simon & Schuster, 2012

Hemming, Henry. *M – Maxwell Knight, MI5's Greatest Spymaster.* Penguin, 2017

Höhne, Heinz. *Canaris.* Secker & Warburg, 1979

Hooton, E.R. *Phoenix Triumphant – The Rise and Rise of the Luftwaffe.* Arms & Armour, 1994

Horne, Alistair. *To Lose a Battle – France 1940.* Papermac, 1990

Hughes-Wilson, John. *On Intelligence – The History of Espionage and the Secret World.* Constable, 2017

Jeffery, Keith. *MI6 – The History of the Secret Intelligence Service 1909–1949.* Bloomsbury, 2010

Jeffreys-Jones, Rhodri. *Ring of Spies – How MI5 and the FBI brought down the Nazis in America.* History Press, 2020

Kahn, David. *Hitler's Spies – German Military Intelligence in World War Two.* Macmillan, 1978

Keegan, John. *Intelligence in War.* Hutchinson, 2003

Kern, Harry. *A Death in Washington: Walter G. Krivitsky and the Stalin Terror.* Enigma Books, 2008

Knightley, Phillip. *The Second Oldest Profession – The Spy as Bureaucrat, Patriot, Fantasist and Whore.* Andrew Deutsch, 1986

Leverkuehn, Paul. *German Military Intelligence.* Weidenfeld & Nicolson, 1954

Macdonald, Bill. *The True Intrepid – Sir William Stephenson and the Unknown Agents*, Timberholme Books, 1998

Mader, Julius. *Hitlers Spionagegenarale sagen aus.* Verlag der Nation, 1974

Mahnken, Thomas G. *Uncovering Ways of War: U.S. Intelligence and Foreign Military Innovation 1918–1941.* Cornell University Press, 2001

Masters, Anthony. *The Man who was M – The Life of Maxwell Knight.* Basil Blackwell, 1984

May, Ernest R. *Strange Victory – Hitler's Conquest of France.* I.B. Taurus, 2000

Miller, Joan. *One Girl's War – Personal Exploits in MI5's Most Secret Station.* Brandon, 1986

Miller, Russell. *Codename Tricycle – The True Story of the Second World War's Most Extraordinary Double Agent.* Pimlico, 2005

Morgan, Ted. *Reds: McCarthyism in Twentieth-Century America.* Random House, 2020

Nekrich, Aleksandr et al. *Pariahs, Partners, Predators: German-Soviet Relations, 1922–1941.* Columbia University Press, 1997

Paillole, Paul. *Fighting the Nazis – French Intelligence and Counter-intelligence, 1935 –1945.* Enigma Books, 2003

Quinlan, Kevin. *The Secret War between the Wars – MI5 in the 1920s and 1930s.* Boydell Press, 2014

Reiss, Curt. *Total Espionage.* Putnam, 1941

Richelson, Jeffrey T. *A Century of Spies: Intelligence in the Twentieth Century.* Oxford University Press, 1997

Ritter, Nikolaus. *Deckname Dr Rantzau.* Hoffmann und Campe, 1972

Sebag-Montefiore, Hugh. *Enigma, The Battle for the Code.* Weidenfeld & Nicolson, 2000

Sebag Montefiore, Simon. *Stalin – The Court of the Red Tsar.* Orion, 2004

Siedentopf, Monika. *Unternehmen Seelöwe: Widerstand im deutschen Geheimdienst.* Deutscher Taschenbuch Verlag, 2014

Smith, Michael. *Station X – The Codebreakers of Bletchley Park*. Channel 4, 1998

Smith, Michael. *The Emperor's Codes*. Bantam, 2001

Smith, Michael. *The Secrets of Station X – How Bletchley Park Helped Win the War*. Biteback, 2011

Stafford, David. *Churchill & Secret Service*. Abacus, 2000

Stehlin, Paul. *Témoignage pour l'Histoire*. Robert Laffont, 1964

Stewart, Graham. *Burying Caesar: Churchill, Chamberlain and the Battle for the Tory Party*. Weidenfeld & Nicolson, 1999

Summers, Anthony. *Official and Confidential: The Secret Life of J Edgar Hoover*. Ebury Press 2012

Tate, Tim. *Hitler's British Traitors*. Icon Books, 2018

Terraine, John. *The Right of the Line – The Royal Air Force in the European War 1939–1945*. Hodder & Stoughton, 1985

Turrou, Leon. *The Nazi Spy Conspiracy in America*. Harrap, 1939

Weiner, Tim. *Enemies – A History of the FBI*. Allen Lane, 2012

Wala, Michael. *Weimar und Amerika: Botschafter Friedrich von Prittwitz und Gaffron und die deutsch-amerikanischen Beziehungen von 1927 bis 1933*. Franz Steiner Verlag, 2001

Wark, Wesley K. *The Ultimate Enemy : British intelligence and Nazi Germany, 1933-1939*. Cornell University Press, 2010

Weiner, Tim. *Enemies – A History of the FBI*. Allen Lane, 2012

West, Nigel. *MI5: British Security Service Operations, 1909–1945*. Bodley Head, 1981

West, Nigel. *At Her Majesty's Secret Service – The Chiefs of Britain's Intelligence Agency, MI6*. Greenhill Books, 2006

West, Nigel. *The Guy Liddell Diaries, Vol. 1: 1939–1942*. Routledge, 2005

Willetts, Paul. *Rendezvous at the Russian Tea Rooms: the spy, the lover and the man called 'M'*. Constable 2015

Yeadon, Glen & Hawkins, John: *Nazi Hydra in America: Suppressed History of a Century*. Progressive Press, 2008

Ziedler, Manfred. *Reichswehr und Rote Armee 1920–1933: Wege und Stationen einer ungewöhnlichen Zusammenarbeit, Ausgabe 2*. Walter de Gruyter GmbH & Co KG, 2006

Ziemke, Earl F. *The Red Army, 1918–1941: From Vanguard of World Revolution to US Ally,* Frank Cass, 2004

Papers and Articles

Andrew, Christopher. *Governments and Secret Services: A Historical Perspective.* Pub. in *International Journal,* Vol. 34, No. 2, *Knowledge and Power* (Spring 1979), pp. 167–186. Canadian International Council

Belot, Robert. *Intelligence Considered as a War Weapon and a Global Power Tool: About the Birth of US Secret Services (1942–1945).* Pub. in *Icon,* Vol. 8 (2002), pp. 55–75. International Committee for the History of Technology

Campbell, Kenneth. *Major General Friedrich Gempp, German Intelligence Leader.* Pub. in *American Intelligence Journal,* Vol. 25, No. 1 (Summer 2007), pp. 75–81. National Military Intelligence Foundation

Charles, Douglas M. *'Before the Colonel Arrived': Hoover, Donovan, Roosevelt, and the Origins of American Central Intelligence, 1940–41.* Pub. in *Intelligence and National Security,* 20:2 (2005), pp. 225–237

Davies, Philip H.J. *Institutionalising Intelligence: The Development of MI6 Internal Organisation and the Whitehall Village Market for Espionage.* University of Reading

Faulkner, Marcus. *The Kriegsmarine and the Aircraft Carrier: The Design and Operational Purpose of the Graf Zeppelin, 1933–1940.* Pub. in *War in History* , Vol. 19, No. 4 (November 2012), pp. 492–516. Sage Publications

Ferris, John. *Whitehall's Black Chamber: British Cryptology and the Government Code and Cypher School, 1919–29.* Pub. in *Intelligence and National Security,* 2:1, pp. 54–91, 1987. Routledge

Holman, Brett. *The Next War in the Air: Civilian Fears of Strategic Bombardment in Britain, 1908–1941.* PhD thesis, University of Melbourne, 2009

Hood, Chalmers. *The French Navy and Parliament between the*

Wars. Pub. in *The International History Review*, Vol. 6, No. 3 (August 1984), pp. 386–403. Taylor & Francis

Hull, Mark M. *The Irish Interlude: German Intelligence in Ireland, 1939–1943*. Pub. in *The Journal of Military History*, Vol. 66, No. 3 (July 2002), pp. 695–717. Society for Military History

Jackson, Peter. *French Intelligence and Hitler's Rise to Power*. Pub. in *The Historical Journal*, Vol. 41, No. 3 (September 1998), pp. 795–824. Cambridge University Press

Jeffreys-Jones, Rhodri. *Antecedents and Memory as Factors in the Creation of the CIA*. Pub. in *Diplomatic History*, Vol. 40, No. 1 (January 2016), pp. 140–154. Oxford University Press

Jenkins, Philip. *'It Can't Happen Here': Fascism and Right-Wing Extremism in Pennsylvania, 1933–1942*. Published in *Pennsylvania History*, Vol. 62, No. 1 (Winter 1995), pp. 31–58

Munshaw, Harvey D. *Extra! Extra! Read all about it: The British and American Press' Coverage of German-Soviet Collaboration, 1917–1928*. University of Central Missouri

Orange, Vincent. *The German Air Force Is Already "The Most Powerful in Europe": Two Royal Air Force Officers Report on a Visit to Germany, 6–15 October 1936*. Pub. in *The Journal of Military History*, Vol. 70, No. 4 (October 2006), pp. 1011–1028. Society for Military History

Overy, R.J. *The German Pre-War Aircraft Production Plans: November 1936–April 1939*. Pub. in *The English Historical Review*, Vol. 90, No. 357 (October 1975), pp. 778–797. Oxford University Press

Paillole, Paul. *L'affaire Aubert*. Published in *Historama, Hors série No. 35*. Orleans 1978.

Pöhlmann, Markus and Lahaie, Olivier. *Le Renseignement Allemand en Guerre; Structures et Opérations*. Pub in *Guerres mondiales et conflits contemporains*, No. 232 (Octobre–Décembre 2008), pp. 5–24. Presses Universitaires de France

Scannell, James. *German Espionage in South County Dublin*. Pub. in *Dublin Historical Record*, Vol. 55, No. 1 (Spring 2002), pp. 88–101. Old Dublin Society

Wallace, William and Phillips, Christopher. *Reassessing the Special*

Relationship. Pub. in *International Affairs*, Vol. 85, No. 2 (March 2009), pp. 263–284. Oxford University Press for the Royal Institute of International Affairs

Wark, Wesley K. *British Intelligence on the German Air Force and Aircraft Industry, 1933–1939*. Pub. in *The Historical Journal*, Vol. 25, No. 3 (September 1982), pp. 627–648. Cambridge University Press

Watt, D.C. *The Anglo-German Naval Agreement of 1935: An Interim Judgment*. Pub. in *The Journal of Modern History*, Vol. 28, No. 2 (June 1956), pp. 155–175. University of Chicago Press

Archival Sources:

UK National Archives, Kew, London: various files mainly from the KV, FO, AIR, CO, CRIM and J series.

US National Archives and Records Administration, Washington: various FBI case files.

Other archival sources consulted include: The Churchill Archives Centre, Churchill College, Cambridge University; The Wellcome Collection Archive, London; London Metropolitan Archives; The Imperial War Museum; Bibliothèque Nationale de France; The National Records of Scotland; The British Library, London; The Media History Library, University of Wisconsin; The Film and Television Archive, University of California Library, Los Angeles; D.C. Thomson & Co., Dundee; Tayside Police Museum, Dundee; and Kent Police Museum, Faversham.

Index